FEMINISM

ENCOUNTERS

TRADITIONAL

JUDAISM

## HBI SERIES ON JEWISH WOMEN

Shulamit Reinharz, General Editor
Joyce Antler, Associate Editor
Sylvia Barack Fishman, Associate Editor

The Brandeis Series on Jewish Women is an innovative book series created by the Hadassah-Brandeis Institute. BSJW publishes a wide range of books by and about Jewish women in diverse contexts and time periods, of interest to scholars, and for the educated public. The series fills a major gap in Jewish learning by focusing on the lives of Jewish women and Jewish gender studies.

For the complete list of books in this series, please see www.upne.com and www.upne.com/series/BSJW.html

Tova Hartman, *Feminism Encounters Traditional Judaism: Resistance and Accomodation*

Anne Lapidus Lerner, *Eternally Eve: Images of Eve in the Hebrew Bible, Midrash, and Modern Jewish Poetry*

Margalit Shilo, *Princess or Prisoner? Jewish Women in Jerusalem, 1840–1914*

Marcia Falk, translator, *The Song of Songs: Love Lyrics from the Bible*

Sylvia Barack Fishman, *Double or Nothing? Jewish Families and Mixed Marriage*

Avraham Grossman, *Pious and Rebellious: Jewish Women in Medieval Europe*

Iris Parush, *Reading Jewish Women: Marginality and Modernization in Nineteenth-Century Eastern European Jewish Society*

Shulamit Reinharz and Mark A. Raider, editors, *American Jewish Women and the Zionist Enterprise*

Tamar Ross, *Expanding the Palace of Torah: Orthodoxy and Feminism*

Farideh Goldin, *Wedding Song: Memoirs of an Iranian Jewish Woman*

Elizabeth Wyner Mark, editor, *The Covenant of Circumcision: New Perspectives on an Ancient Jewish Rite*

Rochelle L. Millen, *Women, Birth, and Death in Jewish Law and Practice*

Kalpana Misra and Melanie S. Rich, editors, *Jewish Feminism in Israel: Some Contemporary Perspectives*

Judith R. Baskin, *Midrashic Women: Formations of the Feminine in Rabbinic Literature*

ChaeRan Y. Freeze, *Jewish Marriage and Divorce in Imperial Russia*

Mark A. Raider and Miriam B. Raider-Roth, editors, *The Plough Woman: Records of the Pioneer Women of Palestine*

# FEMINISM ENCOUNTERS TRADITIONAL JUDAISM

## Resistance and Accommodation

### TOVA HARTMAN

BRANDEIS UNIVERSITY PRESS

*Waltham, Massachusetts*

Published by University Press of New England

*Hanover and London*

BRANDEIS UNIVERSITY PRESS
Published by University Press of New England,
One Court Street, Lebanon, NH 03766
www.upne.com
© 2007 by Brandeis University Press
Printed in the United States of America

5  4  3  2  1

Library of Congress Cataloging in Publication Data
Hartman, Tova.
Feminism encounters traditional Judaism : resistance and accommodation / Tova Hartman—1st ed.
    p. cm.—(Brandeis series on Jewish women)
Includes bibliographical references and index.
ISBN-13: 978-1-58465-658-6 (cloth : alk. paper)
ISBN-10: 1-58465-658-1 (cloth : alk. paper)
ISBN-13: 978-1-58465-659-3 (pbk : alk. paper)
ISBN-10: 1-58465-659-X (pbk : alk. paper)
1. Women in Judaism.  2. Jewish women—Religious life.  3. Feminism—Religious aspects—Judaism.  4. Orthodox Judaism.  I. Title.
BM729.W6H375 2007
296.082—dc22    2007014837

*This book is dedicated*
*to my daughters*
*Nomi, Racheli, & Shira*

# CONTENTS

There was a period of my life in which I spent much of my free time sitting in meetings of synagogue ritual committees, trying to make change. Having spent years straddling a self-imposed wall between my Orthodox religious observance and my immersion in feminist theory, the center was ceasing to hold. Increasingly, I needed my religious environment to reflect the values that had brought such profound clarity and dignity to my personal experience and worldview. When my oldest daughter prepared for her bat mitzvah, I was forced to confront the realization that there was no shul in which I wanted to hold this celebration. There was no shul that went out of its way to create increased opportunities for women's public ritual participation, while remaining within the parameters of Orthodox Jewish Law—(for example, calling women up to the Torah for aliyot, having women read from the Torah, as well as lead certain segments of the service)—all *within* the community, not in a separate women's prayer group.

In response, my family began to make separate services for specific events, and I became extremely active in the ritual committee of the shul. Year in and year out, I made the case for making change from within; year in and year out, this case was met with something beyond resistance: a kind of unbreachable stone mehitza. At a certain point I realized that I had become *that* person: the nudge, the troublemaker, the pest: *Can't you accept there have been some improvements? Isn't that good enough? Why aren't you ever satisfied?*

I remember very clearly my last ritual committee meeting at a popular synagogue. The floor was open for people to propose changes in shul policy. The mehitza should be down the middle; women should lead Kabbalat Shabbat. The responses to these suggestions surprised me less for their content than for the edge of their tone: *The shul will fall apart. We'll become like the Conservatives. We've pushed the line as far as we can push it: women here teach Torah, and that is more than they do anywhere else. Nobody wants it—you're the only person who cares about this.*

I had walked out of many such meetings. But this time I walked out and kept walking.

There was no glory in this. Like activists everywhere, my activism reflected a deep love of and commitment to the system with which I passionately grappled. I love praying in a community; I love going to shul. An overwhelming loneliness came over me with the recognition that I was speaking what seemed to be a language that only I understood. Though some people listened, or tried to, and perhaps even expressed sympathy, no one was willing to take the step of actually bringing about change, or significantly incorporating feminist values, within an existing shul. Many of these were people who advocated radical views in other areas; in some cases, fiery political activists who worked tirelessly for social change. These were people who demanded that Judaism represent and live up to the highest ethical standards; yet they seemed actively, almost intentionally, invested in keeping the ethical claims of feminism at arm's length from their ritual life or religious experience.

At the same time, I felt that if I wanted this so deeply, others must too— I can't be *that* much of an oddball.

Meanwhile, I stopped going to shul altogether. I would sit at home on Shabbat and *fantasize* about going to shul. I would read the paper and set the table for lunch. And then something started to shift. It began to sink in: the depths to which people in these establishment shuls really did not want to change. My bitterness dissolved and a calmness overcame me as I realized, they don't have to change. I don't have to convince them of anything; *I* have to make a change. Did I care enough, and did I have the courage to try? I dropped out of the discourse of pleading and persuading—indeed, dropped out of conversation with mainstream Orthodox shuls altogether—and moved my energies into the sphere of doing. It was a paradigm shift for me and, I think, for anyone who would speak to me. I exchanged questions for challenges: This is my dream, this is my vision. I reached out and simply made myself available to others with shared frustrations, commitments, and values. There had been other attempts in Jerusalem and America to expand the horizons of what was considered possible for women in Orthodox public prayer.[1] Rabbi Mendel Shapiro had written a responsum, published in the *Edah Journal,* in which he made a halakhic case for women receiving aliyot and reading publicly from the Torah. Based on his verdict, he held services for his daughters' bat mitzvahs. Some other individuals followed suit, and when Shirah Hadasha eventually started, many others relied upon this responsum for halakhic permission. These important precursors sought to create and legitimate prayer groups that would allow occasional alternatives to mainstream prayer. They all nurtured my sense of not being totally alone. At the same time, I knew that what I needed and wanted to work with others toward creating was not an occasional refuge, but an ongoing, living *community* of prayer.

After two meetings in my living room, we rented space in a local community center and began. Fifty people came to the first meeting; within a month, our corps of greeters, (one of the elements reflecting the shul's appropriation of traditionally "feminine" values like domestic hospitality to the public ritual setting) were regularly welcoming upward of two hundred guests.

The process that I went through personally in the collaborative effort of founding a new, alternative model for Orthodox worship reflects the central thrust of this book, which examines vital contact points between feminism and tradition. This evolution is another stage in a continuum that can be traced back to the founding in 1997 of the Jewish Orthodox Feminist Alliance (JOFA). JOFA brought Modern Orthodox women together to raise consciousness about feminist issues within Orthodoxy, and to engage in activism as well: pressuring rabbis to address the agunot issue, for example, and developing and lobbying for the implementation of feminist-informed curricula in religious schools. JOFA gave Orthodox women with feminist sensibilities a sense of community and of institutional legitimacy; it thus facilitated the increased acceptance of feminist values within the religious conversation.

The shul is an embodied (and ongoing) experiment in the creativity that can happen when tradition and modernity conjoin. This book similarly is an exploration of the discoveries that can be made when two forms of knowledge, values, and commitments that are not necessarily compatible in all respects—but that are each compelling—instead of trading barbs are made to gaze upon each other with the sympathy of fellow travelers. In this mutual investigation, what quickly becomes apparent is that things are both more difficult and more interesting than originally presumed. Attempts to reconcile tradition with feminist values through interpretive acrobatics begin to seem not only facile or forced, but insidious in their potential to cover up infrastructures of oppression and personal pain. We come to realize that not everything can be reinterpreted, not everything can be made to fit. There is real value but also real constraint in interpretation's ability to affect the lived experiences of religious women. As a result, we are forced to look more deeply into both feminism and tradition. It is in this second round of interrogation that discoveries can be made that open up serious possibilities for living as a feminist and an Orthodox Jew.

This initial process of reengagement, the manner of bringing feminism and tradition into dialogue with each other, and re-engaging in a conversation with tradition without abandoning one's commitment to feminist values (the same process that led to the founding of the shul) is described in chapter 2, "Facing the Legacy of the Canon." Based on feminist responses to another canon, the work of Freud, I extrapolate three basic stances that may be relevant, resonant, and helpful in cultivating a strong feminist position vis-à-vis the traditional Jewish canon. What happens when one is compelled by two traditions? At times they are mutually exclusive: as a result, we question our own reality, silence parts of ourselves, and submit to the tradition, allowing it to define us even as it contradicts our embodied experience. I sensed increasingly that synagogues were not making good-faith efforts to respect women's dignity: their policies, their unspoken assumptions, their very architecture— all proved inimical. Another response to this experience of mutual exclusivity is the rejection model; that is, divorcing ourselves from tradition. In Freudian literature this option is represented by Dora, who ultimately left Freud. My personal analogue was the period in which I stopped going to shul altogether. What I eventually arrived at in my own life was another possibility that some feminist Freudians arrived at as well: reengagement. There are many different ways to reengage, and in a sense the chapters that follow each explore a possible contact point for reengagement. Even the more theoretical pieces are not structural analyses of texts or ideas, but investigations of lived experience: what are the areas of a person's life in which two compelling traditions can be engaged without privileging one over the other?

During my shul committee years, one of the terms consistently leveraged against me as a reason for maintaining non egalitarian or anti-egalitarian policies within the traditional synagogue, was *tzniut,* or modesty. As both a religious value spoken about with increasing fervor, and a legal category defined and defended with increasing rigor, *tzniut* has seen a radical ascendancy in prominence within the discourse of contemporary Orthodox Judaism. My second chapter, "Modesty and the Religious Male Gaze," uses a feminist lens to unpack this discourse, while at the same time demonstrating that exiting religion does not necessarily equal an exit from the oppressive male gaze it channels. The concept of modesty, properly formulated, may ultimately be helpful in countering this gaze and its ill effects on both the men from whom it emanates and the bodies of the women it settles upon.

During the time that I was considering starting the new shul, floating the idea with family, friends, and acquaintances, I was consistently surprised by the vehemence (and, in some cases, the sheer antagonistic bile) of the responses I received. Normally mild-mannered people, people who knew me and cared about me—*because* they cared about me—felt the need to impress upon me in no uncertain terms the dangerous wrongness of what I was considering: *Don't you dare. What are you doing?* and *Who do you think you are?* were common refrains. Some took the tack of dismissive condescension: *Nobody needs it, nobody will show up, this isn't for anyone except yourself. If it were needed, somebody would have done it already.* Some invoked institutional intransigence and power: *How can you do something new in Jerusalem? The rab-*

*bis will attack you and everybody will be too intimidated to come.* Some used veiled threats of ostracism: *If you don't like the way we do things, go to the Conservative movement.* Some went closer to home, suggesting that my three girls would be humiliated, held as outcasts within the religious school system. Others raised the specter of an actual physical threat: *You'll be endangering yourself and your family. You'll be stoned.*

Though it still shocks me to recall the visceral force of these responses, I came to understand them better while working on my sixth chapter, "Roles, Rules, and Responsa: The Backlash Against Feminism." I came to see, for example, how all of the responses I received are in fact tropes around which rabbinic authorities have shaped Orthodox discourse vis-à-vis feminism since the early twentieth century. Claims of inauthenticity (especially through comparisons to other movements), impugning of motives, questioning the validity or even reality of explicitly stated needs; and finally, the consolidation and naked usurping of power through intimidation and threats—the reliability with which these motifs pervade Orthodox groupthink is no coincidence, as I demonstrate through an examination of the rhetoric of several rabbinic responsa.

This exercise of rabbinic power is far from theoretical—as I came to understand firsthand when starting the shul. At our planning committee meeting, two groups walked out. One demanded to know, Who was the rabbi that was sanctioning all of this innovation? We didn't have one. For the first time in my life the roles were reversed: I was part of the group being left behind as disaffected committee members walked out the door.

It was the first time, but it was far from the last.

In fact, at that same first meeting, a second group walked out. They had a different complaint: they demanded that the shul be completely egalitarian. For someone committed to remaining to some degree within an Orthodox framework, this issue is probably the stickiest. While some areas exhibit halakhic flexibility (such as those for which I had been arguing all those years, and which we ultimately adapted in the shul), others are rooted in ancient precedents that yield far less easily to innovation. These others would provoke far more sweeping and definitive renunciation among those attuned to the nuances of Jewish Law. Among these sticky, less flexible issues is the liturgy itself, the androcentrism of which has for decades been a rallying call for Jewish feminists and a top priority for change among liberal Jewish denominations. In chapter 4, "The Paternal Voice in Liturgy," I suggest a rethinking of Jewish liturgy from a feminist perspective. If we take the form of prayer as an inherited given, and preclude changing the words as an option, what are we left with? I found myself forced to reconsider my relationship to the paternal voice—the male essence that figures so prominently in these texts—in the broader cultural discourse and in the psyches of real men and women. In this chapter, I suggest some new ways of reconfiguring and relating to the male voice in prayer.

Chapter 5, "The Hands of Rabbis: Orthodox Women and Niddah," focuses on another well-documented area of feminist religious criticism: the menstrual rite. Through a series of interviews I outline a range of reengagement strategies practiced by Orthodox women that is honest, creative, and nuanced.

In my concluding chapter, "Go Away and Change," I speak explicitly about the creation of the shul, and some of the conflicting messages I received throughout that process. Calls to "work within the system" were seemingly contradicted by challenges like, "If you want something changed so badly, go change it" (which I understood was a thinly veiled invitation to "go *away* and change it," to leave the system and leave those upholding it alone). Women's putative responsibility for bringing the ethical claims of feminism to bear upon societal institutions, for bringing about the kinds of changes that would improve their situation, is a frequent motif within feminist literature, argued both across the feminist/antifeminist line, and among prominent feminist thinkers themselves. In this chapter I examine the different sides of the issue and suggest some of the problems and possibilities for Orthodox feminist change.

For me, joining with others to start the shul came out of a commitment to Jewish tradition and a belief in the possibilities of feminism and tradition. We felt isolated in a Jewish world that wanted to keep feminism and Orthodoxy separate. We knew in some way that we had to leave the model we had known to work together to create something new. I could not continue to teach feminism to my university students and sit behind a sexist mehitza in the back of shul. I needed to show my daughters that in the face of adversity, I tried *something*. I needed to live a life at least somewhat less divided, a life that much more whole.

## ACKNOWLEDGMENTS

I feel fortunate to be among colleagues and friends who have patiently read and commented on my work: Rachel Adler, Yehuda Gelman, Elie Holzer, Alick Isaacs, Judy Klitzner, Steve Klitzner, Jonathan Malino, John Moskowitz, Avinoam Rozenack, Avi Sagi, Alieza Salzberg, Daniel Schwartz, and Shira Wolosky.

Thank you, Valeria Siegelshifer, a brilliant research assistant, for poring over every line of this book, double-checking sources and making important substantive contributions.

To my dear childhood and adult friend Nancy Richler, I am grateful for your critical and loving reading of my work.

At University Press of New England, Phyllis Deutsch believed in the work from the beginning and encouraged me to develop many of my ideas more fully. To Ann Brash, thank you for your careful line editing.

Thanks to Nomi Marmon, my graduate student who worked together with me in researching *Mikveh* and *Niddah*. Our article was published previously in the journal *Gender and Society*.

The chapter "Facing the Legacy of the Canon: Affirmation, Rejection, and Reinterpretation" is a revised version of a previously published article in *New Trends in Jewish Educational Research*.

To my teacher, mentor, and friend Carol Gilligan, who continues to encourage me in my work, your astute comments have been extremely helpful to me. Your observations continue to goad me into seeing things more clearly; and our ongoing conversation is a vital source of insight, discovery, and growth.

To my mother Bobbie Hartman, my soul mate of personal and intellectual endeavors, whom I have stood beside in *shul* since childhood, absorbing religious intuitions from which many of my values, interests, and concerns are derived: thank you for your steadfast support, day and night. Thank you to my father David Hartman, my lively morning *chevruta*, rebbe, for all your encouragement, for your religious teaching, for helping me reopen Jewish traditional books, and in particular, for reading over many of the chapters of this book and commenting line by line.

To my siblings, Dvorah, Donniel, Adina, and Ranan, who have been my cheering squad, lovingly supporting me in my religious and personal journey, there are no words to describe my gratitude.

To Tamar Miller, who davened through many chapters of this book with unending patience, reviewing ideas, editing, laughing, and crying together, thank you for continuously encouraging me with devotion and love.

To Marc Brettler, who offered hours of assistance during the final stages of the book's preparation: thank you for your patience and encouragement. It has been wonderful to begin to work together.

To my dear friends from Shirah Hadashah: together we began to create a religious space to express our spirituality, to sing, dream, cry, laugh, and hug—in other words, the beginnings of a praying community. Together we learned the painful and wonderful process of celebrating compromise, without giving up on our vision. Our *shul* is a work in progress and a labor of love.

To Charlie Buckholtz, who has been my editor, *chevruta,* and dear friend for the past four years, I am deeply indebted to you. I appreciate your creativity in helping to develop, deepen, and express the ideas and insights at the heart of my work. You were instrumental in every stage in the birthing of this book.

Most of all, I am grateful to my daughters, Nomi, Racheli, and Shira, who gave me the courage to raise them with religious integrity and the strength to build a meaningful, loving, and religious home together. They are the deepest inspiration in my life and my work. This book is dedicated to them with all my love.

FEMINISM

ENCOUNTERS

TRADITIONAL

JUDAISM

# 1 FEMINISM AND MODERN ORTHODOXY

Nearly twenty years, ago after completing my M.A. in Jewish philosophy, I began teaching in a religious girls' school in Israel. During six years of teaching adolescent girls, I became increasingly aware of my role as an agent of socialization—and progressively troubled by the disconnect between the tradition I was expected (and wanted) to pass on and the critiques of the tradition that were beginning to coalesce in my own thinking. Eventually the contortions of identity that this disconnect required became too painful, and I decided to move into a field that I hoped might be less charged. For a time, I did not want the challenges and uncertainties of struggling with what had become somewhat disparate identities—my integrity as a woman *and* as a traditionally religious Jew—to impact adversely upon the lives of young girls.

I delved into graduate study in psychology, with a focus on feminist theory. These studies at first provided me with the balance of personal resonance and intellectual detachment I had sought. I was now learning about the "womanhood" and "motherhood" of other cultures, which I quickly discovered to be ensconced in their own muffling set of "oughts" and "shoulds." I was learning, in other words, about the orthodoxies of *other* cultures. Academic feminism gave me a lens through which to make sense of my experience as a woman without forcing me to tackle certain incongruities in my religious experience. Though in my mind a revolution was taking place, my religious life remained largely cordoned off from this upheaval. Ironically, the distance from religiosity an academic setting provided made the questions that had plagued me as a teacher seem less pressing. Amid the intensity of graduate work, I did not think about these questions as much. While it is true that the passion for Torah I had when I was younger cooled significantly during this time, my acquiescence made it easier to adhere to the normative framework of religious observance, which was, after all, second nature: my personal status quo.

At the end of my doctoral studies, I was gearing up to do a relatively abstract dissertation on some specialized elements of feminist theory. At that point, my adviser, Carol Gilligan, staged a classic intervention. Her words still reverberate through my mind, and through all the work that I have done since, culminating in this book. She advised me to go back to Jerusalem, to Orthodoxy, to my home—a kind of *lekh lekha* (Go forth) in reverse. "Tova," she said, "where you have your real questions, you will do your best work." My teacher of feminism directed me to reengage with my Modern Orthodoxy. I took her advice. I went back to Orthodoxy, not as a mode of praxis (which I had never left), but as a lived and living tradition. Through the process of reengaging with Modern Orthodox Judaism, I have discovered the extent to which I am part of a culture that stands starkly at the crossroads of powerful trends. This book is both an explication of the Modern Orthodoxy I encountered and an attempt to highlight these nexus points: the places and the ways in which feminism and Modern Orthodoxy encounter each other.

---

I am aware that there are multiple feminisms and multiple versions of Modern Orthodoxy and a diverse range of people who claim citizenship and authorship in each. Still, on balance, most strands of Modern Orthodoxy define their Modernity, and their Orthodoxy, in a way that makes it very difficult for feminism to enter into its bloodstream, much less to exert a religious claim. There is good reason that feminism has been viewed by most traditional people as a threatening oppositional force. In its critique of patriarchal societies, feminism has in various forms sought to challenge and undermine presumptive religious truths deeply embedded within patriarchal hierarchies. As a religious feminist, I have at times found myself on the defensive within feminist circles for maintaining "old-fashioned" customs that must certainly break my spirit as a woman. Feminism posits that religion is largely to blame for the cruelties of patriarchy, so being religious is often construed as inherently antifeminist.

Feminist critiques of religion evince powerful, critical insights, but do not, I think, tell the whole story. At times, these critiques blur the distinctions between the people in power who make decisions and speak in religion's name, and the intangible, unbounded spiritual-human root of religion itself (see Buber 1923; Soloveitchik 1966 and 1986). At its best, the religious spirit is supple, searching and fluid, and impossible to monopolize or contain. It holds the potential to resist and/or transcend patriarchal power and structure. The religious spirit cannot be boiled down to a set of doctrines or practices; it is more than the sum of its commitments and beliefs. It is constituted by a lived experience of a dense network of relationships—with community, with history, with liturgy, and with God. Thus it also resists the kind of analytical deconstruction that certain feminist theories have offered. Feminism, while offering a cogent assessment of traditional religions' many pitfalls, has not acknowledged the religious spirit embedded within traditional religious communities and institutions. This disregard leads to a kind of communication gap between antireligious feminists and their religious sisters, whose choice to remain so blatantly under patriarchal authority seems baffling. The nonreligious often cannot accept or perhaps do not perceive what in the eyes of many religious women is a simple, intuitive truth: feminism has not thus far offered a positive spiritual framework that stands up against the richly textured experience of religious life (see Ahmed 1992).

Feminism's antagonism to traditional religion often blocks us not only from fully understanding those who have made the decision to remain within tradition, but those who have chosen to leave. This leaving invariably entails more complexity and pathos, in both its motivations and its consequences, than many theorists would lead us to believe. Lives are often indelibly scarred by the void left in tradition's wake, which no modern source of meaning can fill. We make a mistake, and indulge a prejudice, when we label those who stay as uneducated, spineless, blindly dogmatic, or slaves of false consciousness. We should, as feminists, stop assuming an imperative to exit the tradition. If we choose instead to engage the tradition—recognizing its jagged edges without either glossing them over apologetically or running away because they're too sharp—we can then begin to expand our sense of what it means to live within a tradition.

The work of reengaging tradition is necessarily a work in progress. There may never be a sweeping resolution, an exhalation of relief, an oceanic sense of oneness. Following Blu Greenberg, one of the foremothers and still leading voices of Orthodox feminism:

> So I live with the conflict. I live with it every day, in a thousand ways that pull me in one direction or another. I have come to realize that the conflict is a sign of my health, not of my confusion; the tension is a measure of the richness of my life, not of its disorderliness. (Greenberg 1981, 168)

Similarly, the process of reengagement that I describe in this book is challenging and murky—but possible. The following chapters offer the beginnings of a corrective stance that allows for tradition and feminism to view each other not—or not exclusively—as antagonists. This "reengagement" with tradition is a process that I believe can be humanly honest and spiritually enriching. It involves a double recognition: on the one hand, that remaining within tradition keeps one in permanent dissatisfaction; on the other, that leaving may present very serious costs of its own. In this recognition I follow and stand with, among others, Phyllis Trible (1995):

To know that one is a feminist and to know that one loves the Bible is, in the thinking of many, at best an oxymoron, perhaps clever as a rhetorical statement but surely not a possibility for existential living. After all, if no man can serve two masters, no woman can serve two authorities, a master called Scripture and a mistress called Feminism. Therefore, my predicament grew as I heard the challenge that Daly and others pose: "Choose ye this day who you will serve, the God of the fathers or the God of the sisterhood. Biblical religion gives us the God of the fathers. In it is no resting place for feminists." If this were true, then I am of all women most wretched, or whatever adjective seems fitting: confused, schizophrenic, misguided, conservative, or just plain wrong." (7)

Trible chose to reengage with her Bible in a high level of awareness of both what she was gaining and what she was giving up. I join thousands of women and men who are compelled by feminism and traditional religion, in hoping to do the same.

––––––––

I began by speaking primarily about feminism's antagonism to traditional religion. In the chronology of my life, however, that awareness came much later. The feeling of conflict between my sense of myself as a religious person—not merely by default, but a person with deep religious affinities and instincts, happy and grateful for the spiritual rewards I felt my own tradition constantly offered me—and the messages about who I was supposed to be as a religious girl, implanted within me an early nebulous unease. As I grew older, my natural resistance to the increasingly insistent "oughts" and "shoulds" provoked a growing antagonism from various sectors of the religious world. This antagonism was so puzzling to me that it was not for many, many years—until I became a mother—that it began to filter into my conscious awareness. I believed so completely in the claims that Modern Orthodoxy made about itself, and in the image of integration that it projected, that the grave divergences I encountered from this inspiring rhetoric I dismissed as anomalies, explained away, or shoved into an obscure mental "miscellaneous" file. My religious role models wore the same clothes as other people, spoke the same language, went to university and waxed eloquent about integrating traditional religious and modern secular sensibilities. What could possibly be missing from this picture—and why did I constantly feel that something was?

Mothering brought these subterranean questions surging into sharp relief. What for my own religious life could (for better or worse) be left nebulous and void, for my daughters' religious development required a higher level of scrutiny (see Apter 1990). I began to see vividly the gaps between Modern Orthodoxy's claims of integration and its actual treatment of, and discourse about, women. In the books my daughters brought home from their Israeli Modern Orthodox schools, the section about how to keep a kosher home featured pictures of mothers in the kitchen, outfitted in aprons, serving the father his meal. When another of my daughters was seven, her grade celebrated receiving their first *siddurim* (prayer books) by creating a model shul. Previously, the boys and girls had prayed together from their seats in the coed classroom. For the party, the room was divided into front and back sections. The boys sang real prayers from the front of the room, while the girls, outfitted in headscarves for the special occasion, sang "Woman of Valor"—the section of Proverbs 31 with which husbands traditionally serenade their wives at the Friday-night Sabbath dinner table preceding the meal.

Feeling this dissonance between Modern Orthodoxy's claims and its actual attitudes and practices, however acute, did not initially give me cause for despair. Because so much of the rhetoric of Modern Orthodoxy was about openness to modernity within the parameters of halakha, and because there was nothing about the changes I wanted that seemed to conflict with halakha, I felt optimistic that there would be room to integrate a fuller appreciation of feminist insight into its perspectives and practices. My initial attempts to test this hypothesis were local; my daughters' principals were my first guinea pigs. Admittedly, I did not always express my optimism in the most diplomatic of terms. The principals listened politely and changed nothing; my daughters begged me never to speak to anyone at their school ever again.

My faith in Modern Orthodoxy was so encompassing that I dismissed the local resistance I encountered as parochial aberrations from the movement's true core. Certainly these were not "Torah True" Modern Orthodox Jews. I turned my attention to the national Modern Orthodox leadership for what I thought would be a more welcoming response. At the time, *Kibbutz ha-dati* (the religious kibbutz movement) was considered the avant-garde of Israeli Modern Orthodoxy. It had been zealous and creative in its fusion of Jewish tradition and national identity, playing a critical role in the widespread acceptance of religious Zionism not only as a fact, but as a positive and healthy development in the life of the Jewish people. Because of the movement's openness, I assumed it would lead the way in listening to feminist insights and values. This optimism turned out to have been incredibly naïve. *Kibbutz ha-dati* has, like most of Modern Orthodoxy, exhibited extreme skepticism and resistance toward any suggestion in the area of ritual life bearing the air of a "feminist" motive.

What is it about certain kinds of knowledge/values that Modern Orthodoxy feels very comfortable about adopting, and others that it does not? What
is it about Zionism that touched the religious imagination and freed the religious spirit of Modern Orthodox Jews? What is it about interfaith dialogue
that certain Modern Orthodox leaders have come to feel so deeply comfortable with—and what is it about feminism that has generated so much am-
bivalence and backlash? These were some of the questions that had begun to
percolate and simmer in my mind, but that have taken many years fully to formulate and express.

As I continued to explore my own discomforting sense of the dissonance
between Modern Orthodox reality and its claims, I came increasingly to understand the power of religious authorities in framing feminism for the Modern Orthodox world, and the extremely conscientious way in which they did
so.[1] Along the way I encountered Third World feminists like Uma Narayan
(1997), who helped me to bring what I was seeing into clearer focus, and to
give it a name:

> This process of designating certain changes and not others as "problemat-
> ically Westernized" is often carried out as if the label was picking out some-
> thing descriptively obvious. Pointing to the fluid, fractured, selective, and
> changing deployment of this "labeling" is one important strategy for Third
> World feminists who face delegitimatization via accusations of "Western-
> ization." (29)

In the process of encountering these kinds of cross-cultural resonances, I
began to realize that the Modern Orthodox resistance to feminism was not incidental, but deeply embedded in its systems and institutions. Even this (admittedly disturbing) realization, however, has not led me to give up on finding
a place for myself—and my family, and my community—within Modern Orthodoxy. Though it has not yet found a way to integrate feminism into its religious vision, I still maintain that it has the capacity to do so. Modern Orthodoxy is no stranger to the balancing act of tradition and modernity. Its
crowning achievement has been its ability to make a place for the legitimate
claims of modernity without losing its sense of religious conviction and its halakhic integrity. Many women throughout the last decade—perhaps more
than some religious authorities would like to acknowledge—have responded
to the challenge and invitation of JOFA to reject the tradition/feminism dichotomy proffered by many communal religious leaders and accord instead to
feminism the kind of respect extended to Zionism and ethics. The antagonism
that many rabbinic spokesmen show to women's attempts to find distinctive

feminine voices within the tradition is daunting. Nevertheless, given Modern Orthodoxy's track record in integrating other aspects of modernity, I believe that the final chord has not yet been struck. For me, the first stage in urging Modern Orthodoxy to move beyond itself in this arena has been to delineate in terms as clear as possible the sources and limits of its resistance to feminism and the ways in which this resistance has expressed itself. With this knowledge, we can then explore the possibilities that might exist for entering a new paradigm.

––––––––––

In order to understand the different layers of Modern Orthodoxy's resistance to feminism it is, I think, worthwhile to look briefly at the relationship of Modern Orthodoxy to both its orthodoxy and its modernity (that is, to "secular" paradigms of knowledge and values). Speaking generally, with respect to the former, what is shared is (1) a sense of deep grounding in the halakhic process; (2) an alignment with centrist and ultra-Orthodox Jews in its organizational, social, religious mood; and (3) its level of respect for/submission to common authoritative sources (see Sagi 2003 and 2006).[2] With respect to the latter, it holds a sense that modernity is not a problem to be solved, but a religious opportunity to be embraced to the extent that it does not transgress the parameters set by halakha. Here is where Modern Orthodoxy has set itself apart from mainstream Orthodoxy—more specifically, in its relationship with "modern" sources of knowledge and values not derived directly or overtly from Jewish tradition. "The Modern Orthodox experiment begins with the assumption that Orthodoxy can preserve its integrity and passion and even be enriched, by its intersection with modernity" (Berman 2001).[3] According to some proponents of Modern Orthodoxy, this encounter should not be enacted passively or defensively; nor should it be seen as an inescapable consequence of the times in which we live. Modern Orthodoxy must not merely stand at the crossroads of modernity and tradition, but should walk the "difficult path" (Berman 2001) of traditional Judaism and Modernity. "*Descriptively* all Orthodoxies are 'modern' in the sense that inescapably they inhabit the modern world. What gives Modern Orthodoxy its name is the fact that its adherents see this as *prescriptive* also" (Sacks 1991, 10). The important question is: How do Modern Orthodox people actually negotiate this complicated, challenging terrain? Or, to put it in one famous Modern Orthodox rabbi's terms: "Modern Orthodox adherents all go to universities; the question is, how do the universities go through them?"

I suggest that in managing the complex relationship between tradition and modernity, Modern Orthodoxy employs two primary strategies: compartmentalization and harmonization. In the former, external secular knowledge is deemed legitimate on its own terms, carrying authority in its areas of specialization; ultimately, however, it does not—and cannot, by definition—impinge on tradition's eternal truths. Perhaps for this reason the trend has been to valorize certain kinds of *scientific* knowledge, which are less likely to make claims of meaning. The overall attitude toward these kinds of "hard" knowledge has been a kind of "render unto Caesar," wherein tradition makes a strategic retreat from areas of specialization in which it cannot claim expertise. This division of labor is both embraced and rigorously monitored: good fences make good neighbors. The compartmentalized mind-set is reflected in Modern Orthodoxy's umbrella slogan, "Torah and Madda" (secular knowledge, though generally interpreted more narrowly as science). The operative word here, I would say, is *and*: outside knowledge, while not forbidden—indeed, while potentially enhancing of religious insight—is defined as inherently separate from and ontologically external to the holy.

Other proponents of Modern Orthodoxy use a language of synthesis, integration, and harmony to describe the ideal relationship between "holy" and "profane" knowledge.[4] Rabbi Norman Lamm, in his Modern Orthodox manifesto *Torah Umadda* (1990), sees in the harmonization of Torah and Maddah "a way to unite his deepest Torah commitments with his growing experiences as a modern person living in a scientific technopolis, in an open and democratic society, and in a culture that, despite all its terrible failings, is vibrant and progressive" (211). Naturally, though, the position here is not that *everything* can be harmonized with a traditional worldview. Some knowledge or value frameworks may be integrated, while others must be deemed outside the pale. Some will be elevated as shining illustrations of how much modernity has to offer religious consciousness, of the ways in which secular knowledge can enhance our understanding and appreciation of our own tradition. Other frameworks will be excluded because they pose irreconcilable conflicts with the corpus and spirit of Torah. This latter category is essentially the back alley to which feminism has been consigned.

In other words, Modern Orthodoxy's integration of secular madda and knowledge is not applied indiscriminately and universally, but selectively. Selection inherently reflects, and expresses, an underlying hierarchy of values. It always begs the question, Why this and not that? Harmonization, then, means only that *some* external values, deemed nonthreatening and/or enhancing of tradition by some consensus of religious authorities, may be incorporated into the tradition. Other values are either rejected outright or compartmentalized, deemed acceptable or even valuable when applied to the secular realm, but inappropriate for mingling with the sacred. We are brought back, then, with a kind of inexorable force—even (or especially) within this paradigm that supports an ideal of harmonization—to a version of compartmentalization that is in fact more subtle, more exclusive, and more highly charged (see Sagi 2003 and 2006).

### Case Study of Harmonization: Ethics

One of the most prominent examples of a body of knowledge that has been seemingly harmoniously incorporated is ethics, a welcome guest of Modern Orthodoxy. The notion of an independent human ethical sensibility has proved so compelling to modern Jewish religious intuition that it has deeply infused and altered the culture and discourse of Modern Orthodoxy. If one were to ask Modern Orthodox doctors, for example, whether they would save the life of a non-Jew on *Shabbat,* they would not hesitate for a moment and would probably look at you as if you were a moral pervert for even asking. It is highly doubtful that in explaining why they would do so, they would invoke the *heter* of *mipnei darkei shalom*—or claim that there is no need for a *heter* at all. Perhaps, if pushed to the wall, they would say something about the inherent value of all human life: if forced to justify this notion in Jewish terms they might mention human creation in the image of God. The point here is that this ethical imperative is taken for granted by the Modern Orthodox mindset; it does not require traditional validation.

This context is important for understanding the implications of Tamar Ross's work. Ross (2004) frames feminism as part of a "dynamic, cumulative process of revelation," and an aspect of revelation that makes ethical claims to which the tradition must respond. She pushes the rabbis to include feminism within their ethical-religious understanding of God's interactions with our universe, reflecting her own deep understanding that it has heretofore been excluded.

> The cumulative understanding of revelation allows us to view the phenomenon of feminism itself—even if it appears to stem from sources outside of Judaism—as a gift from God. In this sense, assimilating feminism into Judaism is no different than the imbibing of Aristotelianism by Maimonidean rationalism or the absorption of certain ideas from Gnosticism and the Neoplatonic tradition by the Kabbalah, among other examples. What we are now beginning to know is being bestowed upon us. We are the beneficiaries of what has gone before us, as we grope toward a new light

reaching out to us from God. Listening to feminist claims with sympathy and understanding need not be thought of as a deep violation of Jewish tradition. Instead, it should be regarded as a spiritual undertaking of the first order (an avodat kodesh or a holy task). (210)

Different kinds of knowledge and values receive varying treatment, and are spoken about in different ways. In the past, as Tamar Ross shows, Aristotelianism and Neoplatonic traditions were seen to contribute to and even elevate the Jewish religious spirit. Today Western ethics and nationalism join this list of contributors. Yet feminism remains the prototypical reject. Modern Orthodox rabbis who claim ethics as their calling card sometimes base their traditional credibility on an extra strictness regarding women and tradition. Left-wing Modern Orthodox Rabbis in Israel who are loath to mistreat foreign Thai workers or Palestinians—"all men are created in the image of God"—have no problem relegating women to the ceilings of their shuls or behind a maximum-security mechitza, far beyond what the halacha mandates. Similar trends can be found among certain groups of religious Zionists. An Israeli religious settlement voted to add an extra prayer for the residents of the Gaza settlements slated for evacuation, but prohibited the addition of prayers for *agunot* and abused women. What is the basis for these kinds of ethical-religious choices? Of course, there is a place to add prayers for specific circumstances, and I am not saying outright which ones should or should not be added. My question is: Who is compelled by what to allow for such innovations? How are selective ethical-religious choices made ? While we are all selective in our ethical perceptions, I am raising the questions about what is kosher and what is not with regard to women and religious life. As Berman (2001) states, "Modern Orthodoxy . . . is a path that requires filtering out the degraded values of the low culture while welcoming the advances in knowledge and understanding being achieved in the high culture." My question remains: Who does the filtering and how?

Ethics, though, is something of a Pandora's box or (to use the term favored by Modern Orthodox authorities in relation to feminism) a "slippery slope." Once the notion of ethics is taken seriously, it becomes necessary to hold tight the reins as to where, how, and to whom these ethics are applied. The first thing is to define who gets to do the defining—and who does not. In the case of Modern Orthodoxy, certain rabbis maintain this metahalakhic right. This group has thus far chosen to exclude feminism from the ethics club, or to allow extremely limited and at times patronizing applications.

I do not say that feminism has been excluded outright from the discourse of Modern Orthodoxy. I would argue that Modern Orthodoxy—even among those who use the language of synthesis and harmony—has not so much rejected feminism outright as compartmentalized it in much the same way that it has compartmentalized science. In its own realm—that is, the secular realm—liberal feminism is affirmed and its values upheld, indeed demanded and fought for. The notion of workplace discrimination or unequal career tracking, for example, generates righteous indignation. Any Modern Orthodox parents whose daughter was denied the right to pursue the career of her choosing, or was accorded second-class status in any way, would fight the case tirelessly, to the highest court in the land, and be lauded as heroes by their Modern Orthodox compatriots. This egalitarian standard, however, by this point nearly taken for granted within the secular sphere, applies in rather curtailed ways, if at all, to religious life. It does not stand on equal footing with religious norms or the ideas that underlie them, and thus rarely has the opportunity to stand in honest dialogue with the traditional voice, much less lay claim to the religious spirit. In other words, good mechitzahs make good neighbours.

To cite one glaring and disheartening example, Rabbi Lamm, a proponent of harmonization, in his book dedicated entirely to this topic (1990), makes only one reference to feminism. It is worthwhile, I think, to quote in full the list of social perversions in which this reference occurs: "Thus for instance, the decade of the '70's was highly hedonistic, with its much touted sexual revolution, experimentalism with dress and amorality (especially its legitimization of homosexuality as an acceptable 'alternative life-style'), general permissiveness, easygoing attitude toward drugs and pornography, open life-style, apotheosis of the self (evidenced by the emphasis on self-gratification, self-expression, and self-realization), youth culture, feminism (in its more extreme manifestations), and so on" (13). Rabbi Lamm attempts to soften his dismissal of feminism by referencing only its "extreme manifestations." Of course, how one defines an "extreme" version of anything reflects assumptions about its basic nature and value. For me, an extreme manifestation of feminism is to apply the strictest standards of *kvod ha-adam* (honoring the dignity of human beings); for example, honoring motherhood by state-mandated salaries to those who stay home to take care of children. Likewise, extreme feminism would be manifest when agunot are no longer an issue because the debate moved from the realm of sympathy to the active change of religious tradition and law by using every legal means available. What are these dreams doing in a list with drugs, promiscuity, narcissism, anarchy, and pornography?

As Rabbi Lamm's statement makes clear, it is not only religious authorities' explicit understanding of tradition that accounts for Modern Orthodox's hostility toward feminism. Just as much of Modern Orthodox discourse about feminism elides halakha in favor of various metahalakhic social and rhetorical strategies, so too is our analysis of this discourse not only, or even primarily, a halachic discussion. Rather, we confront the modes of thinking that *underlie* Modern Orthodoxy's account of the ideal relationship between modernity and tradition. In one sense, feminism offers a different spin on the discussion about ethics above, as it treats Modern Orthodoxy's stance toward ways of thinking/being not necessarily native to Jewish tradition. There are other trends of Western thought that the tradition has simply absorbed and that form part of the lens out of which it sees. I am going to outline one of these trends, emphasizing that it draws as much from modern, Western, patriarchal intellectual history as any Jewish intellectual tradition.

### Case Study: Autonomous Man and the Relational Ethic

Modern Orthodox thinkers have to a large extent assimilated Western liberal ideals and values in their religious philosophies, especially the ideal of human autonomy and self-realization of the individual. "The Modern Orthodox person must see him/herself as committed to deal with specific issues, such as: authenticity, autonomy, historical consciousness, and individualism" (Ravitsky 1996 and 1999). Thus for example, Rav Soloveitchik (1983) did not hesitate to integrate some of modern philosophy's views of autonomy into his phenomenology of Halakhic Man. The latter is described as having similar characteristics to "Mind Man": he is creative and spontaneous, and he protects his own individuality. Human autonomous creativity becomes a condition for holiness: "If a man wishes to attain the rank of holiness, he must become a creator of worlds. If a man never creates, never brings into being anything new, anything original, then he cannot be holy unto his God. That passive type who is derelict in fulfilling his task of creation cannot become holy. . . . The most fundamental principle of all is that man must create himself. It is this idea that Judaism introduced into the world" (108–109).

Although operating from different philosophical premises, Y. Leibowitz (1976) establishes a strong connection between the performance of mitzvot (commandments) and the achievement of a form of human autonomy as its outcomes. Thus for example, after having set the mitzvot as antithetical to human natural tendencies and needs, he writes: "The man who lives in the world of Halakha . . . designs his life, namely he is autonomous in the exact meaning/sense of the word. He is free, he determines the law of his life, and only the autonomous creature deserves to be called Man" (60; my translation).

In emphasizing the importance of autonomy, Soloveitchic and Leibowitz both integrate elements of the neo-Kantian tradition, which locates the human being at the center of the universe (see Sagi 2006). It is this same tradition that led psychologists like Erikson (1968) and later Kohlberg (1976 and 1981) to develop models of identity formation that posit autonomy as synonymous with maturity and valorize decision-making that transcends relational considerations as the highest level of human moral development. The Lonely Man of Faith meets the Lone Ranger.

Feminist theory has called into question the assumptions, presumptions, and contentions of autonomy as a universal human value. It has posited alternative models of morality and identity, based on women's experience, that hold relationship as a central concern. It does not ask questions like: How can I leave home, separate from my parents, and make decisions independent of societal pressures? Rather, it asks: How do I connect to my past? How can I grow in connection to the friends, relatives, traditions, and institutions that figure so prominently in my life?

Similarly, as a feminist psychologist, I strongly question the total affiliation of modernity with autonomy posited by many Modern Orthodox Jewish thinkers, and their consequent framing of the salient modern issue as human autonomy versus divine heteronomy. The elevation of Autonomous Man as *the* figure of modernity, who must be wrestled with and reconciled, does not reflect some native Jewish truth so much as the assumption of a very specific paradigm of modernity. In other words, one of the problems of Modern Orthodoxy is not merely that it is too Orthodox, but that it is too modern; that is, that it has assimilated too deeply into an extremely Western vision of what modernity means.[5] Furthermore, given the orthodox manner in which Modern Orthodoxy tends to go about sanctifying those aspects of the profane it deems worthy of inclusion, these ideas about what constitutes "modern" become reified, rigidified, and highly resistant to challenge or evolution.

Whether modern liberal thought was taken on critically or by osmosis, it can hardly claim any more inherent religious validity than alternative modern modes of thinking and being. It should seem obvious to point out that of course there is no one strain of modern thought that embodies "Modernity" per se. The radical feminism of Catherine MacKinnon (1987, 1989, and 2005) is as representative a modern phenomenon as the liberalism of John Stuart Mill (1806–1873), just as Carol Gilligan's ethic of care (1982) presents as valid a model for identity formation as Lawrence Kohlberg's (1976 and 1981) stage theory of moral development. The Modern Orthodox establishment has sided with the idea of the autonomous individual standing before God, à la Kantian ethics rather than relational feminists' ethics. Yet I think the latter is at least as relevant for the traditional mind-set. Modern Orthodoxy has chosen to side, in other words, with the modernity of which feminism is a critique, and that has resisted this critique in powerful ways since its inception. It is fair to ask: When Modern Orthodoxy resists feminism, is it speaking from its Orthodoxy or its orthodox assumptions about modernity? Similarly, I think it is fair to say that part of the feminist critique of Modern Orthodoxy derives from its critique of a certain model of modernity as much as of the patriarchal aspects of the religion per se.

Ironically, then, feminism may fulfill the promise of a certain formulation of Modern Orthodoxy that speaks of modern knowledge and value systems as restoring to the tradition parts of itself that have been attenuated or lost throughout the course of history. For example, feminism might help us to reaccess the relational ethos of traditional Judaism, so that feminism has perhaps the potential to reclaim religious sensibilities that were lost, or superseded by modern Western notions and ways of being in the world. Modern Orthodoxy's austere alignment with the autonomous strain in modernity has left it closed to these possibilities.

---

As liberalism has served as a philosophical basis for Modern Orthodoxy's resistance to feminist knowledge and values, so can another source of resistance be found within the psychological dynamics of Modern Orthodoxy's self-image and -understanding. I am referring to what some theorists call "negative identity"; that is, I know who I am by who I am not (see Chodorow 1978 and 1989; Kimmel 1997).[6] Much of Modern Orthodoxy has constructed its self-conception upon notions of who it is not, and in so doing has carved out a narrow stretch of identity that cuts it off from many potentially enriching spiritual and intellectual resources.

For example, in order to maintain its leftward, "modern" credibility, Modern Orthodoxy on the whole negates the backwardness of ultra-Orthodoxy, rather than appreciating and allowing itself to embrace its religious passion. To uphold its rightward, "Orthodox" flank, it denounces the more liberal movements, as well as many forms of social progressivism that those movements have taken seriously and that therefore bear their unkosher scent. Feminism has found itself for decades caught in this ideological crossfire. This negative identity may help to account for Modern Orthodoxy's taking such an aggressively defensive stance against feminism, rather than the more open, sifting approach that it has exhibited with respect to philosophy and ethics. Notwithstanding the aspects of feminism, outlined above, that challenge directly some of the assumptions of traditional life, it may also be true that Modern Orthodoxy finds it difficult to approach feminism independent of other movements that have integrated it into their religious identity, and whose rejection has become a key precept of Modern Orthodoxy's sense of self.

Once we understand the place that feminism has been assigned within this (negative) model of religious identity, certain confusing trends become suddenly transparent: for example, the vehement, not infrequently vitriolic responses of religious authorities to seemingly innocuous requests of women, say, for modest increases in ritual participation or other public roles, like prayer groups. There is also use of nonhalakhic reasoning in halakhic decision-making, even in cases of personal desperation that could seemingly be halakhically resolved. Thus it becomes religiously legitimate for a nineteenth-century rabbi to leave a woman languishing in marital limbo, not because of an irresolvable halakhic quandary, but because to release her would too closely resemble the Reform:

> I will say one more thing which to my mind is exceedingly important. . . . if we who are zealous for the word of God will imitate the heretics to negate the institution of *gittin* and *halitsa* by means of conditional *kidushin*, even if we would say that it is being accomplished in a permissible fashion, nevertheless what will "the reformist rabbis say: behold those Orthodox (rabbis) have conceded that their laws are no good and the temper of the times cannot tolerate them . . . and they have thereby conceded that the temper of the times is mightier than antiquated laws. And what can we possibly say in response? Is there, God forbid, a greater desecration of the God's name? Consequently in my opinion conditional kidushin should not be instituted under any circumstances. (Twersky 1998, 10)

And it becomes legitimate a hundred years later for a major Orthodox authority with strong influence within the Modern Orthodox world to quote this precedent favorably in order to prohibit women from performing ritual acts because they resemble other movements, even though he admits there is no halakhic prohibition: "Rav Hoffman clearly evaluatated the proposal practically and axiologically. Accordingly, he concluded that even if one could practically design conditional *kidushin* and avoid violating the particulars of halakha, nevertheless it would be absolutely wrong to do so because etiologically it would signify ideational assimilation" (Twersky 1998, 10).

It is important to recognize that any movement, any sociological minority, relies upon negative identity for some aspect of its self-definition. This is certainly true for the other denominations of Judaism, and to a certain extent is implicit in the very work "denomination." The question that must be asked is:

Why has Modern Orthodoxy chosen to stake such a great part of its negative self-definition on a rejection of feminism in religious life? It is true that an important feature of a feminist reengagement with Modern Orthodoxy involves questioning the *prominence* of negative identity within self-definition. This analysis derives from a broader feminist critique of patriarchal models of identity formation based on separation, individuation, and self-sufficiency.[7] One of feminism's strong motifs has been to offer an alternative model of identity formation based on continuity and relationship.[8] With respect to communities, this motif translates into an attempt to encourage the cultivation of a positive collective identity. For Modern Orthodoxy it would mean an identity based less on such questions as: Who are we separate from and how? How can we reify those differences into attitudes and norms? Instead, identify such questions as would depend on: Who are we connected to? How can we draw upon these connections to enhance our identity, while at the same time maintaining a functional, bounded sense of self?

In this way, the challenge of feminism to Modern Orthodoxy is far deeper than a challenge to specific aspects of halakha, or even to the halakhic process as a whole. It advances a different kind of stance in the world (albeit one that, as mentioned above, recovers certain aspects of the tradition that have been attenuated or lost): it prioritizes the cultivation of relationships with various different "others" as integral to one's own sense of self. What I am calling for, then, goes far beyond a feminist "reading." I envision a Modern Orthodoxy that allows itself to be claimed by feminism, reengaged and religiously reinvigorated in the encounter.

———

What I propose, then, is not a halakhic debate. I do not offer a phenomenological structure of how to join feminism and Orthodoxy or advocate any particular solutions for halakhic change. I have no equation or recipe. In my own life, in order to give my daughters a model of religion that I could live with and wanted them to live with, I found it necessary to join with a group of people to build a shul and a community that I could pray in, even if that meant leaving certain loyalties behind (see Apter 1990). Any feminist reengagement of Orthodoxy will likely involve these kinds of decisions to venture out into communal fringes—decisions that are inevitably painful both personally and socially but, if my own case is in any way illustrative, that also have real potential for positive outcomes. Still, I do not pretend that I had any organizing principle for making these decisions in my own life. To propose a methodology for others to do so would be not only presumptuous but impossible. It is certainly far from the intention of this book, which is rather to survey and examine some of the ways in which the encounter between feminism and tradition take place, and to contemplate some ways in which that encounter might be reenvisioned.

I do not present this encounter as a revolutionary agenda, and I do not feel that it represents a radical departure from normative Modern Orthodoxy. Indeed, to say that the capacity for some creative adaptation within the parameters of a rigorous legal system is what has given postbiblical Judaism its time and space-spanning vitality in the first place (and is constitutive of the very term *rabbinic*) and would be unlikely to raise too many red flags among Modern Orthodox Jews. In Zionism and ethics, I have discussed two modern examples of precisely such acceptance and incorporation of new knowledge and value frameworks within the tradition.

What becomes striking then, is again not the exercise of rabbinic creativity by religious authorities to validate and encompass forms of knowledge and value derived elsewhere, but rather the selectivity with which this creativity is applied, and the discourse within which the process of selection is configured. Indeed, I would go so far as to question whether it is precisely the rabbis' awareness of their powerful agency in shaping tradition that has generated their adamant rejection of feminism: not only because their awareness of their power is what makes them so reluctant to share it, but because their selective faculties caused them to question, very reasonably, the potential impact on their values and culture of feminism's sweeping claims about the need to create the world anew.

Despite this resistance, the religious world of Modern Orthodoxy has not remained static. In the past twenty-five years there have been significant advances in opportunities for women's learning. Thousands of women study Talmud intensely and have achieved remarkable levels of knowledge. It is Modern Orthodoxy's signature response to the feminist challenge. There are programs that train women to become *Yo'atzot Halakha* (Jewish law consultants). It is hoped that these programs will expand and become ever more deeply rooted and accepted in the community. Perhaps these advances indicate the beginning of shared authority in the religious world. The common assumption, however, that increased learning will necessarily lead to greater self-determination and ritual participation—or even that small advances betoken the inevitable coming of greater participation—is not that clear. Granted, there has been a major shift in Orthodox policy with far-reaching implications for the lives of religious women. Nonetheless, during this same period, attempts by women to increase their ritual participation or roles in public life have been overall adamantly resisted. Often, the discourse used to put down these requests employs rhetoric strongly redolent of *nashim da'atan kalah* (women are weak-minded). It is neither women's knowledge that is questioned nor the halakhic validity of what they propose. Rather, it is their motivation—that is, their *use* of knowledge—that is scrutinized, suspected, and impugned (see chapter 6).

---

Amid all this talk about being claimed by feminism, and in the face of so much resistance, the question arises: Why remain within tradition at all? Daphne Hampson (1990), articulating the thoughts of so many modern women, asks this question with the utmost seriousness and cannot come up with a compelling answer: "The question then as to whether feminism and Christianity are compatible is that of whether the equality of women is compatible with a religion which has come from a past patriarchal age" (11). Her quest yields a brilliant synopsis of why there is in fact no way to integrate feminism with patriarchal religion. She says goodbye to her faith—Christianity—and in the scope and power of her argument leaves little room for any self-respecting woman to remain.

It is difficult to refute Hampson's arguments, many of which I find personally compelling. I find it impossible not to empathize with her choice. I can only point out that there are many people who, like myself, are aware of these arguments, find them compelling, and nonetheless continue to identify with tradition—its communities, values, and norms. I stand with the tradition because it speaks to a deep sense of who I am; I affirm my free choice to stay or go, while noting that the language of choosing is not sufficient to describe the claim it makes on my identity. This ontological claim calls upon me not to abnegate tradition but totally and continually to reengage with it. Disparities between tradition and other claim-making frames of knowledge and values do not force me to exit but rather, on the contrary, to continue to gaze deeply into both.

In this I am not alone. There are many different kinds of people who define themselves as Modern Orthodox. Having surveyed the approaches of some of those who speak for Modern Orthodoxy and have contributed to the shaping of its attitude toward feminism—while exhibiting great difficulty perceiving or accepting the religious possibilities that feminism offers—it has become apparent that some Modern Orthodox people are actually beginning to walk along additional paths. There are many people, men and women, who do not want to change the way others practice Modern Orthodoxy but seek new paths for themselves. Yet they do not want to leave: they are willing to live with jagged edges; they are staying and building religious communities, and making more room for themselves and others. It is through this process of individual and communal reengagement that I have found myself, to my own surprise and delight, on a path toward the possibility of a whole life within Modern Orthodoxy.

# 2

## FACING THE LEGACY OF THE CANON

### AFFIRMATION, REJECTION, AND REINTERPRETATION

What happens when subjective experience collides head-on with deeply rooted social norms based on "objective" religious truths? This question confronted me with increasing frequency and intensity in the years before I finally made my break from mainstream synagogue life. I remember one Friday evening in particular on which, filing out of a packed and popular Jerusalem shul, I approached the rabbi. The seating structure of the shul was such that the men cannot see the women, and the women watch the men's backs as they lead prayer and read from the Torah. I told the rabbi that I felt like an extra piece of furniture and asked why it would not be possible to divide the seating in a more balanced way. He replied that this was the only way to preserve the sanctity of the space; if the men were able to see the women, the inherent holiness of the synagogue would be compromised.

Others gave different answers, though rarely any that satisfied my nagging discomfort. Some said: Don't you know that as a woman you are on a higher spiritual plane than the men, and therefore need less active involvement with the technicalities of ritual worship? When I would ask, "if I were Rosa Parks and this were a bus, would you still make me sit in the back?" the common response was that having a Torah Scroll in the room makes it different; and furthermore, if you really understood what a Torah Scroll means, you wouldn't feel that way, you wouldn't ask the question.

I tried, for a while, not to ask the question. I tried seeing it their way. But ultimately, the contortions and leaps this kind of seeing demanded of me—the front is not the front, the back is not the back—proved to be too much. Instead of quelling my restless questions, these somewhat Orwellian answers fed and fueled them. My questions became fruitful and multiplied. When is it okay to notice that something is not right? Who gets to define what a problem is?

Of course, presuming you to be crazy if your grasp of reality differs from that of those in power is not a practice exclusive to traditional Judaism. With the rise of a feminist sensibility and its infiltration, in subtle ways, into even very traditional cultures, this dynamic has become a common feature of modern religious life. One of the most pressing questions facing us when approaching the Jewish canonical texts is the missing voice of women. Yet this absence is but one facet of the larger issue of the role and status of women in Judaism. The status quo concerning women has been challenged in most religious communities, each of which has focused on particular aspects of the issue. The developments in feminist theory and practice influenced directly and indirectly the thoughts, hopes, and expectations of Jewish women. Concerns for equality have taken many forms. Some have seceded from the traditional community. Others, following the lead of "liberal feminists,"[1] have demanded to become full members, bringing about institutional changes in various Jewish movements. Women at the crossroads of modernity and tradition began to reexamine their traditional roles and began experimenting with new ones. Traditional representations of Jewish women were no longer acceptable.

In facing our canonical tradition, we are faced with a dilemma. Should religious texts, be treated with awe, accepted uncritically at face value? To what extent can they be reinterpreted and engaged critically? And at what point does such a critical approach prevent us from relating to the tradition as a real and viable one? This predicament is not peculiar to the Jewish religious tradition. Cultural images and norms inherent in other traditions have posed challenges to a variety of fields.[2] Those engaged in the human sciences are also grappling with a patriarchal culture and how it has affected the self-perception of women.[3] Can these scientists engage in disciplines that at best did not hear the voices and experiences of women and that so often relegated women to the role of the "other," less developed half of the human species, with less developed bodies, less developed minds, and a less developed moral sense.

In this chapter I shall present three possible models that can be used to read a religious canon: the reaffirmation model, the reinterpretation/revisionist model, and the rejection model. These models are based on three approaches that women scholars of psychology have applied to the canon of Sigmund Freud, the father of psychoanalysis. Although theology and psychoanalysis on the face of it seem to be very different disciplines (and I am sure that adherents of both traditions will balk and object to the comparison), both created canonical writings that carried with them authority over their adherents. Freud's students and indeed the whole field of psychoanalysis constituted a community of the faithful in which Freud's writings were the canon. It had all the characteristics of a religious community. The psychoanalytic community saw in the interpretation of Freud's writings a key to the innermost secrets of the human psyche, and the sectarian tendencies of this guild manifested itself in the clear demarcation of the insiders from the outsiders. There were believers and heretics. Those who questioned Freud's teachings were excommunicated from psychoanalytic societies.[4]

In addition, both entailed definitions of the self in general and of woman-hood in particular. In the religious tradition various prescriptions of behavior, the allowed and the forbidden, were in large part based upon a presumed understanding of the essence of womanhood. Freud's theoretical construct as well was based on his understanding of the psychology of women. For the women among Freud's disciples, the canon posed a special challenge. Their acceptance of Freudian doctrine was not always easy to reconcile with their experience as women. This dissonance caused unrest among women in the community, which led to various challenges to the canon.

### Reading Freud through the Reaffirmation Model

The psychological legacy of Freud is extensive. This chapter will not pro-vide an extensive survey of Freud's understanding of women and woman-hood.[5] Instead I shall discuss the three aforementioned models as possible re-sponses to Freud's presentation of womanhood. The first model will review the specific case of his patient Emma Eckstein, her subsequent response to him, and the implications this case has on reading, interpreting, and relating to his canon.

Emma Eckstein, a patient of Freud's, suffering from female "hysterical symptoms," underwent an operation on her nose at the hands of Dr. Fleiss, Freud's close friend and confidante. Freud had recommended the operation in keeping with his and Fleiss's theory of the nasal origin of sexual disturbances. The operation was not a success; in fact, complications ensued and Eckstein suffered a near fatal hemorrhage. Freud writes to Fleiss often concerning Emma's condition:[6]

> Eckstein's condition is still unsatisfactory. . . . She had a massive hemor-rhage . . . there were two bowls full of pus. . . . suddenly pulled at some-thing like a thread, kept on pulling. Before either of us had time to think, at least half a meter of gauze had been removed from the cavity. I felt sick. . . . I do not believe it was the blood that overwhelmed me—at that moment strong emotions were welling up in me. So we had done her an in-justice . . . how my intention to do my best for this poor girl was insidi-ously thwarted and resulted in endangering her life. (March 8, 1895)

Freud is dismayed by the results of the failed operation on his "poor" patient. He is remorseful. Soon, however, he becomes encouraged when Emma shows signs of improvement. In particular it is important for him that she still re-mains a faithful patient.

Things are finally going well with Eckstein, as they could have without the detour three weeks ago. It does speak well for her that she did not change her attitude toward either of us; she honors your memory beyond the undesired accident. (March 13, 1895)

Surgically, Eckstein will soon be well, but now the nervous effects of the incident are starting: hysterical attacks at night and similar symptoms which I must start to work on. It is now about time you forgave yourself the minimal oversight, as Breuer called it. (March 15, 1895)

The half-meter of gauze left in her nose had become a "minimal oversight."

She [Eckstein] is doing well; she is a very nice, decent girl who does not hold the affair against either of us and refers to you with great respect. (March 28, 1895)

At this point Freud's description of Eckstein changes radically. She is no longer the poor girl whom he has to pity. In fact the roles have reversed. The victim has turned into the villain.

She, my *tormentor* and yours, appears to be doing well. (April 27, 1985, emphasis mine)

Not only has she become Freud and Fleiss's tormentor, it will be "proven" that she brought about her own suffering and bleeding. Her psychological state caused the bleeding. The "minimal oversight" was insignificant in Eckstein's almost fatal hemorrhage.

First of all Eckstein. I shall be able to prove to you that you were right, that her episodes of bleeding were hysterical, were occasioned by *longing,* and probably occurred at the sexually relevant times (the woman out of resistance has not yet supplied me with the dates). (April 26, 1896)

So far I know only that she bled out of longing. She has always been a bleeder, when cutting herself and in similar circumstances; as a child she suffered from severe nosebleeds; during the years when she was not yet menstruating. She had headaches which were interpreted to her as malingering and which in truth had been generated by suggestion; for this reason she joyously welcomed her severe menstrual bleeding as proof that her illness was genuine, a proof that was also recognized as such by others. She described a scene from the age of fifteen, in which she suddenly began to bleed from the nose when she had the wish to be treated by a certain young doctor who was present and who also appeared in the dream. When she saw how affected I was by her first hemorrhage while she was in the hands of Rosanes, she experienced this as the realization of an old wish to be loved in her illness, and in spite of the danger during the succeeding hours she felt happy as never before. Then, in the sanitarium, she became restless during the night because of an unconscious wish to entice me to go there; since I did not come during the night, she renewed the bleedings, as an un-failed means of rearousing my affection. (May 17, 1896)

Her story is becoming even clearer; there is no doubt that her hemorrhages were due to wishes; she had several similar incidents among them actual simulations in her childhood. (June 4, 1896)

As far as the blood is concerned, you are completely without blame. (January 17, 1897)

These letters reveal Freud's story to Fleiss as he gradually reconstructs Eckstein's illness as one in which she is the agent of her own pathology. She has always been a bleeder. "Eckstein's bleeding in the succeeding letters undergoes a process of hermeneutic transformation until it appears to be self-generated . . . [b]y reconstructing Eckstein's bleeding episodes as hysterical expressions of longing" (Sprengnether 1990, 33–34). Emma resisted telling Freud the dates of her period. Freud interpreted this negatively, claiming she was hiding important information from him. This resistance was however short-lived and very limited. All in all, Eckstein continues to regard Freud in the highest light throughout. Afterward, she trains with Freud to become an analyst herself, working with Freud to expound his—and now her—"truth." Although her life had been put in danger by Fleiss's surgical incompetence, she was to remain one of Freud's most important challenging and faithful patients. She "was to reveal to Freud the interweaving of sadistic fantasy and reality in her mental life. Emma Eckstein had shown Freud the way of the future for both his theory and his professional relations, from shifting from being a patient to an analyst and taking on her own patients for psychoanalytic treatment" (Forrester 1992, 136).[7]

Emma had been degraded, humiliated, and was the victim of medical violation. She had been through physical pain, as a result of a doctor's mistake. In Freud's terms, she moves from a poor patient to a "tormentor" and a hysterical woman who bled to gain affection. The problem is not due to medical incompetence or what was done *to* her; the problem is *within* her. "Freud prepares the ground for a diagnosis of hysterical bleeding, as if to say: her pains are unreal, and the hemorrhages which may have appeared to come from your operation were in fact psychologically caused—they were hysterical in origin, deriving from repressed wishes, not unskilled surgeons" (Masson 1992, 72). Emma had to accept this analysis of her condition in order to become one of Frued's professional colleagues. She goes on to write with him and develop his theories—the very theories that pathologized her, the very theories that ignored a half-meter of gauze left in her nose. Emma to a large extent accepted Freud's perception of who she was. Not only did she have to suppress her feelings, she had to acknowledge that her pains and her bleeding were actually proof of the theory of hysteria.

The result was that she had to go out of relationship with aspects of herself in order to be in relationship with Freud and his theories (see Gilligan 1990 and 1992).[8] She accepted his authority, his reality, and his perception of her experience as proving the basic theory. In order for her to be a part of the structure, in order for her to continue to be a partner in the theoretical framework, she had to accept its definitions of herself. By accepting them, she had to renounce her inner feelings and pain. This approach, the traditional approach, places authority exclusively in the texts and in the writers of the canon. If there is a contradiction between the subjective experience of the patient and the theory, the "problem" lies with the patient. She will be taught that her experience is faulty, and that the problem is thus within her. One does not question the veracity of the theory. The truth is manifest; women must fit themselves to it. In this model the texts are holy ones, immutable, incarnations of the truth. They must be taken at face value. In fact, they define reality. There is no reality other than the wisdom of the sage.

### Reading Freud through the reinterpretation/revisionist model

An adherent of the reinterpretation/revisionist model may well have an appreciation, even at times a commitment, to the existing canon. She will, however, read this canon critically. She may ask questions based on her own subjective experiences. In the case of psychoanalysis those questions concern the way women and girls have been described or ignored by the canon. Some women have challenged the canon's definitions of health and development. These critiques are not necessarily internal to the system: that is, they need not derive from an internal contradiction between the different writings; they may also emerge from new data, new experiences, from hearing and legitimizing new and different voices. The underlying assumption is that there may be flaws in the canon. Questions and critiques are legitimate. These perspectives provide a new lens through which the canon can be read and interpreted. The awareness that a problem exists and the attempt to find an answer within the psychoanalytic tradition and texts is what characterizes the reinterpretive model.

The underlying question is: How can Freud's writings continue to be considered canonical, taken seriously, used as authoritative in spite of seemingly inherent problems (in particular, his perceptions of womanhood)? Freud after all went beyond claiming psychological and biological differences between the genders. He attached values to these differences. Men not only have different superegos but better ones, which privileges them with a more developed sense of morality. According to Freud, women's bodies are inferior: they lack the desired genitalia, and knowledge of this inferiority expresses itself in negative character traits that girls and then women develop (see Freud 1925 and 1931). Feminist psychoanalysts assumed the task of reconciliation between feminist theory and psychoanalytic theory (see, for example, Mitchell 1974). This model incorporates a number of different strategies that address the complex balance of commitment and criticism.

One such strategy is to contextualize Freud. According to this view Freud was inevitably influenced by his historical and cultural context. The reader must then distinguish between the essence of his writing and those aspects that derive from sociocultural influences.

> Out of the strains of sexual life, the political contradictions of an autocratic, feudal court, a rigidly hierarchized society in a rapidly industrializing city, from the particular tension of integrated but rejected Jewry, came probably both widespread neurosis and a high level of particular type of artistic productivity. Certainly its inhabitants saw Vienna this way. . . . Against this background, against these preoccupations, Freud's work on femininity can be set. . . . The prevalent sexual situation, the attitude to femininity, the political position of women were the factors that provided a framework for his questions. (Mitchell 1974, 435)

Because Freud is a product of his culture his readers must distinguish in his theory those pronouncements about women that reflect prevalent attitudes in the society in which he lived from those pronouncements and attitudes that are the essential building blocks of his theory. This strategy then first looks to Freud's times, in order to understand the prevailing attitudes about women and how these became part of Freud's theory and practice. The assumption is, had Freud lived in another time, his theory of gender would be different. The objective then is to determine exactly how. Various hypotheses have been offered for a different picture. The question is whether the whole theory will collapse or whether it is possible to remain true to the general guidelines while changing those elements that are culturally prescribed.

Another strategy distinguishes between two periods of Freud's writing, the "early Freud" and the "late Freud."[9] These two periods in Freud's writings on women are defined to a large extent by the different interpretations Freud gave to hysterical symptoms and to neurosis in his women patients. Originally, Freud believed that the origins of neurosis and hysteria lay in early sexual trauma, usually at the hands of a relative. Later, Freud maintained that those symptoms resulted from the fantasies and imagination of children. He recanted the seduction theory and succumbed to the norms of early twentieth-century Vienna (Masson 1985). "Sexual assaults such as Freud described them in the 1896 papers have been entirely relegated to the fantasy life of the child, or the lies of hysterical women" (Masson 1985, 123). "The stubborn, independent, unsuggestible hysterics who resisted Freud and were his teachers will give way to 'Freud's women' as psychoanalysis internalizes the structures of patriarchy" (Gilligan 1997, 156). "Freud suffered emotional and intellectual isolation as long as he held to the reality of seduction. In accepting the reality of seduction, in believing his patients, Freud was at odds with the whole medical establishment. An act was replaced by an impulse, a deed by a fantasy" (Masson 1985, 113).

At different periods in his life, Freud claimed different things about the psychology of women. This perspective privileges Freud's initial theory, claiming that it is the "true Freud." Any subsequent changes resulted from sociopolitical conditions. The proponents of this reading can thus claim that Freud was initially pro-woman. He listened to women and took their narratives seriously. Women were his teachers about the psychology of women. When he made the connection that bodily symptoms of hysteria were physical expressions of mental ideas, he began listening to what the patient said and observing how she expressed herself. The way to cure is by engaging in a relationship with one's patient in which her experiences are respected and believed (Breuer and Freud 1893–1895).

In this view there is no one Freud. They differ according to different periods and according to context. Freud's writings about women are often contradictory, and there is no reason to grant the problematic texts precedence over the others. For feminist psychologists the nonmisogynist texts are the ones that should be privileged. In this vein theorists such as Shulamith Firestone (1971) call for a partial, piecemeal acceptance of Freud's theory. Furthermore, Mitchell claims that we should not confuse description with prescription. Therefore, "in trying to understand the psychology of women, Freud took into account the specific cultural demands made upon them. It was not his concern whether they were right or wrong, for in this respect he was neither a politician nor a moralist" (Mitchell 1986, 339).

Chodorow, a feminist psychoanalyst, chooses another strategy: revising the existing theory by modifying and reinterpreting it where necessary. She recognizes some of the theory's errors and biases but believes that it should be salvaged because of its essential validity and explanatory power.

> It is a serious mistake, however, to conflate this delimitation of the contribution of psychoanalysis to feminism with a dismissal of its importance. People everywhere have emotions that they care about, connections to others, sexual feelings, and senses of self, self-esteem, and gender. People everywhere form a psyche, self, and identity. These are everywhere profoundly affected by unconscious fantasies as well as by conscious perceptions that begin as early as infancy. Psychoanalysis is the method and theory directed toward the investigation and understanding of how we develop and experience these unconscious fantasies and of how we construct and reconstruct our felt past in the present. Historically, this method and theory have not been applied in a socially or culturally specific manner, but there is not a basic antagonism between psychoanalytic thinking and social specificity. . . . My own project . . . continues to be a project in psychoanalytic feminism, to engage and weave together strands of feminism and of psychoanalysis. (Chodorow 1989, 4–5)

Chodorow claims that feminism can use psychoanalytic theory to explain the social organization of gender. She continues:

> Feminism also wishes to change the social organization and psychology of sex and gender. Its basic argument is that gender and sexuality, whatever the biology that helps to inform these, are created culturally and socially; they are not immutable givens. Therefore, feminism demands a theory of how we became sexed and gendered. Freud has given us such a theory. He has given us a rich account of the organization and reproduction of sex and gender, of how we are produced as gendered and sexed. (168)

Chodorow's defense of the use of a revised psychoanalytic theory does not negate the claim that Freud's writings are in fact misogynist and sexist. Psychoanalysis in both components—theory and practice—is oppressive to women. Chodorow addresses this failure:

First, we have to acknowledge that this criticism is not entirely wrong; Freud was indeed sexist. He wrote basically from a male norm and ignored women. He repeated cultural ideology in a context where it can be mistaken for scientific findings. He talks, for instance, about of women's lesser sense of justice, of their jealousy, shame, vanity, and lack of contribution to civilization as if these were clinical findings, but then claims that these are "character traits which critics of every epoch have brought up against women." He finds it perfectly natural that girls would find their own genitals inferior. . . . Moreover, the evidence seems clear that psychoanalytic theory has been used against women, for instance, when they were labelled frigid because they did not have what turned out to be a non-existent vaginal orgasm, when they were called masculine for wanting careers. (Chodorow 72)

In sum, this revisionist model does not want to throw out the baby with the bathwater. Some say there is only a bit of water, others a tubfull, but all agree that there is a baby. These students of Freud's say he should be read critically. There is no need to justify what appears offensive; rather, we must see in what way these aspects of Freud's writings can be reinterpreted—either by relegating them to a specific time in history, or by relegating them to different periods in Freud's writings. In addition they can be understood by Freud's acknowledged lack of understanding of women.

Freud himself repeatedly stated that his ideas regarding female psychology were incomplete and required further investigation. However, in spite of his caution, the early theory became solidified. . . . In spite of his genius and invaluable contributions, he did not have enough information regarding early preoedipal development in girls, something that he pointed out himself. (Cherazi 1987, 22)

These authors claim that Freud had many important, true insights, but that these insights were misapplied to women. These disciples of Freud say that if they add missing aspects and reinterpret his theory it can and should remain canonical. It will not, of course, be canonical in the same holy sense as the first model where revision is not possible, but it will be important enough to write about, to study, and engage with.

In sum, within this model interpretation is viewed not as uncovering a stable authoritative meaning of the text but rather in a Gadamarian (Gadamer, 1986) sense of "fusion of horizons." In such a model the significance of a text cannot be separated from its meaning. The meaning of the text is produced via an active confrontation and rereading by a reader who brings her sensibilities to bear upon the text.

*Reading Freud through the Rejection Model*

"Dora had listened to me without any of her usual contradictions. She seemed to be moved; she said good-bye to me very warmly, with the heartiest wishes for the New Year, and came no more." Thus comes to an end Freud's analysis of one of his most famous patients, whose case is the topic of *Dora: An Analysis of a Case of Hysteria* (1905).

Dora, a young woman, complains about being used as a pawn, an "object of barter." Her father hands her over to "Herr K," whose wife in turn would be free for himself. Dora refuses to cooperate. Herr K. attempts to embrace Dora twice, and Dora's expression of disgust is seen by Freud as repressed fantasies. It is a sign that she has problems and is sexually frigid. Her disgust is analyzed: it is a sign of pathology because she did not enjoy Herr K.'s advances. During the course of therapy, Freud attempts to convince Dora that his analysis of her true feelings is correct. He interprets her "failure" to experience excitement by Herr K.'s embraces as evidence of pathology and hysteria. He further claims that her repeated noes only represent her desired "yes" ("No signifies the desired yes"; Freud 1905, 76). However, Freud writes "Dora persisted in denying my contention" (77).[10] Dora's persistence in holding on to her own reality and not submitting it to Freud's truth leads her to part ways with Freud. Dora, in a sense, is the counterpoint to Emma Eckstein. The case has been taken up by many researchers of Freud as an example of a woman who resisted accepting a truth about herself or her identity that did not emerge from her inner truth.[11] Just as Dora gets up and leaves, many others have felt it necessary to part ways with Freud.

The implication of Dora's case is that a new psychology must be written to understand human experience and human development. A psychology that labels the sincere subjective truth of a woman as pathological, must be rewritten. It is difficult, unscientific, and undesirable to revise a theory that at its very heart is discriminatory, prejudiced, and inaccurate. Furthermore, a psychology that excludes women is probably not very accurate when it comes to men either. A new theory had to be created to understand "human development." A new theory might be written in relation to the old and might acknowledge the impact of the old. The old theory could still be studied in the context of a history of ideas; nonetheless, something radically new must be written.

This new model incorporates the school of thought that rejects the attempt to revise the problematic theory. Heilbrun (1988) cites Mary Jacobs's insightful comment: "This involves moving from seeing the problem as located within the person if they deviated to seeing the issue as based within the theories themselves. To propose a difference of view, a difference of standard—to begin to ask what the difference might be—is to call in question the very terms which constitute that difference" (40). And Lerman (1986) writes: "Some psychoanalysts are extremely eager to have the glaring problem of psychoanalysis with female development rehabilitated without recognizing that the problem lies at the very heart of the theory" (00). In other words, the issue then is to negate the existing theory, to show its biases, its essential flaws: "The issue is not one of elaborating a new theory of which woman could be the subject or the object but of jamming the theoretical machinery itself, of suspending its pretension to the production of a truth and of a meaning that are excessively univocal" (Irigaray 1977, 78).

This model highlights how building upon a faulty theory will shake the foundations of any new theory. A theory that is contaminated will inevitably contaminate what is written using fundamentals of the faulty presuppositions. In the attempt to fit into the existing theory, major or even minor revisions at the core must still accept the basic tenets of the existing problematic canon. Women, in attempting to fit themselves into a theory that at best marginalized them, whose no was interpreted as yes, would have to go out of relationship with themselves, with what they knew about their own reality, in order to be in relationship with the supposed truths of the canon and its sages. This distortion means removing oneself from definitions, even revised ones, that interpret "the human psyche." "Women come to question the normality of their feelings and to alter their judgments in deference to the opinion of others. . . . Thus a problem in theory became cast as a problem in women's development" (Gilligan 1982, 7 and 16).

This model seeks to show that the problem is in the theory, thereby providing the possibility of saying no. It claims that there is a point where reinterpretation is not the way to proceed in order to understand human development. It does not deny the importance of Freud's writings, but it shows how distorted they were in too many instances. Writing about women as subjects and not objects demands "jamming the theoretical machinery"—creating a new psychology written in "white ink."[12]

In sum, as Dora leaves, she not only rejects Freud's perception; she must begin to write her own story with her own words—perhaps "in a room of her own." Dora dreams that her father is dead. She receives a letter from her mother telling her of the death, and begins an arduous journey home, arriving after everyone has left for the cemetery. Then, climbing the stairs, she "went calmly to her room, and began reading a big book that lay on her writing table" (Freud 1963/1905, 140). Initially Dora forgets this final dream segment—and while Freud focuses on the encyclopedia as signifying Dora's secret pursuit of sexual knowledge, the detail of the writing table suggests that *Dora may now have come to the realization that the encyclopedia does not contain her story and that if she wants her story, her sexual experience, to become knowledge she may have to write it herself* (Gilligan 1997).

## Religious Tradition

The predicament of women facing the psychoanalytic tradition can be translated or is analogous to the predicament of women facing a religious tradition. The complex relation of women psychologists to the legacy of Freud can serve as an example to educators of a religious tradition. As educators, they have the burden and obligation of reproducing or rejecting their tradition, the attitudes of which toward women have been shaped by a patriarchy. And these attitudes pervade the most basic components of the tradition: "The problem runs throughout the course of Jewish history, penetrating the basic theological suppositions of Judaism; its imagery of women and men, its liturgy, its conceptions of the Jewish people and community, its understanding of God as father and King" (Heschel 1983, xl). The core of the problem is: Who is the woman that is written about? In whose image has she been created? With which paintbrush is she painted? What is her designated role and what may she do? In what may she partake and what is forbidden? What is her telos as a human being, as a religious person, and as a woman? In what way is she a member of the society? Is there a monolithic view of womanhood, of the rights and obligations of the woman throughout history?[13]

The role and status of women within the Jewish tradition can be understood through two main perspectives: (1) the normative and legal status of women as prescribed by the legal corpus of Jewish law, the *halakha;* and (2) the images, narratives, and metaphors in the nonlegal components of the tradition, including *aggada,* works of medieval kabbalah and philosophy, and other genres of literature that have been produced throughout the generations.

There is almost no written record of women's perceptions or evaluations of their male-legislated roles. The rare occasions when women's voices are documented, they are recorded by and described through the eyes of male witnesses. If there was a female underground, no trace of it remains. The question of whether Jewish women ever resisted male notions of womanhood and to what extent they internalized their traditional roles will remain unknown and unknowable: works by women (assuming such were produced) were rarely transmitted and never canonized (see, for example, Ozick 1983).

Torah study is perhaps the most important value informing traditional Jewish culture. It is more than an intellectual pursuit; it represents a primary religious moment of intimate encounter with divine revelation. Becoming a scholar of Torah and especially of Talmud was the highest religious aspiration; it is no wonder, therefore, that the scholar became the main authority figure in the community. The institution of the yeshiva—an intense, all-encompassing educational environment—was created in order to produce and nurture this ideal type (see Helmreich 1982; Halbertal and Hartman Halbertal 1998). The yeshiva was not only the main institution of higher learning; it was also a constitutive experience of the intellectual elite. Because of the centrality of this ideal to the tradition, it is vital that we consider the exclusion of women from this area of life (until very recently) in order to gain perspective on the experience of women in Jewish society. In this society, the exclusion of women from Torah study, more than anything else, meant the marginalization of women.

Because this culture was so immersed and influenced by the ongoing interpretation of canonical texts, the institutional exclusion of women from yeshiva life and Torah study prevented women from becoming full and active partners in the life of community. (This exclusion is analogous to the denial of citizenship to women in the Greek polis where the life of the active citizen was regarded as the highest fulfillment of human potential.) Not only did this policy inhibit women from fulfilling their culture's highest achievement; it also blocked them from reaching the positions of authority granted to scholars.

The justification of the prohibition against teaching women Torah extended beyond formal legal reasoning into the domain of myth and ideology. The halakhic ban on teaching women the Oral Law reflected and reinforced a specific psychological portrait of women that for generations provided the ideological rationalization for this policy. Women were seen as the "weaker sex," particularly in terms of their intellectual limitations and sexual proclivities. The stereotypical woman was the victim of her passionate nature. She was vain, sexually vulnerable, and inherently incapable (because of her female "essence") of mastering the intellectual and spiritual disciplines necessary for pursuing the ideal of Torah scholarship. One of the classical justifications of this policy is found in the Mishnah, tractate Sotah (20a):

R. Eliezer says: Whoever teaches his daughter Torah teaches her obscenity.

This Talmudic suggestion makes its way into the law. Maimonides, a twelfth-century luminary writes:

> The Sages have warned us that a man shall not teach his daughter Torah, as the majority of women have not a mind adequate for its study but, because of their limitations, will turn the words of the Torah into trivialities. (Maimonides, M.T. Laws Concerning the study of Torah)[14]

The negative stereotype that justified women's exclusion from the community of scholars and from fulfilling the cultural ideal of the *talmid hacham* (Torah scholar) was reinforced by a positive female ideal that complemented the male ideal of the *talmid chacham*. This ideal emphasizes the virtues of self-sacrifice and self-denial of the woman who is totally devoted to her husband and sons so that they may pursue Torah learning. The archetypal story describing this ideal is about Rachel, the wife of the great second-century rabbinic scholar, Rabbi Akiva.

> R. Akiva was a shepherd of Ben Kalba Sabua. The latter's daughter [Rachel], seeing how modest and noble [the shepherd] was, said to him: "Were I to be betrothed to you, would you go away to study at an academy?" "Yes," he replied. She was then secretly betrothed to him and sent him away. When her father heard about this, he drove her from his house and made a vow forbidding her to have any benefit from his estate.
>
> [R. Akiva] departed and spent twelve years at the academy. When he returned, bringing with him twelve thousand disciples, he overheard an old man saying to her [Rachel]: "How long will you lead the life of a living widow?" "If he would listen to me," she replied, "he would spend another twelve years [at the academy]!" He [R. Akiva] said: "It is with her consent that I am acting" and he departed again and spent another twelve years at the academy.
>
> When he finally returned he brought with him twenty-four thousand disciples. His wife heard [of his arrival] and went out to meet him. When her neighbors said to her: "Borrow some respectable clothes and put them on," she replied: "*A righteous man regardeth the life of his beast*" (Proverbs 12:10). On approaching him, she fell upon her face and kissed his feet. His attendants were about to thrust her aside, when [R. Akiva] cried out to them: "Leave her alone! All that is mine and yours is hers." (T.B. Ketubot, 62b–63a.)

Rachel's self-sacrifice and devotion to Akiva was and continues to be the archetype of ideal womanhood in traditional Jewish society (see Rappaport, Penso, and Hartman Halbertal, 1996).

Because the issue of Talmud Torah is so crucial, I shall focus on three models of approaching a foundational story—that of Beruriah—relating to the place of women in the community of learning. My discussion does not aim to analyze the legal status of women learning Torah (see, for example, Brown 1997; Wolowelsky 2001). I shall examine three models that can serve as paradigms for relating to traditional texts. I am using this story as an example of the issue of women learning and the different readings possible. As Emma learns of herself, as Dora resists learning about herself, and as Mitchell (1974) and Chodorow (1978 and 1989) negotiate with the texts, so too can different readings lead either to compliance, resistance, rejection, or negotiation with the message of the story of Beruriah. Beruriah, the wife of Rabbi Meir, lived in the second century and was widely recognized as a learned and well-versed woman. We learn about her from different talmudic sources.

In the Talmud Erubin (53b-54a) it is written:

> R. Jose, the Galilean, was once on a journey when he met Beruriah. "By what road," he asked her, "do we go to Lydda?"—"Foolish Galilean," she replied, "Did not the sages say this: Engage not in much talk with women? You should have asked: By which to Lydda?"

In this story Beruriah admonishes R. Jose, who attempts to engage her in a more lengthy discussion than is necessary. The story can also be interpreted to mean that R. Jose is asking her to come with him (the emphasis is on *we*). She rejects his offer and continues to admonish him, using classical statements of the sages to prove that discussion with women is prohibited because of modesty. She is here an example of a learned and modest woman. The Talmud continues with another story about her:

> Beruriah once discovered a student who was learning in an undertone. Rebuking him, she exclaimed, Is it not written *Ordered in all things and sure?* If it is *ordered* in your two hundred and forty-eight limbs it will be *sure,* otherwise it will not be sure?

Here Beruriah is rebuking a Talmud scholar for not learning in the correct manner. Again the Talmud brings in Beruriah as being superior to a Talmud scholar.

In a third and fourth story, we see Beruriah differing with her husband's interpretation of Biblical verses.

There were once some highwaymen in the neighborhood of R. Meir who caused him a great deal of trouble. R. Meir accordingly prayed that they should die. His wife, Beruriah, said to him: How do you make out that such a prayer should be permitted? Because it is written, Let *hatta'im* cease? Is it written *hot'im*? It is written *hatta'im!* Further look at the end of the verse: *and let the wicked men be no more.* Because the sins will cease, there will be no more wicked men! Rather, pray for them that they should repent, and there will be no more wickedness. He did pray for them, and they repented. (Berachot 9b–10a)

A certain *min* said to Beruriah: It is written: *Sing O barren thou that didst not bear.* Because she did not bear is she to sing? She replied to him: You fool! Look at the end of the verse, where it is written, *For the children of the desolate shall be more that the children of the married wife, saith the Lord.* But what then is the meaning of "*a barren that did not bear?*" Sing O community of Israel, who resembles a barren woman, for not having born children like you for Gehenna. (Berakoth 10a, emphasis mine)

Beruriah in the Talmud is the exception to any of the rules concerning women's intelligence and abilities to study. She is portrayed as having superior intellectual and moral attributes, superior to many of the scholars or rabbis.

Although Beruriah is portrayed in the Talmudic tradition unambiguously, later sources depicting the way her life ended open deep questions about the tradition's actual view of her. The Talmud mentions cryptically that R. Meir fled because of "Beruriah's deed." Rashi (1040–1105), the commentator on the Talmud, recounts the following story concerning "the deed:"

*Some say it is because of the story of Beruria:* Because she once made fun of the saying of the sages: "Women are weak-minded." R. Meir (her husband) said to her: "By your life, you will end up admitting [the truth of] their words." He then commanded one of his students to seduce her for the purpose of sinning. The student enticed her for many days until she submitted and when she found out [the true story], she strangled herself. Rabbi Meir then left for Babylon out of shame. (T.B., Avodah Zarah, 18b)

Met with the dissonance between the "weak-minded" woman and the woman whose erudition is superior to that of men, what is our legacy of Beruriah? Gleaning from the models for reading inside the Freudian canon I shall present three similar kinds of possible interpretations of the story of Beruriah and their subsequent relationship to the creation of the tradition.

## Reading Beruriah through the Reaffirmation Model

In reaffirming the traditional role of women, proponents of the reaffirmation model will use the story of Beruriah as an example of a woman whom we are *not* to be, whom we do not want to be. The tradition claimed that women were not to study Talmud, they were not to be a part of Judaism's intellectual and cultural endeavor. This endeavor is designated for men only. It is based on the different nature of women. *She* is different, she is "da'ta kala" (weak-minded); not only are her intellectual capabilities inferior, her psychology is different, and she is ruled by uncontrollable sexual urges. Her difference is an excuse for her exclusion. This image should never be challenged. Women must internalize these truths about themselves. If a woman has any doubts about this description of womanhood, she should go look at what happened to Beruriah. She is an example of a woman who crossed the barrier that should not be crossed. "Beruria came to a bad end . . . her sin was the direct result of her abnormal scholarship" (Adler 1983, 14).

Beruriah is taught then as a warning to those who think they can challenge the truths laid down by the tradition about women. She carries the shame of what happens when one thinks she is special and can do something not pre-scribed by the tradition. The story of Beruriah is a way to make women them-selves reaffirm their exclusion from the "beit midrash" (the hall of study). The alternative to the normative model of womanhood is Beruriah herself, who defied the "natural" place of the woman. Her role in life, her self-understanding was not to enable her spouse to study (like that of Rabbi Akiva's wife), but to herself partake of the holy of holies. Her true nature, however, could not be suppressed for that long. After scratching the surface, she herself realized her true nature and was taught a lesson.

As women, we must learn the lesson of Beruriah. As Emma learns of her true nature from the psychological tradition, women after her learn about the nature of hysteria, the relationship between physiology and psychology, the relationship between the all-knowing sage and the perception of self. Women learn of their intellectual capabilities and their psychological predispositions from the prohibitions about women's learning in general and from the story of Beruriah in particular. There is no room for resistance. The circle is closed; the aberration is temporary. The story that was posed to undermine the challenge to the system by the image of Beruriah shows that Beruriah is a "woman like all women"; she is "weak-minded." The disorder that Beruriah seemed to present has been returned to order.

## Reading Beruriah through the Reinterpretive Model

Contextualizing Beruriah's story in history is one way to deal with the problematics of its message. Such a contextualization accepts the previous reading but empties it of its direct authority and legitimacy in defining the nature of womanhood. Instead, it rereads the text. There are many ways to reread and revisit a text. I shall point out one such possibility where Beruriah is an example of a learned woman first and foremost. All statements about women's inferior intellectual abilities are shaken by the very existence of such an extraordinary intelligent woman. She is mentioned in the Talmud in the context of her exceptional religious/moral/modest and intellectual capabilities, which are often superior to those of her male counterparts.

The tradition is thus aware of women's abilities. This tradition can be contrasted to those that speak derogatorily of women. Beruriah is the exception to the rule that sheds light on the rule as well. She runs counter to tradition, demonstrating "that patriarchy was never absolute and controlling but only one element in a multitude of conflicting voices" (S. Heschel 1983, xxii). The story of Beruriah and her husband can be taught as a voice in the tradition that poses a deep criticism of men in general—and R. Meir in particular. Men's cruelty in reaffirming their exclusivity brings about death. It teaches us how threatened men were in the face of "real" competition to their male hegemony and to what extremes they were willing to go to uphold this hegemony. The story of Beruriah is an aberration, where the tradition criticizes a man who feels so threatened by a woman's knowledge that he will push her to suicide and make his student transgress a *halakha* (that is just as much punishable by death), simply to preserve male exclusivity. The text specifically states that she withstood the advances many days. She commits suicide when she hears it was her husband who set her up. The breach of that trust sent her to her own death. She is the heroine in the story.[15] Yet R. Meir as well is the subject of the story. His zealousness to maintain the supremacy of the patriarchy is subject to deep criticism, and he must run away. He fails to maintain his world order and was displaced by his cruel effort to affirm his place.

This reading, unlike the first one, is a message to *men* to *allow* women's voices and strengths to surface. The attempt to silence will lead to the silencing of voices altogether, and men as well must then be silenced and exit. The story unmasks one of the ultimate heroes of the tradition, Rabbi Meir, who failed, who is shamed by his need to shame another. Men trying to prove that women are "weak-minded" become themselves weak-minded, blinded to all reality except to prove a point. The strong male is portrayed here as weak and manipulative. Beruriah, at the end had the dignity, grace, and strength to kill herself. (She may also have killed herself because she knew the law regarding infidelity and punished herself according to Jewish law. It is interesting that she strangles herself, which is the prescribed punishment for infidelity. The story of Beruriah thus ends with the text continuing to compliment her.) The great Rabbi Meir—whose crime should be punishable as well—merely and meekly runs away.

This model thus suggests a reading of Beruriah in which she is consistently regarded as a supreme intellect. It stresses the dangers of men trying to force their supremacy. At the end, there is no place for men either. All will be destroyed when men attempt to silence women.

The importance of rereading Beruriah is that it keeps alive another voice in the tradition. There are other paradigms besides the dominant one. Maintaining the complexity of the different readings enables "an acknowledgment of the structural possibility within the culture that a woman could achieve such knowledge of Torah as to be authoritatively cited in an important question of ritual practice . . . a counter hegemonic voice that recognizes the reality of some women's intellectual and spiritual accomplishment" (Boyarin 1993, 183).

### Reading Beruriah through the Rejection Model

The story of Beruriah is an example of the distorted imagery of women. These texts reveal that this tradition was written by men for men. There is a narrative of history that has excluded women. Man is the subject, women is the "Other" (see de Beauvoir 1949):

> De Beauvoir's analysis provides a key to women's silence within Judaism, for, like women in many cultures, Jewish women have been projected as Other. Named by a male community that perceives itself as normative, women are part of the Jewish tradition without its sources and structures reflecting our experience. Women are Jews, but we do not define Jewishness. We live, work, and struggle, but our experiences are not recorded, and what is recorded formulates our experiences in male terms. (Plaskow 1990, 3)

In whose interest is this story told? It is told in order to maintain the world order and culture created by men. The expulsion of women from Torah learning meant that the culture was written by men to serve men's interests and power. In the interest of the patriarchy women could not be granted entrance or any shared power.

> Once a group is defined as inferior, the superiors tend to label it as defective or substandard in various ways. These labels accrete rapidly. . . . Women are supposed to be ruled by emotion. . . . Dominant groups usually define one or more acceptable roles for the subordinate. . . . Functions that a dominant group prefers to perform are carefully guarded and closed to subordinates. Out of the total range of human possibilities, the activities most highly valued in any particular culture will tend to be enclosed within the domain of the dominant group; less valued functions are relegated to the subordinates. Subordinates are usually said to be unable to perform the preferred roles. Their incapacities are ascribed to innate defects or deficiencies of mind or body, therefore immutable and impossible of change or development. It becomes difficult for dominants even to imagine that subordinates are capable of performing the preferred activities. More importantly subordinates themselves can come to find it difficult to believe in their own ability. (Miller 1976, 6–7)

The exclusion of women is based on a system of dominants and subordinates. The dominants have decided that women will have no part in the important endeavors of its culture. The learning of Torah is a right that has not been given to women. Moreover this "right" is one of the central components of the culture. The exclusion of women from Torah study means that they are excluded from the major religious discourse. They are excluded from writing the culture, from creating and re-creating their tradition. They thus must inherit a tradition that they have had no part in creating. At times they may be granted certain rights, in some groups more than others, but they are not privy to the central component of the very creation of their culture. The highest religious achievement and goal of their religion is barred for them.

There are, of course, "reasons" for this exclusion. Beruriah is the example of a woman who thought she could partake in what was granted only to the dominants; her story, however, maintains the stronghold of the dominant group. It is interesting that the Talmud itself testifies to the existence of voices from the underground. In this case, a woman known for her Torah scholarship negates the classic rabbinic denigration of women's rational capacities. The conclusion of the story nonetheless turns the voice of resistance against itself, by forcing Beruria to face the reality of her female nature and thus acknowledge the truth of the rabbinic claim about women's inherent weakness. The tradition's message is thus clear:

The horror of her end, the extraordinary lengths to which the text goes, even defaming one of its greatest heroes to achieve its purpose, is once again a symptom of the extraordinary threat that the learned woman represented to the Babylonian and later European rabbinic culture, a power that threatened to upset the whole applecart of gender relations and social organization and that had to be suppressed, therefore, by extraordinary means. (Boyarin 1993, 189)

This model stresses then that the tradition leaves no choice but rejection; its divisions between the privileged class and the nonprivileged class, its discrimination with all of its ramifications, cannot be merely mended. A tradition that has excluded woman's voices and experiences from its creation cannot merely accord a few extra privileges to women. It must be fundamentally changed.

Lowering the mehitzah a few inches or permitting a woman to say the blessing over bread in her home on the Sabbath are acceptable changes as long as they can be justified according to the rules and methods of halachah and so avoid any challenge to its inviolability. Yet that approach hardly represents a feminist perspective, inasmuch as it perpetuates women's dependence on a legal system conceived and operated entirely by men. Regardless of how many laws can be "legally" changed there remains the very real probability of hitting a stumbling block, such as the very existence of the mehitzah altogether. (S. Heschel 1983, xliv)

Separating men from women and then granting men the powers to affirm their superiority are symptoms of a tradition that cannot be mended by piecemeal engineering.[16]

## Conclusion

I have presented these three models as independent and mutually exclusive models. Theoretically these models stand as independent and distinct. In life, however, they are often intertwined. We can glean from the above three models the following options.[17] There is a serious and large community that adheres to the first model. There is an extensive body of literature, although not always monolithic, whose main theme repeats itself: the role of woman is to enable her husband to achieve the highest religious telos in the community. If it is written, it reflects a truth. There is no legitimacy in the subjective experience of the girl or the woman. If she does not fit into the mold, then the problem is within her. She will be reeducated and taught to conform, not only to conform behaviorally but to accept the whole gestalt. The veracity and legitimacy of the texts is unquestionable. The definitions of her womanhood are clear. She learns about them from the canonical texts.

The third model takes these texts more or less at face value; therefore they must be on the whole rejected. The texts may be taught as a study in cultural history as it is a culture that has impacted history and still impacts large portions of the Jewish people. It is however, inherently flawed. It defines the women's role as enabling men to achieve religious, spiritual, and intellectual excellence. In this capacity she is righteous and blessed. If this role is at risk of being challenged, then it becomes the justification for exclusionary practices. The tradition is sexist, at best excluding the women's perspective. While there are remote glimpses of alternative images of woman, these voices are also peripheral. Too often the tradition is misogynist, degrading to women as people, to their minds and bodies, and to their spirit.

In short, it is an unjust system, discriminatory in its cultural images, its description of woman, of her nature, and of her spiritual and intellectual capabilities—all of which affect her legal status, her sense of self. How can one maintain and develop a sense of self if the definitions of self are incongruous with her inner world? How can a woman reading herself in the tradition "maintain a coherent inner world within an outer world that is patriarchal? How can women breathe psychologically within this civilization?" (Gilligan 1997, 151). Above all, it is a culture written by men for men, women have had no part in the creation of this culture. These texts should be studied to understand how it came to be that women's status is as it is, to understand what must be overcome in order to begin to write their own story in various forms. "We need to know the writing of the past, and know it differently than we have ever known it; not to pass on a tradition but to break its hold over us" (Rich 1979, 35).

The second model remains with the tradition in an attempt to salvage it. It revisits the tradition with different lenses. It claims a link with a long tradition of reinterpretation. As in the feminist psychoanalytic position, there are many facets of the second model. The common thread, however, is the drive to continue to study the texts and to appreciate their formative role in the shaping of the tradition; the model stresses the subjective analysis of the reader and enables her to continue the long history of interpretation and reinterpretation. These different ways can include realizing women's voices more prominently within the tradition or revising the system in light of women's experiences. The impetus may stem from a commitment to the tradition, to an appreciation to what it has contributed, or "simply because of habit or sentimental attachment, or . . . because they want to remain faithful to what for them has been an experience of truth" (Berger 1979, 92–93).

This second model is the most compelling one in Jewish education. It challenges its adherents to be in a constant state of engaging and reengaging with the traditional texts. Revisiting them through different lenses creates a dynamic dialogue with the tradition.

> Readers as diverse as Adrienne Rich and Harold Bloom have arrived, by various routes, at the conclusion that re-vision constitutes the key to an ongoing literary history. Whether functioning as ephebe/poet or would-be critic, Bloom's reader, as "revisionist," strives to see again, so as to esteem and estimate differently, so as then to aim correlatively. . . . For Rich, revision entails "the act of looking back, of seeing with fresh eyes, of entering an old text from a new critical direction." (Kolodony 1985, 258)

Following Rich and Bloom, this revisionist model enables the reexamining[18] of texts with "fresh eyes." This model offers the possibility of maintaining a serious, live, and ongoing dialogue with the canonical texts, but in a critical fashion. Whether through examining a historical and cultural context, using the various sources to explicate others, or simply reinterpreting, this model empowers its adherents to continue to relate to their tradition as significant. Rereading is legitimate; in fact, the text as it is written and the different forms in which it is written, enables this multitude of interpretations.

Those who waver between the problematics of the traditional images and seek alternative images may also ask a fundamental question: Can one leave the tradition, reject it and still assume—that one can write and create in an intellectual vacuum and create *yesh mi'ayin*—ex nihilo. Can Dora in fact write her own story? How isolated is the room of her own? The milk from women's breasts that will produce Rich's white ink has been suckled by children growing in this world.

> Many of us are under the impression that all we have to do is not enter a church, refuse to practice the sacraments, and never read the sacred texts in order to be free from the influence of religion in our lives. . . . This does not solve the problem of how significant is the influence of religion upon culture. Thus we are all imbued with the many Greek, Latin, Oriental, Jewish, and Christian traditions, at least, particularly through the art, philosophy, and myths we live by, exchange, and perpetuate, often without our realizing. The passage from one era to the next cannot be made simply by negating what already exists. (Irigaray 1993, 23)

This perspective claims that Judaism is patriarchal in a larger patriarchal world. The underlying belief is that if we can point to these places that are not endemic to the tradition but that only reflect prevalent attitudes and beliefs vis-à-vis gender, we can reread our texts and reclaim them. "If Judaism is patriarchal I do not believe there is any nonpatriarchal space to which I can go to create a new religion. It is true that women who move outside traditional religions dispense with the need to deal with certain arguments and institutions that drain feminist energy" (Plaskow 1990, xiii).

Facing the culture does not only entail the examination of the rights or lack of rights given to minorities. The missing voice of women in the creation of their tradition has far-reaching implications. If women's perspectives have not been integral to the creating of the tradition, then how does the tradition continue to be viable and compelling to generations of people who maintain that this perspective is crucial? Exploring these three approaches to the texts opens a discussion about how to deal with women's place in the present or the future, as well as our relationship to our past, to our canon. These three options and the comparison with the psychoanalytic tradition speak to women's predicament and our ability to adopt, reject, and negotiate with the traditions that have shaped and written our identity.

In a sense, those who reaffirm, those who reject, and those who reinterpret Jewish tradition are all challenging contemporary religious communities. But only reinterpreters constitute a community that is bound together not by their solutions to different religious problems but by accepting the validity of the questions. The reaffirmation model says I am crazy for having such questions; the rejection model says I am crazy for thinking they could ever be answered. Reinterpreters stand together in the problem, irrespective of the solutions pursued or proposed. This formulation puts Shirah Hadashah, for example, in community with both full egalitarians as well as those who do not feel comfortable altering synagogue ritual, but who do allow the issue to permeate their consciousness.

# 3 | MODESTY AND THE RELIGIOUS MALE GAZE

One of the main sources of resistance to egalitarian shifts within Modern Orthodox synagogue life is found in the discourse of *tzniut* (modesty). This conversation takes a number of different forms, and in the process of starting Shirah Hadashah we encountered all of them—and some we had not previously known or thought of. *Kol Isha,* the sensuality of a woman's singing voice, *Mechitza* the physical divider that separates the sexes in the synagogue, and the saying '*Kol K'vuda Bat Melech Penimah,*' the dignity of a princess is internal—all reflect an anxiety about how increased women's public activity, with its heightened level of intermingling and exposure, will affect the social dynamics of the congregation. Of particular concern is how it will impact the spiritual lives of the community's men. Moreover, the various terms in the lexicon of modesty are all employed to a more or less common end: to discourage women from legitimating, much less expressing, spiritual needs within the communal context.

This discourse participates in a broader conversation about modesty, not only within Modern Orthodoxy but cross-culturally as well. Many traditionalist religions perceive a breakdown of traditional values and norms in mainstream Western society. Nowhere is this critique sharper than around issues of sexuality, in particular, the public display of women's bodies. For women, this often involves exhortations from (usually male) authorities to accept and/or reaffirm their roles as sexual gatekeepers, with rhetoric running the spectrum from exultation of the unique feminine sanctity that requires hiddenness; to appeals to take responsibility for the spiritual well-being of their male counterparts; to threats of punishment (both this- and otherworldly) if rigorous modesty standards are not upheld. The claim is often heard that Western society only wants to undress its women so that they can be made available for the pleasure of men. (Indeed, this criticism resonates deeply with many feminist cultural analyses.) Traditional religions often present themselves as an alternative to this dissolute culture of rapacious debauchment, as a place of resistance to Western imperialism, and a safe haven. They claim to neutralize the West's obsession with women's bodies, focusing instead on the person in her entirety. In response to the West's undressing of women, fundamentalist religions urge women to cover up and reclaim what has been taken from them: a lost sense of honor, dignity, and integrity.

This discourse operates under the general heading of "modesty," and various current manifestations of Orthodox Judaism partake in it. In analyzing how modesty is framed within Orthodox Jewish discourse, much can be learned about underlying ideologies regarding women, men, and relations between the sexes. To this end, I shall examine the discourse of modesty within the Orthodox Jewish community, both providing background on how the concept has been variously constructed throughout history and analyzing its current usage in a fast-growing genre of texts devoted exclusively or primarily to this topic.

In the course of my analysis, I shall demonstrate that, despite being framed as the antithesis of Western values, religious discourse, and even practice, preserves *precisely* those unsavory elements with which it claims to be at war. Presented as a return to integrity, religious discourse actually strips women of even the most basic bodily integrity, constructing them as a collection of parts. The essentials—a pervasive male gaze observing, evaluating, deconstructing and compulsively speaking about women's bodies in such painstaking detail—all remain in force. The changes the religious discourse makes— from any substantive perspective and certainly from the perspectives of the women upon whom its authority exerts force—are quite superficial and ultimately little more than cosmetic.

### Background

A plethora of books have been published within the last ten years that deal extensively with the issue of modesty (*tzniut*) from both Jewish legal (halakhic) and philosophical perspectives. Conventional wisdom within the Orthodox Jewish community has assigned a simple explanation to this trend: the recent fervor surrounding *tzniut* represents a necessary response to the progressive erosion of even the most basic standards of modesty within contemporary Western culture. According to this logic, the spike in the discourse is a gesture toward making sense of a rapidly changing world. Most important, it is an act of resistance: a stopgap attempt to protect their communities from the corrosive effects of an exhibitionism that in modern secular culture has become more or less the norm.

It is precisely in this context that many Orthodox women have taken up the mantle of *tzniut* as a vehicle of neofeminist empowerment (Manolson 1997). A similar attitude can be found within the discourse of modern religious Muslim women, who view themselves in a position analogous to that of Orthodox

Jewish women. During the 1979 revolution in Iran, Iranian women from the middle class decided to wear the veil in solidarity with women in the working-class. In this case, wearing the veil was an act of resistance and protest (Mohanty 1988). In the face of a corrosive and corruptive Western ethos, one that seems interested only in uncovering women for the pleasure of men, the act of covering oneself is framed as a subversion of the dominant culture's insidious designs on women's bodies—an embodiment of female power and pride.

> Partly in reaction against Western liberation and Western ideals in general, women in many parts of the Islamic world are self-consciously adopting forms of dress by which they can identify with Islam rather than what they now see as the imperialist West. Islamic dress . . . signals for many an identification with a way of life that they are increasingly convinced represents a more viable alternative than that offered by the West. (Smith 1987, 242)

Here then, one finds a coherent explanation for the swelling discourse of *tzniut* in the Orthodox world, which in recent years has steadily escalated in frequency, fervency, and pitch. On its surface, the discourse is compelling: the clear-cut wickedness of the encroaching enemy whose express intent is to undress their women and girls; the heroism of the stand taken against him; and finally, the ideal of *tzniut* itself. Downplaying people's more superficial attributes in favor of their inner qualities emerges as a defining value within Jewish sources—one not only worthy, but critical to pursue. The following quote is taken from an essay found in a textbook from an Orthodox girls' secondary school:

> The quality of a person is his/her inner life, because "this is the entirety of a person" (Numbers 32). A person is not a collection of limbs: eyes, arms, etc. A person is not the external attributes by which, more often than not, he/she is characterized . . . but rather, the fullness of his/her personality and the integrity of self. And it is the development of the self which is the fundamental task incumbent upon all of us. (Ariel 2000, 62)

From here, an idealized model of *tzniut* emerges that figures modesty as the process though which one achieves a kind of profound spiritual self-actualization. Combined with the promises of personal empowerment and cultural subversion outlined above, one can better understand why *tzniut* has come to be identified as such a compelling virtue among contemporary Modern Orthodox women.

This model, however, presents a host of internal contradictions that, even if noticed, are rarely pointed out. In fact, a closer look at these sources of *tzniut* (which are often presented as answers to questions posed by modern Jewish women) causes other, deeper questions to become increasingly exposed. One need not challenge or even discuss the philosophical merits of modesty per se; what is striking is how little these ideals have to do with how, both historically and currently, modesty has been constructed by religious authorities and texts.

First of all, the call to look inward for the true indices of one's identity and growth—rather than to, for example, our body parts—bears reexamination. If this ideal is appealing, it is appealing precisely because of its universal applicability, the implicit equivalency of men and women's respective inner lives, and the types of relationships with self and others this spiritually democratizing focus evokes. This attractive idea begins to seem disjointed, indeed disembodied, when one begins to consider, for example, common usage. In contemporary Orthodox Jewish jargon, the term *tzniut* is used to apply (perhaps not exclusively but primarily) to the responsibilities of religious women and girls, through their behavior and especially through their dress, to mute the inexorably arousing effects of their feminine presence on the overweening sex drives of the men around them.

How did *tzniut* make this harrowing transition from spiritual aspiration to muffling mechanism for the repression of female physicality? Why is it that in the essay from the textbook quoted above (Shwartzbaum and Sadlan, 2000), the proclamation of the universal transformative potential of *tzniut* is followed directly by the question, "Is the essence of a woman her body or her soul?" without a parallel inquiry into the implications of modesty for men? The question of why such a one-sided leap is considered even logical—to say nothing of valid—is not only unanswered; it is never asked. Furthermore, why is this textbook required reading in schools for Orthodox women and girls and not in male institutions of Jewish learning? Why is the vast majority of the literary output dealing with *tzniut* addressed to a female audience and marketed (in light of the above, quite shrewdly) almost exclusively to a readership of women? And finally, why, in the vast majority of cases, are the writers of these publications not women? Why, for example, of the thirty-one articles that constitute this textbook, are twenty-seven authored by men?

Foucault (1980) suggests a compelling explanation for similar trends of heightened cultural output, expressing amusement about a society that spoke endlessly, floridly, and provocatively about its sexual repression. Orthodox women can perhaps detect a similar (if inverted) irony in the case of religious men speaking incessantly, and with great specificity—down to the finger, at times even the joint—about which areas of a woman are most arousing and why—all in the name of decrying the insidious inroads of prurience and lasciviousness into their communities. In one recent book, the subject of *tzniut* is broken down into chapter headings, each of which takes the name of a different female body part to be explored in meticulous halakhic detail (Aviner 1983; Ellinson 1992). Another contains illustrations of problematic body parts—collarbones, for example—in increasing states of undress: methodically mapping the halakhic status of the neckline's progressive plunge (Falk 1998). As Foucault writes: "What is peculiar to modern societies, in fact, is not that they consigned sex to a shadow existence, but that they dedicated themselves to speaking of it ad infinitum, while exploiting it as the secret" (1980, 35).

Following Foucault, one must hold out the possibility that to speak so stridently and ceaselessly of the need to cover itself reflects a kind of fervent immodesty that may well be a symptom of the very "problem" it proposes to address. Indeed, it seems increasingly likely that the current discourse is being defined by men—both rabbis and laypeople—in whose tone can be detected a heightened level of stimulation that reflects, one suspects, not only an antagonism to Western immodesty, but an implicit surrender to its corrupting effects. In order better to understand the current usage of *tzniut* within Orthodox culture generally (and particularly within rabbinic discourse), it is necessary to look more closely at the means and motivations by which Judaism has historically understood and implemented the value that women be covered—and at the means by which contemporary Western society currently and systematically demands its women to be uncovered.

## Motivations for Covering

### SHAME AND CONTAINMENT

One paradigm that for centuries served as an anchor for the justification of keeping women covered equated the female with raw physicality, consequently projecting her as the embodiment of a dangerous and chaotic sexuality that, for the good of civilization, required constant reining in. Many traditional sources speak explicitly of the need for women to cover themselves out of shame. One finds a pointed example in a canonical rabbinic literary compendium: "Why does the man go out bareheaded but the woman with her head covered? He said to them, it is like one who has committed a sin, and he is ashamed in front of others: therefore she goes out covered" (Bereshit Rabba, chap. 17). This midrash is taken from a list in which the "sin" referred to is the sin of Eve causing Adam to eat from the Tree of Good and Evil, which is equated with spilling his blood and ushering death into the world. This inter-

pretive tradition extends the shame of Eve's original act to all women throughout all time, and in so doing transforms it into an essential condition of womanhood. Whatever quality caused Eve to sin, and whatever consequence the
sin exacted upon her ontology, lives on in her female progeny like a dominant
spiritual gene.

It only follows that someone living within a haze of primordial shame
would want to cover herself when going out to face the world "she" has defiled.
It follows even more strongly, of course, that such a person would not want to
go out at all. It also follows that her male counterparts, direct descendants of
Adam, would find it in their best interest to keep her circumscribed. For if the
sin of Eve indeed is not merely history but a live present threat, in constant
danger of being reenacted, then suffice it to say, the temptress must be contained.

It is thus that Aristotle, having gone to tortuous lengths to prove the biological and ontological inferiority of women to men, considered it "natural"
that women be debarred from citizenship and active participation in his "final
and perfect association," that is, the polis. "The male is by nature superior, and
the female inferior; and thus one rules, and the other is ruled; this principle,
of necessity extends to all mankind"; "The male is by nature fitter for command than the female, just as the elder and full-grown is superior to the young
and more immature"; "All classes must be deemed to have their special attributes; as the poet [Sophocles] says of women 'Silence is a woman's glory,' but
this is not equally the glory of man" (Aristotle, *Politics*, book 1, part 5). "For the
female is, as it were, a mutilated male . . . for there is only one thing they have
not in them, the principle of the soul" (Aristotle, *On the Generation of Ani-
mals*, book II: 3 737a).

A dominant strain of both ancient and medieval Jewish thought identified
woman schematically with physicality, with matter—this in explicit opposition to man, whose true nature could be found in his intellect and/or soul. De
Beauvoir put it sharply and succinctly: "Woman has ovaries, a uterus; these
peculiarities . . . circumscribe her within the limits of her own nature. . . .
Man superbly ignores the fact that his anatomy also includes glands" (de
Beauvoir 1949, xxi). Man in contrast perceives himself as the "inevitable, like
a pure idea, like the One, the All, the Absolute Spirit" (146).

This Platonic paradigm, espoused by Philo and reclaimed with a vengeance
by Maimonides, regarded woman as animalistically oversexed, incapable of
controlling her base urges, whereas the "real man" was seen as impenetrably in
control, serene governor of all things physical—including, but not limited to,
his own body. Woman's putative vulnerability to her sexual urges served not

only as a sign of her inferiority to man; it embodied precisely the type of base physicality he was to contain. It is in the service of this containment that much of the relegation of woman to the private sphere, and the demand that she cover herself extensively when in public, can be understood. The traditional view of woman as a sexual temptress (Eve, Delilah, Salome) is portrayed in secular culture in films such as *Fatal Attraction* and *Presumed Innocent* and the bitch characters of soap operas (Bordo 1993). The "depiction of women as continually and actively luring men to arousal . . . work to disclaim male ownership of the body and its desires. The arousal of those desires is the result of female manipulation and therefore is the woman's fault" (Bordo 1993, 6).

It is a result of this strain of containment within Jewish tradition, and the misogynistic legacy it has left behind, that feminist critics of traditional Judaism can find substantive basis for their claim that vis-à-vis Jewish men, "woman looms as a potential source of pollution and disorder whose life and impact on men must be regulated" (Baskin 1985, 14); that "it is difficult to conclude anything other than that women are a source of moral danger and incitement to depravity and lust" (Plaskow 1990, 184–185); and that the laws of female covering and containment "contribute to a sense of female inferiority and male superiority" (Swidler 1976, 138).

## SAMSON THE NEBBISH: THE RELIGIOUS MALE GAZE

If the Platonic dichotomy of man-as-spirit versus woman-as-matter (see Boyarin 1993) rings somewhat archaically in modern ears, that is because, as a strain of thought—and hence a justification for the comprehensive covering of women—it has more or less fallen out of style. To say it was abandoned would be an overstatement; as a trend of thought it still exists with varying levels of authority within different communities and cultures (and of course within countless extant texts). Overall, though, its prevalence has waned, replaced as modesty's raison d'être by none other than its inverse. The tendency to view men as volatile compounds of primal longing and hormonal lust, and women as inertly dignified creatures of a higher evolutionary stripe—favoring relationship, disdainful of baseness, and immune to stark physical desire—is a trend with a pedigree equal to that of its predecessor.

The central dynamic within the contemporary Orthodox world, defining how and why women's bodies are covered, is one that feminist critics isolated and taxonomized with respect to Western culture almost two decades ago. It is within the strictures and specifications of an all-encompassing "male gaze" that women's bodies are evaluated, regulated and defined—not only with respect to the men watching them, but for themselves (Mulvey 1989).

Standards of beauty describe in precise terms the relationship that a woman will have to her own body. They prescribe her motility, spontaneity, posture, gait, the uses to which she can put her body. They circumscribe the dimensions of her physical freedom. And of course, the relationship between physical and psychological development, intellectual possibility, and creative potential is an umbilical one. In our culture, no one part of a woman's body is left untouched, unaltered. No feature or extremity is spared the art, or pain, of improvement. . . . From the age of eleven or twelve until she dies, a woman will spend a large part of her time, money, and energy on binding, plucking, painting, and deodorizing herself. (Dworkin 1974, 113–114; see also Bartky 1990; Bordo 1993 and 1997)

In a profound and disheartening sense, then, it is largely through the male gaze that women's relationship to their own bodies, and the bodies of other women and men—to physicality itself—is defined: "In contemporary patriarchal culture, a panoptical male connoisseur resides within the consciousness of most women: they stand perpetually before his gaze and under his judgment. Woman lives her body as seen by another, by an anonymous patriarchal Other" (Bartky 1998, 34).

The specific makeup of the male gaze, and its implications for women both privately and socially, depend, of course, on who is doing the gazing. Religious society puts at the center of its gaze a fear of what *halakhically* proscribed thoughts and acts will be provoked by the viewing of women's bodies. Cover up, says this gaze, so that I will not be led into sinful thoughts. The gaze-based ethos informs virtually every aspect of male/female relationships within Orthodox society. For example, the structure of the synagogue is configured primarily in one of two ways: either with men sitting in the front and women sitting in the back, separated by some sort of divider; or with men sitting on the ground floor and women up in a balcony, free to gaze down upon men. When one rabbi, whose synagogue was modeled upon the former design, was asked by the author if he would consider placing the divider lengthwise, so that men and women would be sitting side by side, both facing the site of ritual activity, he replied that if he, or any man, could see any woman, the sanctity that he had worked so hard to cultivate in his place of worship would be lost.

It is important to emphasize that this rabbi did not invoke halakhic considerations in his response. In fact, from a strictly legalistic perspective, it is possible to divide a synagogue such that men and women stand side by side in prayer. This rabbi's response expresses a metalegal fear of the inexorably sexualizing effect upon men of having women within view, and an equally met-alegal contempt for the claims of women against this perspective's marginal-izing effects. In the structure of the synagogue, then, we find an entire archi-tecture built around a radical sensitivity to men's needs and the assumption that women have no needs that would require comparable sensitivity. It is pre-cisely this axiomatic absence of sexual hunger attributed to women that casts the entire crippling burden of desire—and the spiritual brittleness and vul-nerability that comes with it—upon men.

Once this premise is accepted, it only follows that the entirety of female en-ergy in the realm of *tzniut* should go toward protecting men from their puta-tive sexual incontinence. Women, who by rights should be grateful at having been passed over for this sad affliction, are expected to count their blessings and enlist themselves sympathetically—if secondarily—in the war against misguided desire by muting whatever parts of themselves men claim to find arousing and therefore threatening. Men, instead of dedicating their consid-erable resources of time, energy, and intellect inward, fix their gaze unwaver-ingly—and here again, Foucault's irony—on the bodies of women. What one finds, at the end of the day, is that the full-time job of managing male sexual-ity has been displaced onto women, freeing their counterparts to more noble pursuits. Given this background, the proliferation of modesty-literature di-rected at women, and penned by men, makes perfect sense. Only men know what men find arousing; women's role is simply to receive this knowledge as it is transmitted to them and demurely accede.

Just as the rhetoric of modesty and the architecture of the synagogue point to the way femininity is constructed within Jewish orthodoxy, so does the re-lationship of modern women to food and to their bodies point to the way femininity is constructed within Western "liberal" culture.

> The rules for this construction of femininity . . . require that women learn
> to feed others, not the self, and to construe their desires for self-nurturance
> and self-feeding as greedy and excessive. Thus, women must develop a to-
> tally other-oriented emotional economy. In this economy, the control of fe-
> male appetite for food is merely the most concrete expression of the gen-
> eral rule governing the construction of femininity: that female hunger—
> for public power, for independence, for sexual gratification—be con-
> tained, and the public space that women be allowed to take up be circum-
> scribed, limited. (Bordo 1993, 171)

We are faced here with a chilling similarity in the way femininity is con-structed in both Orthodox and secular contexts. Women's needs and desires are defined by men, their voices muted, and the public space allowed to them utterly circumscribed.

It emerges, then, that all this talk of *tzniut,* of which women are the ostensible subject, actually has very little to do with women at all. Women are subjects, really, in only one sense of the word: royal denizens, loyal subjects of an inscrutable king, waiting submissively for the next decree to be handed down about how best to hide themselves from an ever-encompassing royal gaze. In every other sense, when it comes to the discourse of *tzniut,* women have been, and remain, objects: constituted neither by the fullness of their being nor the rich integrity of their inner selves, but by the potential effects of their various body parts upon the spiritual lives of men. The situation is in some ways analogous with pornography, where women are the main characters yet are totally treated as objects, and where the apparatus is largely composed by men: directors, producers, consumers, and defenders.

What effects might such a lopsided dynamic have on women's images of themselves, and—equally important—their images of men (as well as men's images of themselves)? As Adrienne Rich observed with respect to pornography, all subject-object relationships inevitably compromise the humanity of both sides. "All objectification is prelude to and condition of slavery" (Rich 1980, 313–320). The abstract ideal of *tzniut,* then, potentially ennobling on its own terms, at this point seems quite remote. It would not be an overstatement to say that *tzniut,* as practiced, works stridently in opposition to its stated goals. Under the bright, surgical lamp of halakhic scrutiny of their bodies—eerily reminiscent of Charcot's treatment of his hysterical woman patients in late nineteenth-century France—and the inescapable spotlight of a gaze that is at turns domineering and fearful, but never less than severe, women are encouraged, both overtly and implicitly, to think of themselves not in terms of their ineffable spirit, of the whole that is greater than the sum of its parts, but of the parts themselves. This dismembering (in every sense of the word) is what has emerged, within contemporary Orthodox discourse, as a working definition of *tzniut.*

Meanwhile, it almost goes without saying that no attention is paid (much less credence granted) to what women may find arousing or distracting or otherwise disruptive to their spiritual pursuits. "Men are systematically conditioned not even to notice what women want" (MacKinnon 1989, 181). This obliviousness evolves for the simple reason that women qua women are considered sexually evolved, and therefore sexually neutral. Consequently, for the purposes of halakhic or literary-philosophical exploration (or any other form of serious male attention) they are sexually and spiritually irrelevant. This view is also found in classical adolescence psychology and sex education classes: "psychologists seem to be colluding with the culture in simply assuming that adolescent girls do not experience sexual desire" (Tolman 1994, 253). "Within public schools . . . in the typical sex education classroom, silence, and therefore distortion, surrounds female desire" (Fine 1992, 38).

> Female pleasure and questions are far less often the topic of discussion. Few voices of female sexual agency can be heard. The language of victimization and its underlying concerns . . . ultimately deny young women the right to control their own sexuality by providing no access to a legitimate position of sexual subjectivity. (Fine 1992, 41)

The rendering of women as purely spiritual, asexual beings makes them halakhically "needless" in more than one sense. The purported vacuum of female desire gives rise to a system of male-female relations that lacks checks and balances—one that, instead of challenging men to purify and refine the influences constituting their gaze, blithely permits them to give in. To the contrary, *tzniut,* as it is currently manifested in Orthodox culture, caters slavishly to this gaze, and therefore in a very real sense nurtures and reinforces it. Instead of being pushed to engage and refine and thus take some measure of responsibility for their sexuality, men are conditioned to attribute it to an inherent and irremediable weakness, and to look to women—those bulwarks of sexual equanimity and restraint—for salvation and relief.

A pointed illustration of this phenomenon was related by a student in a girl's post–high school seminary. A young male teacher, before giving an evening lecture, placed a bowl of pastry in the center of the table. As the girls reached for the pastry, he stopped them, explaining that they had to wait until the end of the lecture. He left the pastry in the middle of the table and taught the class. At the end, as the girls finally began to eat, he said dramatically: "Remember how distracted you were by those pastries? That is exactly how I feel when you do not dress modestly" (interview with author).

Male desire is primal and overpowering; men, themselves, are therefore constructed as powerful and primal, and any woman concerned with her safety—to say nothing of her purity—should be as strict as possible about covering herself as protection from this primordial force. A young woman from another post–high school seminary related the story of one of her rabbis who, on a field trip, informed his students that if they really knew what men were thinking when they looked at them, they would all dress in sackcloth.

Male sexuality is constructed as such an overpowering force that men themselves have no real hope of controlling it; more often than not, they end up slavishly and skittishly in its service. Another seminary student told how one of her teachers described the relationship of a man to a woman as analogous to the relationship of a Holocaust *musselman*[1] to a crumb of bread. Women, then, called up in their role of nurturer, empathizer, the embodiment of Support—a whole supporting cast of mothers, daughters, girlfriends, sisters, wives—are drafted into its service as well. Recent research on teachers in Modern Orthodox girls' schools (Hartman and Summit, forthcoming) reveals that religious teenage girls are taught, in no uncertain terms, that it is up to them to ensure that the boys they meet in youth group activities (the schools themselves are gender-segregated) will not sin.

It seems, then, that the Orthodox representation of these differences has reached the point of caricature, and that these caricatures, imbued with the authority of both religious wisdom and natural law, have come to dictate halakhic policy and social norms. What we are left with is the reification of an extreme model of male sexual brutishness/helplessness; a dismissal of women as sexual agents; and an unbridled fervor for covering them under suffocating blankets of spiritual-psychic anxiety not their own.

### NO RELIEF: THE WESTERN MALE GAZE

It is hardly surprising, given the above, that an increasing number of Orthodox women have, to varying degrees, decided to cast off traditional standards and practices of *tzniut.* Many of these women have turned elsewhere for models of thinking about and enacting female sexuality and gender relations—models that resonate more deeply with their intuitive sense of themselves, their world, and God. In this turning outward, liberated, postfeminist Western society has been the obvious choice. Its liberal flexibility vis-à-vis gender roles, the strides of feminism in opening multitudes of personal and professional options for women, and a general atmosphere of sexual openness all seem to hold out the hope for a type of freedom these women have not previously known: the freedom to discover and express resonant voices within themselves that traditional norms have demanded they suppress. Often these women experience a kind of honeymoon with Western culture, which is experienced as a panacea for all the ills of a suffocating past: a feeling akin to that of shedding heavy clothing on a hot day; or, in more severe cases, to a mental patient throwing off her straitjacket after years of being wrongly detained. The new freedom and comfort are palpable, and for all practical purposes, little more could be asked.

But for many women, what eventually follows is a kind of subtle, dawning realization that what they have come to is, in some very fundamental ways, disconcertingly similar to what they thought they had left behind. They find that feminism did not arise only out of rabbinic misogyny, but out of a series of profound imbalances endemic to modern, secular society. They discover by observation and instinct what many feminist critics have noted and affirmed: Western culture, for all its freedom and openness, for all its very real strides in opening up an unprecedented range of possibilities with respect to women's roles, nonetheless still enforces a strict regime of gender oppression when it comes to their bodies. Their bodies are still objectified and apportioned according to the needs and desires of an equally insatiable male gaze.

> There is no need for arms, physical violence, material constraints. Just a gaze. An inspecting gaze, a gaze which each individual under its weight will end by interiorizing to the point that he is his own overseer, each individual thus exercising this surveillance over, and against himself. (Foucault 1977, 155)

> Women are no longer required to be chaste or modest, to restrict their sphere of activity to home, or even to realize their properly feminine destiny in maternity: normative femininity is becoming more and more to be centered on woman's body—not its duties and obligations or even its capacity to bear children, but its sexuality, more precisely, its presumed heterosexuality and its appearance. (Bartky 1998, 41–42)

In contrast to the traditional view of women, the Western gaze does not attempt to conquer and suppress the male sex drive by covering women up, but rather to glorify the drive and hence conquer women by insistently stripping them down. The Western male gaze, then, rather than trying to attenuate male sexual craving, remains openly brazen in its bodily longings and base types of desire. Society demands that women service these desires by dutifully uncovering themselves, publicly and privately, and by remaining uncovered as on-call objects of pleasure for the effortless consumption of men. "[T]he process and content of women's definition as women, as an under-class, are the process and content of their sexualization as objects for male sexual use" (MacKinnon 1989, 140). "'Woman' is defined by what male desire requires for arousal and satisfaction and this is socially tautologous with 'female sexuality' and 'female sex'" (MacKinnon 1989, 131).

Once uncovered and made available, the woman's body comes under a kind of surgical scrutiny that is again a direct reflection of male desire run amok. In its treatment of women's bodies, Western society can be likened to a massive procrustean bed—or, as the rabbis called it, a Bed of Sodom—upon which body parts that obtrude beyond the punishing parameters of an anorexically narrow male gaze are tucked, starved, stretched, suctioned, or summarily lopped off.

> Thanks to the second wave feminist analysis of beauty culture, we can see that fashion gives us corsets, hose, high heels, underwire bras; "health and beauty" industry gives us paints, powders, dyes, silicon, liposuction; "nutrition" centers offer diets and other ways to become smaller and less present while remaining in continual states of paralyzing obsession; mental health industry offers Xanax, Valium, and Ativan; and advertising tells us "you've come a long way, baby," pretending to offer freedom by actually turning the key on a new form of imprisonment. Femininity now, as in the second wave and before, is about constriction (Shoemaker 1997, 112)

Meanwhile, male sexual desire is essentialized, naturalized, romanticized—even sacralized—and those men who enact it are granted a cultural carte blanche. Bordo (1999) in this context points to the American adoration of athletes, which often continues even after they commit serious crimes. It is precisely because of this unchecked validation of male potency that it is possible to sympathize with the actual confusion expressed by young men in situations of date rape, while nonetheless demanding that they be held accountable and punished. Their claims of uncertainty in the communications surrounding the act, and of bewilderment with respect to the subsequent accusations levied against them, should not be taken merely as cynical strategies to elude punishment. Rather, they should be considered very seriously as telling indicators of how boys are being educated to view themselves and their expectations of performance vis-à-vis the opposite sex:

> This culture places boys in a double bind. We fabulously reward those boys who succeed in our ritual arenas of primitive potency . . . but at the same time, we want male aggression to bow to civilization when a girl says "no" and to be transformed into tender passion when she says "yes." (Bordo 1999, 242)

One finds a classic example of this training and its perversely harmful effects in Freud's treatment of the Dora case (1905), in which the aggressive sexual attacks against her by Herr K were considered normative sexuality, and her inability to derive pleasure from these unwanted advances were labeled a pathology: Every arena becomes a masculine testing ground: After a day's work we "work out," so that in the evening, with our wives or lovers, we can "get the job done" with our "tools" and thus calm our "performance anxiety." (Kimmel 1996, 331)

This recipe for maleness is obviously toxic and hardly benefits most actual boys and men in their relationships with each other (to say nothing of the women among whom they live): "As men grow up to deny their emotional needs, as they learn to live out myths that we have absorbed about 'how men are supposed to be,' we hardly appreciate the 'injuries' we do to ourselves through being cut off from our emotional lives" (Seidler 1997, 50).

Meanwhile, the role of women as sexual gatekeepers of traditional gender relations—is replicated with only slight modification within modern Western society. Most date rape workshops, for example, are marketed to and attended primarily, if not exclusively, by women (see Bordo 1999). They focus on teaching women to say no in a way that is convincing and firm—not only to their partners, but to themselves. It is here that we can locate the practical consequences of the Western gaze in its relentless and systemic drive to strip women of a sexual identity that is independent of male desire and consequently of a sexual volition as well. This hollowed-out self-image is what Michelle Fine (1992) calls "the missing discourse of desire" in women's sexuality. Men who meet cultural standards of virility often feel, to the contrary, that directing their sexual attention toward a member of the opposite sex is equivalent to giving her a blessing.

-----

Given the plight of women's bodies in Western culture, traditional society may in fact muster a nostalgic appeal. Better your body be plastered over and cast to the margins, one might argue, than stripped down and laid out across a Bed of Sodom. Far from marginalizing women's bodies, however, the Orthodox male gaze has of late placed it front and center on the cultural stage. This trend of religious men speaking incessantly about women's bodies with great passion and specificity (this discourse being carried out under the pretense of "modesty") evokes with very little nuance Freudian ideas about sublimation, and the cultural irony so aptly noted by Foucault.

These claims can be demonstrated quite concretely by turning to a source often overlooked in research regarding traditional gender relations. Within the Orthodox world, matchmakers are a remarkably knowledgeable source of information about the current state of male and female psyches. In particular, this is perhaps the one place within Orthodox society where male desire is made explicit. It might be expected, given traditional values and sensibilities, that while attractiveness would certainly play a role in projecting the desir-ability of potential mates, religious prohibitions about viewing the female form—in person or in any medium—would mean that the specific ins and outs of women's bodies would not be factored in. In fact, matchmakers know that the vast majority of the men they fix up, not only know what a women's size 4 is, but set it as the absolute maximum they will consider for their po-tential soul mate—a deal-breaker on par with religious worldview–affinity and childbearing capability. Religious young men order from these match-makers detailed specifications of women's figures as if ordering fast food. Ob-viously, modesty has not served to cover the bodies of Orthodox young women from the voracious Western gaze, much less protect them from the pervasive sexualization of women's bodies criticized by feminists and religious Jews alike. As for the girls themselves, the Orthodox community, in both the United States and Israel, maintains one of the fastest-growing rates of eating disorders among young women. Consultants are being brought into teenage eating disorder clinics and adolescent psych wards to negotiate the demand for increasingly strict levels of kosher food. Mothers alarmingly tell of their daughters' putting off dates (which are all geared single-mindedly toward marriage) for three months in order to go on starvation diets. Interestingly, this is one area in which, despite many philosophical points of contention, the difference among ultra-Orthodox, Modern Orthodox, and secular women is negligible. Unknowingly, it seems, religious and secular women of all stripes have finally managed to carve out some cultural common ground: all are lan-guishing under the same disfiguring cultural gaze. Their ideologies may seem disparate, but their bodies are all suffering the same plight.

It seems clear that an affinity between Orthodox and Western perspectives, despite the air of ecumenical achievement, raises the specter of new, poten-tially menacing threats to the minds and bodies of women and men. The heart of what is held in common by the sexual discourses of Orthodoxy and the West is that the discourse itself is shaped almost exclusively by males, and ac-cepted by women as if by divine fiat. This lopsided disconnect itself would ap-pear to be the source of all the various forms of corruption to which the dif-ferent systems of gender give rise—ultimately as harmful to men as it is to women, and ultimately serving neither. The fact that the male gaze travels in only one direction—and the way that this solipsism allows and encourages men not only to see women, but to see themselves, as well as the way in which it causes women to hypersexualize both their own bodies and their ideas about men—is itself an essence of immodesty, a paradigm of promiscuity and coercion from which other distortions arise.

In fact, the Biblical imperative that serves as the source for the Jewish paradigm of *tzniut* speaks directly in opposition to this imbalance: *hatzne'a lechet im elohekha*. (Micha 6:8: Walk modestly with your God). The choice of preposition here is telling and precise: not under, not behind, but *with*. Clearly implied here is that inherent to any true model of modesty is an equality, a "*with*ness," between the partners involved. And if indeed we are, as men and as women, given the condition of modesty, fit to walk with God, is it possible to conceive that we are unfit to walk modestly *with* each other? Men and women are here enjoined equally in the responsibility to view themselves not according to the images of each other that we have generated through generations of cagey anxiety and misguided notions, but in the far more fearless and forgiving gaze of the divine. Thus we must open ourselves to the possibility of a modesty discourse that is *not* solipsistic and top-down, that places limitations upon an encompassing male gaze, and takes into consideration the implication of a female gaze that does more than simply respond to male needs. Instead of blithely accepting that women and men are from two different planets—and then suiting them up as babies in their little pink and blue space suits, assuming that this is simply the natural course—we must examine the ways in which we are responsible for what has happened. We have been outfitting our sons and daughters for different journeys to different atmospheres—some of which make it very hard for them to breathe (see Bordo 1999). We must consider how, in our well-intentioned attempts to equip them for survival, we often unintentionally send them throttling off into dizzying orbits that serve neither their own deepest spiritual needs, nor the personally meaningful, practically expansive, and communally redemptive imperatives of *tzniut*. In short, we must create another cosmology, wherein men and women inhabit the earth together—our synogogues together—not as two different species, but as one holy community, together embodying the directive of walking with God.

# 4

## THE PATERNAL VOICE IN LITURGY

*There have been numerous prayer book commissions.*
*Why is there no prayer commission?—A. J. Heschel*

There has perhaps been no greater testing ground—or battle-ground—for the coexistence of feminism and Modern Orthodoxy than the realm of synagogue ritual, and in particular the language of prayer. Traditional liturgies of all faiths, with their ubiquitous Fathers and Kings, have long been targeted by feminist critics as blatant purveyors of patriarchy. Jewish prayer has not been spared this scrutiny or this critique (Plaskow 1990; Adler 1998). The Reform and Conservative movements championed egalitarian worship as part of a broader liberalizing agenda in response to the feminist movement's ethical-religious claims. The mehitza was taken down, women were counted as full participants in the community of prayer, and the language of worship was adjusted in different ways to neutralize, or at least balance out, the highly masculine imagery of the traditional liturgy.

Orthodoxy has on the whole resisted these egalitarian trends and rejected outright the possibility of similar liturgical change. One reason for this might be categorized as formalistic or halakhic. While some of traditional religion's more overt patriarchal features are subject to evolution within the bounds of Jewish law (women's prayer groups, better seating arrangements, access to the Torah scrolls during Sabbath services), the language of prayer was imbued by the rabbis with a highly sacred status and a "built-in" legal mechanism to resist any change.

In addition to refusing to make change internally, many Orthodox rabbis have criticized severely the other movements for their halakhic (and in some cases overtly antihalakhic) choices. Orthodoxy itself has been charged with moral blindness and cultural paralysis. This thick accretion of double meanings, political recriminations, and cultural codes has done much to obscure, and at times contort, some of the core issues underlying the call for egalitarianism in prayer (see chapter 6). Rarely recognized, emphasized, or even acknowledged within Orthodox rhetoric is the deeply religious impulse at work here, the seriousness with which both prayer and language are being taken by those advocating for change (see Plaskow 1990; Adler 1998), and the deep desire for prayer—to find a place for oneself within Jewish prayer—that such advocacy reflects.

First and foremost, this advocacy reflects a belief that language conveys meaning and exerts a formative impact on the person who uses it. It acknowledges that just as language has the power to heal, it has the power to hurt; just as articulation has the power to create and shape reality, omission has the power to erase. The presence of the masculine is so strong within Jewish prayer, and the omission of the feminine so glaring, that *not* to ask the question of how this language might impact its speakers, as well as the society in which they live, begins to seem a barefaced omission in and of itself.

Second, this advocacy reflects a belief that prayer is a vital human activity and a profound response to the human condition. This stance can be seen as an optimistic, if somewhat ironic, take on the common notion of religious language projecting human images upon the divine. It also seems in concert with a cursory reading of Jewish liturgy, which is laden with human experience. It seems to constitute a response to the needs and aspirations of the Jew both as an individual human being and as a member of a people. It encompasses seminal historical events, pressing present needs, and longings for future individual and communal dignity, sovereignty, and redemption. As such, it reflects a total understanding and vision of what it means to be a human being standing before God.

This dimension of prayer is fleshed out explicitly, and granted clear legitimacy, in a poignant exchange found in the Babylonian Talmud. Here the Men of the Great Assembly argue with two prophets:

> Rabbi Yehoshua ben Levi said: Why were they called the Men of the 'Great' Assembly? Because they restored the crown to its original state. Moshe came and said: "the great, powerful, and awesome God." Jeremiah came and said: Aliens are destroying in his sanctuary! Where is his awesomeness? He therefore did not mention "awesome" [that is, in his prayer]. Daniel came and said: Strangers are enslaving His children—where is his power? He did not say "powerful." (Yoma 69b)

This exchange is especially fascinating and relevant for our purposes, as the claims of subjectivity upon the prayer experience are brought specifically to bear upon the issue of liturgical change. The prophets Jeremiah and Daniel are living in a time in which the Holy Temple has been destroyed, foreign armies and religions have taken over the land, and masses of Jews have been murdered and/or sent into exile. Faced with the destruction of God's temple, the discrepancy between the political-religious reality they are experiencing and the words that have been formulated by Moses seems too great to bridge. Each one of them, focusing on a different aspect of the destruction (perhaps the aspect that touches them the most) can no longer use the adjective that no longer describes the God they know. Their response is incredulous. They are unable to follow the traditional liturgy, attributed to no less a figure than Moses himself, because the current social-historical context renders it noncredible. Their response is to alter the text-based primacy according to the theological implications of their subjective perception of the world in which they live, where neither God's awesomeness nor greatness can readily be found.

The Talmudic exchange continues with the entrance of the Men of the Great Assembly, who according to tradition took charge of rebuilding the Jewish community in Israel after the Babylonian Exile, following the destruction of the First Temple. The Men of the Great Assembly offer an alternative solution to the problem of the liturgy no longer reflecting reality.

> But then they [Men of the Great Assembly] came and said: On the contrary! Therein lie his mighty deeds that he supresses his wrath, that he extends long-suffering to the wicked [who oppress them]. Therein lie his awful powers, for but for the fear of Him, how could one single nation persist among the many nations? (Yoma 69b)

Rather than change the words, the Great Assembly keep them and reinterpret their meanings. Even this alternative solution, however, tacitly acknowledges the basic fissure between liturgy and contemporary reality. In other words, everyone agrees that there is a problem, and the dispute is about how to solve it.[1] This reading is bolstered significantly by the way in which the Talmud concludes the exchange, justifying the prophets' actions with an explicit and theologically compelling rationale:

> Now, the Rabbis [that is, Jeremiah and Daniel], how did they act thus, to abolish the institution that Moses instituted? R' Elazar said: because they knew about the Holy One, Blessed be He, that He is truthful. Therefore they would not speak falsely about him. (Yoma 69b).

The feminist tension, then, between the words of the liturgy and subjective experience of reality as filtered through a contemporary lens, turns out not to be an exclusively feminist tension at all—or even a particularly modern one. Indeed, it appears rather to be merely the most recent manifestation of a tension with which the ancient Rabbis themelves grappled and toward the resolution of which they offered two different approaches.[2]

A later instantiation of the value and halakhic weight of subjectivity in prayer—and validation of the tension between subjectivity and the received liturgy—can be found in Maimonides' letter to Ovadyah the Convert. Ovadya, whom Maimonides praises as "the knowledgeable and righteous convert," asks a question about the nature of conversion itself: To what extent does the spiritual transformation of conversion join one not only to the Jewish present and destiny, but to Jewish history and genealogy? At the moment of conversion do and can converts project backward and consider themselves retroactively as always having been a part of the Jewish People? This issue is given pragmatic relevance in practical halakhic questions concerning matters of blessing and prayer. In Maimonides' paraphrase,

> your question regards matters of blessings and prayers, in private or public: Should you say "our God and the God of our fathers," "who has sanctified us through his commandments and commanded us," "who has chosen us," "who has given our father an inheritance," "who has taken us out of the land of Egypt," "who has performed miracles unto us," and all similar matters?

A number of prayer and blessing formulations invoke the historical relationship of God with the Jewish People, both generally and with respect to particular events. In voicing these formulations, supplicants similarly invoke their own continuity with the historical communities who upheld the human side of this relationship. Should the converts place themselves on this continuum? Maimonides' emphatically affirmative response reflects not only his attitude toward converts, but toward prayer. Interestingly, he does not settle the matter with a formalistic answer: the prayer language is fixed, you must not diverge from it, end of story. Rather, he reinterprets the meaning of "father." While we may tend to think of father as a biological category, in fact, Maimonides explains, it encompasses (at least in Abraham's case) the meaning of teacher or "spiritual father" as well.

> You should say them all [that is, all of the traditional prayer formulations] in the prescribed manner; do not change a thing. Rather, just like any native Israelite prays and blesses, so too you ought to bless and pray. The principle of the matter is that it was Abraham, our father, who educated the whole of the people, and enlightened them. Therefore, whoever converts up until the end of generations, and whoever unifies the name of the Holy One blessed be He, as it is written in the Torah, is a student of Abraham our

father, may he rest in peace. They are all members of his household. Just as he caused the people of his generation to return through his words and teaching, so too has he caused all future converts to return by means of the commandments [he related] to his sons and household after him. It follows therefore that Abraham, our father, may he rest in peace, is a father to his worthy seed who follow in his ways, and a father to his disciples, and every future convert. (Maimonides' letter to Ovadyah, p. 65)

What is perhaps most striking here is the extent to which Maimonides recognizes the validity of the question being asked. In going to such great reinterpretive lengths to explain that Abraham can in fact be viewed and spoken of as a father figure to converts, he tacitly, but powerfully, legitimates the desire and need for the language of prayer to reflect the personal experience and self-image of the person using it.

In the above, Maimonides appears to represent the approach of the Men of the Great assembly to dissonance in prayer. The first response is an attempt to keep the words as they are and do the work of finding oneself within them. What follows, however, appears to side somewhat more with the prophetic side of the debate:

However, [concerning statements such as] "You who have taken us out of Egypt," or "you who have performed miracles to our fathers," if you wish to change them and say "who has taken Israel out of Egypt" and "performed miracles to Israel," you may do so. (ibid.)

Here Maimonides appears to represent the prophetic response to subjectivity: if the convert finds within the words of prayer a dissonance too acute to resolve through reinterpretation, it is permissible to change the words in order to make them reflect his/her subjective reality more accurately. One is not required to do so, but one is allowed. It is important to emphasize here that the reason for this leniency is not because the objective reality of the convert is at odds with the liturgy. Indeed, the Rambam is strident in claiming that objectively speaking, the convert fully joins the Community of Israel in every respect, and has no need whatsoever for liturgical change. "[I]f you do not change," he says, it is of no consequence.

Since you have entered under the wings of the Shekhinah and joined Him, no difference exists between us and you. All the miracles were done as it were to us and to you... There is no difference whatsoever between us and you. Because the Torah was given to us and the converts, for it is written: "One ordinance shall be both for you of the congregation, and also for the stranger that sojourneth with you, and ordinance forever in your generations: as ye are, so shall the stranger be before the Lord" [Numbers 15:15] (ibid.)

The permission to change the liturgy, in other words, is given strictly for the purpose of facilitating a greater sense of connection between the subjective self-image of the supplicants and the words they use to pray. Thus the two responses to subjectivity and dissonance found in the Talmudic passage examined above find another expression in Maimonides' letter to Ovadyah. What we noted in the Talmudic case is true here as well: while the two responses give varying degrees of weight to such considerations as communal stability, historical continuity, and literal truthtelling, both validate equally the need for the liturgy to reflect a recognizable and coherent sense of self.

————

So too in our own time: this history-spanning conversation can be found intersecting again in the dissonance many feel with exclusively masculine prayer language. As history and consciousness have evolved, our ethical sensibilities have been refined and expanded in ways that stand in opposition to some traditional viewpoints. This ethical evolution bears significant theological consequences that in turn create the kinds of disjunctures between traditional norms (for example, liturgy) and current perceptions of reality that give rise to the kind of tension the Talmud so cogently and pointedly—and fearlessly—evokes. In the modern era, the scope of the human has expanded to include types of people who previously had been categorized as lacking in basic human or humanizing criteria. Perhaps feminism's single greatest accomplishment has been to insist upon the full humanity of women—translated by Jewish feminists into an affirmation that women were present at the Revelation of Sinai and included in the covenantal bond (*brit*). (Plaskow 1990) Not to incorporate this new consciousness into our prayer seems, again, not merely a suspicious omission or moral blind spot, but a stance at odds with the very nature of prayer itself, the way in which prayer is meant to reflect each individual's experience. Such a stance works to weaken Jewish prayer, making it potentially less relevant, less resonant, less credible, and less effective in whatever ways one deems prayer to exert its force.

The wholesale resistance to liturgical change begins, then, to seem at least as misguided as attempts to alter and update the ancient texts. A. J. Heschel (1956) expressed this tension with his usual eloquence: "Those of us who are anxious to omit no word out of reverence for the treasures of the liturgy are paying a high price for their loyalty. Judaism is faced with a dilemma, with a conflict between two requirements: the loyalty to the order, and the requirement of kavanah" (35). Here we find Heschel reformulating in modern terms the ancient Talmudic tension between the prophets and the Men of the Great Assembly. Both of these religious personalities felt and validated the requirement for *kavanah* (intention) in prayer. The primary difference is that the latter gave a countervailing weight to the value of loyalty, the legacy of history, and the structure of tradition. This value pushed them to keep the text but delve deeper into its nuances and possibilities, reinterpreting the words so that they could be spoken with integrity.

The move to reinterpret, extremely common when applied to legal texts, can serve as a model for what I propose with respect to masculine prayer language. As in the Talmudic case, I would argue that the disjuncture between the received prayer language and the contemporary reality has become so acute that something must be done. When one begins to take the full humanity and dignity of women seriously, using the traditional Jewish liturgy—in which women are at best ignored, and all God-imagery is male—becomes, in Peter Berger's terms, a "mind-wrenching effort" (1979, 89). Tamar Ross (1999), a Modern Orthodox religious philosopher, summarizes the problem boldly and succinctly in the title of her article (1999) on prayer and feminism: "Can we still pray to our Father in Heaven?"

––––––––

Granted, there are many different motivations that go into calls for change, both among, and without those who choose to take a stand: "There are many thoughts in the human heart" (Proverbs 19:21). There has been a systemic refusal, however, on the part of religious authorities (who tend to pigeonhole all who express a desire for something different as childish upstarts or calculating political operatives) to recognize that at least one prominent motivation in the call to change is simply the desire to pray as a dignified human being, and to pray Jewishly. The profound inner knowledge that the traditional prayer environment constitutes an assault on women's dignity, an assault so distracting as to become an acute impediment to prayer, is what informs much of the dissatisfaction with traditional prayer and the attempts to make change. Indeed, it has led some to leave traditional prayer behind, in favor of silence or alternative models of worship. It has led others to experiment with new kinds of language: to change the words.

I appreciate the creativity and viability of these approaches for change, and I sometimes feel envious of the freedom they bespeak. My investment in halakha, however, precludes me from embracing the change they suggest. I mean this in two ways. First, as mentioned above, in the language of prayer we run up against some very ancient and impassable halakhic boundaries: "*Kol ha-meshaneh mi-matbe'ah she-tav'u chachamim bivrachot lo yatza yeday khovato*" (One who changes the liturgy formulated/fixed by the Sages, does not fulfill his obligation) (Berachot 40b). While there are areas in which innovation is possible, in which elective prayers can be created and added, much of the core prayer, and its surrounding blessings, was invested with great sanctity and great authority, a kind of immovable gravitas.

But there is another reason for resisting the renovation of traditional prayer language, a reason having more to do with personal intuition than with traditional authority (though perhaps the tradition was informed by this intuition as well). Using the traditional liturgy allows us to participate in a relationship with Jewish communities that spans time and space, that is at once transcendent and intensely intimate. In traditional prayer we are participating in a historical religious drama of the covenantal community, we are part of the Jewish historical process. Fixed liturgy enables us to partake in something larger, older, greater than our immediate reality. As A. J. Heschel (1954) writes: "The purpose of prayer is not the purpose of speech. The purpose of speech is to inform; the purpose of prayer is to partake. It is good that there are words sanctified by ages of worship, by the honesty and love of generations" (16 and 33).

I am sympathetic to Heschel's religious impulse to view prayer as a portal to profound experience, to participation in holiness and history, rather than as an instrument of personal expression. Although I appreciate his perspective that prayer is not exclusively or even essentially a personal act, I also contend that it is mediated by the very real and experiential tension between wanting to partake in something greater, and recognizing that the words we use, no matter how saturated with honesty and love, may nonetheless create a spiritual environment that compromises human dignity. And while I also agree with him that ultimately "it is precisely the function of prayer to shift the center of living from self-consciousness to self-surrender" (57), feminism helps us to understand there is no pure center. Every act, even religious acts, acts of self-surrender, takes place within a context. The contexts in which we pray determine our ability to feel comfortable and safe enough to expose ourselves in the ways that prayer demands—certainly for the kind of transcendent prayer experience to which Heschel refers. In what elements of the context in which we pray do we need to feel secure so that we will then be able to surrender to the experience of prayer itself? What kind of safety is required, and how is it defined?

This deep religious tension, which finds expression in many aspects of traditional Jewish life (characterized at times as the tension between subjectivity and objectivity, or between the spirit and the letter of the law) lies at the heart of calls for a liturgy that includes women's voices and upholds women's dignity. I will now address a potential source of discomfort underlying this entire discussion. The discomfort lies not in framing questions or offering solutions but in the very premise of asking the question: By so rigorously engaging the imagery of God in prayer, do we not risk giving too much weight to representation and losing sight of God's ultimate transcendence—the ineffability and unknowability of the Divine? Even if we were to adjust our impressions about the implications of "male" and "female," is there not ultimately something dubious about any project expanding and reifying our sense of God's gender and gendered-ness?

To better understand the implications of attempts to balance the representation of God's gender, it may be illustrative to examine a case in which this tendency is played out in the extreme, and feminine imagery is used exclusively. Some women who rejected patriarchal religion in toto still searched for an outlet for the religious impulse. They found it in a pre-monotheistic time when women's voices and images were celebrated in goddess-cults. Adrienne Rich (1976), finding the lack of feminine representations in religious language to have a profound effect upon our religious imagination, and our very sense of self, poses the question: What would or could happen if feminine images of the deity were incorporated into our religious lives?

> [Female images of the divine] express an attitude toward the female charged with awareness of her intrinsic importance, her depth of meaning, and her existence at the very center of what is necessary and sacred. She is beautiful in ways we have almost forgotten, or which have become defined as ugliness. Her body possesses mass, interior depth, inner rest, and balance. She exists not to cajole or reassure men, but to assert herself. . . . Let us try to imagine for a moment what sense of herself it gave a woman to be in the presence of such images. If they did nothing else for her, they must have validated her spiritually, giving her back aspects of herself neither insipid nor trivial, investing her with a sense of participation in essential mysteries. (93–94)

I too wonder about the potentially transformative effects feminine imagery could have, individually and culturally. I also resonate with its implicit insight that Jewish monotheism, notwithstanding the theological claims it makes to the contrary, did not obliterate the pantheon of idols but merely pared it down to one: the masculine image of the divine. Why was feminine imagery cleansed from Jewish prayer, and the masculine so meticulously preserved and valorized? Beginning again with the goddess seems as legitimate as remaining with the masculine image of God.

Notwithstanding the truth embedded within this claim, Cynthia Ozick (1983) argues compellingly that the type of approach articulated by Rich to the masculine God problem (and she extends this criticism to include the addition of any "female anthropomorphic imagery" to Jewish tradition) presents, from a Jewish perspective, a much greater one: a reversion to outright paganism. "What?" she asks, incredulous.

> Millennia after the cleansing purity of Abraham's vision of the One Creator, a return to Astarte, Hera, Juno, Venus, and all their proliferating sisterhood? Sex goddesses, fertility goddesses, mother goddesses? The sacrifices brought to these were often enough human. This is the new vision intended to "restore dignity" to Jewish women? A resurrection of every ancient idolatry the Jewish idea came into the world to drive out, so as to begin again with a purifying clarity? The answer slanders and sullies monotheism. (122)

Ozick's objection seems informed by a Maimonidean discomfort with anthropomorphic language in general. "There is great danger," Maimonides famously claims, "in applying positive attributes to God" (Maimonides 1953, 222). The deepest truth about God is that we are not God, and any human naming diminishes God. Thus, to paraphrase Ozick, the more humanity we ascribe to the divine, the more we try to create God in our image rather tirelessly striving for the opposite—the more we try to approximate the divine in human language rather than emphasize Its ultimate Otherness from humanity or language—the further we regress into the morass of pantheism from which it was the Torah's great purpose to extricate us.

Ozick raises, but then discards, the point that the divine is presented by the Jewish tradition in language, and not in a neuter language but one that is overwhelmingly masculine. She does not find this element of anthropomorphism theologically problematic, or even, it seems, significant. She does not see it as connected to, much less causative of, the prevalent (and legitimate) complaints about "the self-esteem of women" (120). Indeed, she rejects the premise that women's marginalized status within Judaism emerges from its theistic language, which she dismisses as a technical issue stemming from the limitations of language itself, "quibbles about the incompleteness of pronouns"

(122). The question, she says, is instead sociological in nature, and it can and should be remedied by sociological (that is, halakhic) mechanisms.

The general point about emphasizing the transcendent otherness of the Divine over Its linguistic-humanistic manifestations is well taken. Maimonides' admonition is a proper corrective to the intensive focus on representation, and Ozick's insistence that to expand upon the embodied conversation is misguided should be held close at hand. Nevertheless, there is a theological purism to both of these approaches that makes them difficult to embrace fully. Notwithstanding a certain compelling theological pathos, depersonalizing God divests religious experience of its relational aspect. True, we avoid committing the sin of anthropomorphism; perhaps, however, this is an instance of the operation being a success notwithstanding the patient's demise. Our desire for a relational God is one who was involved in history, revealed to us, who intervened on our behalf, made covenants with us; put demands on us, suffered in our pain: the God of our fathers and mothers. As poor as our language is, it is the currency we have inherited with which to connect to this Jewish God: "The Torah speaks in the language of human beings." Against Maimonides' abstract philosophical Divinity stands a tradition of divine immanence and relationship that affirms the value and significance of the words with which we conduct that relationship.

Plaskow (1983), moreover, responding to Ozick from within this latter tradition, affirms the theological validity, indeed necessity, of feminine imagery within a monotheistic framework. "If God is male," she asks, "and we are in God's image, how can maleness not be the norm of Jewish humanity?" (228). She dismisses concerns about regression to paganism as alarmist, arguing: "Rationally, it seems contradictory to argue that the Jewish God transcends sexuality, that anthropomorphism—while necessitated by the limits of our thought—is not to be taken literally; and at the same time to insist that a broadening of anthropomorphic language will destroy the tradition. Using sexually dimorphic images may be the best way to acknowledge the limits of language and God's fullness, so that the inclusion of women becomes, at the same time, an enrichment to our concept of God" (229). Again we are left with, if not a definitive argument for changing the language of prayer, one that is viable, compelling, and worthy of serious consideration. And so again our resistance to this approach is informed by the limitations imposed by tradition, at times inscrutable and at times yielding valuable insights for modes of reengagement. If we desire to maintain a relationship with both tradition and the God of tradition, who encourages us to imagine Him in the language He gave us to use, there would appear to be little alternative.

Where does this argument leave Orthodox feminists? Because of our commitment to stand with tradition and halakha, we cannot simply change the language of prayers; because we embrace feminist values, neither can we fully say these prayers in good faith. Something has got to give; the center cannot hold. What I suggest is that although there is great difficulty in changing the gendered terms, it may be possible, following the model of the Men of the Great Assembly, to reexplore some of the associations we bring to them, to reconfigure some of the meanings we assign to them. Can we, in other words, deconstruct what we mean when we say God? Granted, He is described in the male form, the father, the all-powerful king and judge. Still we can only understand what *He* means from our particular cultural vantage point. In order to access the supernal realm, we must delve into the structures of our own consciousness: we must think about our relations, how we understand fathering and other male images. Must a Father in Heaven be understood and experienced in prayer as an overbearing authority figure? Must a king be a man in a beard with a staff, passing down inscrutable decrees? Perhaps "He" is more open and adaptable than we give Him credit for.

David Hartman, in his foreword to Yochanan Muff's *The Personhood of God,* makes a similar argument to a broader theological end. He describes two alternative constructions of the divine: one that in essence deletes the human messiness of this conversation by eschewing altogether the notion of a relational God; and one that accepts the biblical premise of embodied God-imagery, and follows its cue, takes it a step further, positing a Jewish God who is involved in, and beholden to, a deep ongoing relationship with the vicissitudes of human understanding and experience.

> Maimonides' *Guide of the Perplexed* guides us in the struggle against idolatry and false conceptions of God. Yochanan Muffs guides us in the struggle against indifference and apathy in religious life. . . . God is not a static, unchanging reality, but a dynamic, evolving *person* actively interacting with human beings in history and with his beloved community, Israel. Here there is no leap to a transcendent God but rather a leap into one's own psychic life with the humanity of God can be understood and, at times, emulated." (Muffs 2005, x–xi)

Only in embracing our own humanity and the psychological dynamics of the human condition will we be able to meet the God of the Bible.

In other words, while the term "God" may itself remain fixed, it does not reify a fixed set of denotations but acts more like a placeholder for an evolving reality and relationship. By extension, we might argue for a similar understanding of other, more gender-specific divine names: to view them not as predigested images of male power but as triggers for us to reflect upon our own evolving gender identities and relationships. Caroline Walker Bynum (1986), the feminist religious historian, opens a different door onto this same conversation; she claims: "[g]ender-related symbols, in their full complexity, may refer to gender in ways that affirm or reverse it, support or question it; or they may, in their basic meaning, have little at all to do with male and female roles." (2). This may ultimately be the message, or one important message, that the Men of the Great Assembly were attempting to convey: that the words of prayer were given, and fixed so firmly into place, for the sake of pressing us to engage in this kind of reinterpretation. In a world that is always changing, something must remain constant. This stable control holds the history of evolving meanings, goads us forward to generate new ones that reflect our own changing psychic and social realities, and continues to reflect these realities back at us for consideration, evaluation, conversation and insight. We may similarly look upon these masculine God terms as alive rather than fixed: gender itself is not a fixed notion. Who "He" is is ultimately up to us.

Before going any further, I would like to acknowledge that this type of approach immediately raises the red flag of apologetics. Admittedly, the meanings of words, while fungible to a certain degree, are not so open as we would like to think. Because language occurs in a social context, there is an aspect of the meaning of words that perforce will be socially determined. Accepting this premise, I merely suggest that it adds an extra dimension of social activism to this quest for personal dignity in prayer. I am not trying to claim that by deconstructing its language, or offering a different understanding of the words, traditional prayer language becomes something that it is not. Simply by viewing the words in a different way we do not redeem them from their oppressive effects. I acknowledge the question, the problem, the struggle with language that presents images of women that we do not recognize (when it presents them at all). My claim is that when we uphold this struggle at the same time that, for other reasons, we accept the immutability of this language, other variables may begin to reconfigure themselves; other insights may ferment and rise into view. These insights do not necessarily constitute solutions, but neither should they be summarily dismissed. They may allow us to appreciate the traditional prayerbook without necessarily justifying every term found within it; they may enable us to see something about these words, and about our lives, that we may otherwise have missed. "Like a hammer, it explodes the stone" (Jeremiah 23:29); the Rabbinic tradition understands this verse to represent the midrashic banging away at texts that yields continuous explosive new meanings. Similarly, when we bang our heads against the rock of the traditional prayerbook, some valuable water does eventually leak out. We are not necessarily left with any less of a headache; yet, a certain deep thirst may begin to be quenched.

---

Accepting the immovability of the liturgy, we are forced, in a sense, to confront it, to stare at it, to meditate on it, and ask deeper questions about what it means. What does it mean when we say that God is a "He"? Is a "He" necessarily something oppressive? Is it a place where women have no place? Might the "He" have more room than we originally imagined; might the "He" have room for us as well? Perhaps it is not the liturgy that necessarily needs to change. Perhaps it is "He" that needs to change.

After all, there are two sides to the problematic of masculine prayer language, a "positive" side, and a "negative" side. For one, "Our Father" actively represents, reproduces, reifies, and deifies the patriarchal male. This identification of maleness with the divine who is viewed positively places masculinity at the pinnacle of human value. Second, and negatively, that masculine God identity leaves no space for women to occupy or even exist. One Hebrew word for God is "Ha-Makom" (The Place) implying the attribute of divinity that is all-inclusive. Exclusively masculine God language contradicts this attribute, cutting in half the part of humanity that can find a place of identification with the divine. Indeed, excluded from this version of God are not only women, but the majority of men, who are not fathers or judges or warriors (at least, not in the traditional connotations of by those terms). How, then, can we remedy this exclusion? How can we feel that God is a Place in which all of humanity, and all the different parts of the human personality, can dwell?

Again, perhaps it is necessary to begin to crack open and explore the meaning of maleness itself. How is it, first of all, that we have come to associate maleness so completely with "masculinity," to the extent in common parlance that the terms have become virtually synonymous? To be "a man" in both Western and many traditional cultures is to embody a set of well-known masculine characteristics (strong-willed, laconic, dominating, self contained, and so forth). If we take just a small step back, we realize that this set need not be so fixed. The conventional constellation of traits that have come to be subsumed within the term *masculinity* are merely one version of what maleness might look like—albeit a version that has become extremely privileged within many societies:

[T]he concept of masculinity is flawed because it essentializes the character of men or imposes a false unity on a fluid and contradictory reality. Masculinity is not a fixed entity embedded in the body or personality traits of individuals. Masculinities are configurations of practice that are accomplished in social action and, therefore, can differ according to the gender relations in a particular social setting. (Connell and Messerschmidt 2005, 836)

This insight about the fluidity of maleness and the multiplicity of masculinities (which within gender studies has achieved the status of a truism) has perhaps not yet or not sufficiently penetrated religious, even religious-feminist thinking, at least within the liturgical sphere. Connell, a leading theorist in this field, helped to coin and popularize the term *hegemonic masculinity* (Connell 1982, 1983, 1987) to denote "the currently most honored way of being a man" (Connell 2005, 832). It "required all other men to position themselves in relation to it, and it ideologically legitimated the global subordination of women to men" (ibid.). The notion of hegemony at work here does not necessarily refer to physical violence as the mechanism for enforcing a particular version of masculinity; it applies as well to "ascendancy achieved through culture, institutions, and persuasion" (ibid.). As the term developed, it maintained and advanced a basic assumption that gender relations were historical; thus, gender hierarchies were subject to change. Hegemonic masculinities came into existence in specific circumstances and were therefore open to historical change (ibid.). For Connell, this aspect of historical flux constitutes a window of optimism for gender identity and gender relations in the future: "there could be a struggle for hegemony, and older forms of masculinity might be displaced by new ones" (ibid.).

Those advocating for and implementing change in the masculine liturgy, while certainly working toward a greater sense of gender equality, might miss this nuanced but critical element of gender dynamics, and by extension a key opportunity for mending gender relations. By accepting the basic male/female dichotomy in conventional masculine/feminine terms, they leave uncontested the hegemonic masculinity that much of the male God imagery has come to connote. Yet, applying Connell's description and critique of hegemonic masculinity to our discussion about male God imagery, we come to realize that even traditionally "masculine" images like father, judge, and king need not necessarily inhere in the connotations about masculinity we generally (and often unconsciously) assign to them. Indeed, as we have found to be true with many feminist-theoretical insights, this new paradigm may help us to see our own tradition clearly. To take just one example from within the Bible itself, the greatest Jewish warrior and king, King David, challenges many of these embedded stereotypes: he is a warrior who is emotional, artistic, flamboyant, psychologically sensitive, and physically small. The cultural-historical overlay of hegemonic masculinity has homogenized our image of kingship and blunted our ability to appreciate the complexity of kingship our own tradition offers.

Similarly, applying this insight to our relationship with prayer may allow us to find new meaning, and new places of identification, with male terms freshly stripped of assumed "masculine" meanings. This insight advances not merely the deconstruction of gender hierarchies between men and women, but the embedded hierarchies within men, many or most of whom do not correspond (or feel they correspond) to the hegemonically masculine ideal. Understanding that men are themselves victimized by this ideal—while admittedly benefiting from it in some respects (what Connell refers to as "internal hegemony") is another benefit of holding onto masculine prayer imagery and looking deeper inside it, working it, and working with it and through it, rather than accepting it and abandoning it to its received meanings.

———

What are some images and meanings with which we might fill these masculine terms once we have neutralized our initial assumptions about what they represent? In approaching this question I draw primarily on radical feminist thinkers like Carol Gilligan (1982), Sara Ruddick (1989), and others who challenge us to break the stylized myths of the inherent gender traits. They insist that "masculine" and "feminine" are not biological essences tied ineluctably to male and female bodies, but themes, voices, ways of being in the world that can be—and regularly are—appropriated by males and females of different types, at different times, to different levels, in different ways. Gilligan (1982), in the introduction to *In a Different Voice,* throws down the gauntlet on the essentialist myth, explaining it as a kind of deep-seated, collective, cognitive error: "The different voice I describe is characterized not by gender but by theme. Its association with women is an empirical observation and it is primarily through women's voices that I trace its development. But this association is not absolute" (2).

When Gilligan speaks of the "care voice," for example, she refers not to gender or generalized representations of either sex but to themes and modes of thinking and being in the world. The association between male and female and their characteristics is simply not that absolute. Likewise, Sara Ruddick (1989) in *Maternal Thinking,* equates maternal thinking with peace thinking, with nurturance and commitment to a tomorrow:

The promise of maternal peacefulness lies in the work and love to which mothers are committed. By virtue of her mothering she is meant to be an initiator of peace and a witness against war. She represents a practice whose aims and strategies contradict those of war, which like mothering is also an organized human activity with moral pretensions. Women and men whose maternal identity is central to their self-respect should, as others, be uneasy militarists and self-possessed peacemakers, whatever their individual proclivities. (221)

The "maternal" is a theme for which women as mothers have been the primary carriers, but that belongs to men as well: when we project onto male-gendered language the exclusive connotations of domineering, aggressive, and so on, and seek to balance it with "softer," more "maternal" imagery, in fact we are merely perpetuating and further reifying the old essentialist dichotomy. In other words there may be an essential and very significant weakness of the "inclusiveness" (that is, the change-the-words) approach to liturgical sexism. Granting its basic legitimacy, there is a de facto consequence to this approach that to some extent undermines the goals it seeks to achieve and perpetuates the problems it sets out to correct. By adding women to the liturgy, what are we doing other than balancing out stereotypical images of masculinity with stereotypical images of femininity? In a way, these kinds of egalitarian counterbalances accept the premises of the patriarchy and play into its hands, exempting us from doing the very difficult this-worldly work of actually rethinking our inherited gender structures.

What is needed, perhaps, is to change the meanings of the words we *do* use. "Our Father" could potentially come to signify not exclusively a ruling and judging God, but a nurturing God; He may come to hold maternal qualities as well. Changing the heavenly spheres depends on changing the meaning we give in this world to malehood and womanhood and the nature of the relationships between men and women. When we change these on-the-ground realities, we will be affecting changes in the heavenly spheres, and vice versa, in a virtuous cycle of *Tikkun Olam* (Repairing the World). I argue that it is only when we expand our definitions of what male and female can entail that our image of God—and of our fellow images-of-God—will truly begin to change.

---

The idea that we represent the divine through the medium of human relationships and institutions and language can be found in the works of philosophers of religion over the last two centuries. As alluded to above, some leverage this insight into a sweeping critique of organized religion. Once we realize that "God" is merely a projection of specific sets of human ideals, culturally defined in its nature and economically motivated in the uses to which it is put (once we reach this point of enlightenment, that is), it becomes clear that we are far better off without Him.

The inclusiveness vis-à-vis prayer language can in some sense be seen as an appropriation of this "projective" thinking into a religious context. Accepting the premise that God is, if not wholly created, then largely understood, in terms of the human language we use to describe Him, projective thinking maintains a commitment to using language which represents and embodies our highest religious and moral values, the current "state of the art" in human consciousness. Peter Berger (1979) offers a compelling critique of projective thinking, embodied in the words of Feurbach, which in a sense might be seen as the basis for the alternative approach to prayer language offered above. Berger explains that while language may indeed be the vessel through which our awareness of God is made manifest, God also maintains an independence from that language, an independence of which we must remain ever aware:

Modern philosophy and science in the wake of Feurbach, are quite correct in seeing religion as a symbolization of the human world. The gods are indeed symbols of Human realities. This insight, important as it is, does not necessarily imply that the gods are nothing but that. Religious experience insists that, over and beyond their capacity to become human symbols, the gods inhabit a reality that is sui generis, and that is sovereignly independent of what human beings project onto it. What is more, religious experience suggests that the opposite understanding of the matter is finally the more important one: the human world in its entirety (including its various symbol systems) is itself a symbol—to wit, a symbol of the divine. In the most literal sense of "symbol," the human world stands for something beyond itself. It is a reflection, a signal, an intimation of another world. If men project their own meanings into the sky, their very capacity to do this comes from the fact that they have a celestial affinity. Feurbach and all his successors have grasped only one side of this dialectic of man-as-symbolizer/man-as-symbol, man-as-projector/man-as-project. To grasp the dialectic in its fullness is ipso facto to begin transcending the boundaries of modern secular consciousness. It also means to reject the reductive option for contemporary religious thought. (112–113)

The weakness of changing the words of prayer, I claim, lies in this kind of Feurbachian reductiveness. Because we see ourselves in some way as the creators of God, we feel that by changing the language we use to describe God, we alter God's essence. Realizing that human reality itself is "a reflection, a signal, an intimation of another world," pushes us to focus more intently on the human realities underlying the words. By giving more weight to the "man-as-symbol," "man-as-project" side of the dichotomy—that is, by focusing more on changing ourselves, filtering that transformation in the way we understand the language we use, and offering it up in our prayer—we can even more forcefully leverage our "celestial affinity" to transform the template in Whose image we were made.

# 5

## THE HANDS
## OF RABBIS
## ORTHODOX WOMEN
## AND NIDDAH

One of the early voices of criticism against Shirah Hadashah came not from other Orthodox Jews, but from a group committed to the absolute value of egalitarianism. They felt that in its negotiation with Orthodoxy, Shirah Hadashah was compromising on this absolute value. Some articulated the question implicit in much feminist thinking, and at times quite overt: why stay with Orthodoxy at all, if it cannot embrace and incorporate egalitarian values? As I mention in the introduction, I find it difficult to dispute that there are many compelling reasons for exiting traditional religious life. Feminist theorists have launched severe, sweeping critiques against the patriarchal structures of traditional cultures. There is, however, an important other voice that must be kept in mind when making this type of argument. Cross-cultural critiques of feminist theory, as well as certain self-reflective strains within feminist methodology, often reveal the presumptuousness some feminists evince in the way that they speak about (and note that I said speak *about*, rather than speak *with*) traditional women.

There are moments when the theoretical perspective that has come to liberate women has bound them up in its own world of assumptions. The movement whose aim it is to return to women their voice has at times overvoiced them. In their deep sense of ethical purpose, certain feminist theorists may be blind to the limitations of their view. Theory becomes so compelling that it simply cannot be imagined to be otherwise: anyone who adheres to the strictures of a patriarchal worldview must inherently be oppressed—regardless of the life experiences of the women living within these cultures (who are in fact rarely consulted, or if they are, rarely taken seriously). In my own work, I have found the glaring omission of traditional women's voices to be a limitation of this type of theory and a weakness in the feminist project more broadly defined: to honor women's lives. While it is often traditional systems and dicta that must be critiqued in order to further this aim, there is a certain element of feminist analysis that must also be scrutinized. We have been speaking about how religious texts often fail to take into account the experience of women, the degradation that comes with this kind of erasure, and the cultural mechanisms that encourage them to feel strange or crazy if they express any such feelings. Yet feminist theory, which comes to counter precisely this trend, demanding that women's experience be taken seriously into account, has also often assumed women's experiences without actually exploring them—without talking to the women themselves. In doing so it risks pigeonholing traditional women into (Freud's famous patient) Doras-in-reverse. Traditional women are often implicitly accused of a similar pathology for *not* feeling oppressed. The feminist reading of their lives is privileged over their consciousness, their subjectivity is undermined, their dignity compromised.

None of this is to deny the force of the feminist critique of traditional life. The demonization and regulation of women's bodies within religious patriarchies has been well documented in various cultures. Women have been subjected to a range of negative characterizations: polluting, dangerous temptresses (Douglas 1966), "inherently different from men's [bodies] in ways that made them both defective and dangerous" (Weitz 1998, 3). As a result, women have been systematically overdressed and undressed, locked indoors and exposed to public humiliation, and even burnt at the stake to placate men's fears about the hyperbolized, often mythologized, dangers their bodies are purported to pose (Arthur 1999; Daly 1999; Eilberg-Schwartz 1995; Polhemus 1978; Sanday 1982; Turner 1996). Menstruation in particular, has many taboos and has been studied extensively from a range of perspectives: psychological, sociological, anthropological, and comparative-religious. Feminist analysis has highlighted the extent of the oppressive strictures surrounding the menstrual taboo—spoken and unspoken, encoded in texts and transmitted orally.

Religious codes, which tend to reify these attitudes into explicit catalogues of restrictive norms, are obvious agents in this systemic silencing of women. The Jewish laws of modesty and *niddah* (the system of ritual purity and immersion) seem to serve as Judaism's version of this familiar patriarchial device. Jewish feminists claim that these laws oppress and degrade women and their bodies because their restrictions imply that women are a "potential source of pollution and disorder whose life and impact on men must be regulated" (Baskin 1985, 14; see also Biale 1984; Hyman 1976; Baum, Hyman, and Michel 1976; Priesand 1975; Swidler 1976). Judith Plaskow (1990) maintains that, based on Jewish sources about women, "it is difficult to conclude anything other than that women are a source of moral danger and an incitement to depravity and lust" (184–185). "It is precisely in this area [of sexual regulation]," says Paula Hyman (1976), "that the second-class status of women within Judaism is highlighted" (110).

This theoretical critique of patriarchal systems in general, and Jewish religious law as a salient case in point—particularly the negative valuations attributed to menstruation and the oppressive practices that arise from it—has unquestionable force. At the same time, it is my claim that the theoretical power of this account leaves unanswered—perhaps unasked—just how religious women themselves live and experience their regimens and commitments: how they both see and do not see the disciplinary structures (see Foucault, 1977) in which they reside and through which they, in very complex and countering ways, define themselves. Any approach that attempts to separate rules from the women who live them is inherently flawed.

It is indeed an unintended irony of some feminist approaches to traditional religion that, because the "readings" of cultural symbols are so compelling, the need to listen closely to the voices of actual people seems, on some level, to be obviated. If such voices are sought out and solicited, there is a strong temptation to theorize them into preexisting categories, rather than to allow them to re-form the categories—or force us to recalibrate our understanding of the symbols. Thus the nuances of individual lives are often obscured. In fact, as potent as the feminist critiques of religious patriarchy are, they have not yet managed to articulate a multivocal account of the experiences of women living within these systems (for exceptions, see Kandiyoti 1991; Kaufman 1993).[1] This absenting of actual women's voices constitutes a conspicuous gap in knowledge, and, consequently, a theoretical weakness.

This chapter will explore case studies (Stake 2000) of Orthodox Jewish women vis-à-vis the practice of *niddah*.[2] Our intention here is primarily cartographic:[3] to map out the lived landscape of *niddah* observance in its provocative complexity and, in so doing, convey something of the richness and sophistication of the women who are constantly negotiating its marked trails and hidden passes, its contours and its cliffs. What emerges, then, is a picture of *niddah* practice as viewed from the perspective of women who live within the Jewish legal (*halakhic*) system. This picture looks very different from the ones deduced or inferred from theoretical analyses.

When thinking about the observance of *niddah*, we kept in mind that ritual acts can be conceptualized in terms of two constituent parts: regulation and attribution. Regulation refers to the behavioral aspects of the ritual; attribution, the reasons given for the behaviors. Steinberg (1997) points out that Orthodox Jewish tradition, and especially *niddah* observance, require fealty to ritual praxis regardless of one's attributions or understanding. He also notes, along with Yanay and Rapoport (1997), that while the practice of *niddah* has remained relatively constant among traditional Jewish women over many centuries, the attributions have varied radically at different times and in different places.

As discussed above, the rules that govern religious women's bodies are often criticized as oppressive methods of domination. In fact, a self-conscious discourse of oppression figured prominently in our participants' descriptions of their experience observing the *niddah* laws. This admission, however, was only part of the picture: they also had many positive comments with regard to the ritual, as well as uplifting things to say about the effects and implications of *niddah* in their lives. What was most striking about the accounts these women gave was the ease and willingness with which they made distinctions: among elements of these practices they found meaningful and/or beautiful; those they found neutral or unmeaningful; and those they found burdensome, unsavory, offensive, or oppressive. As we shall show, it is the simultaneous validity of this multiplicity of responses—so often set in opposition—that in fact constitutes their vibrant discourse of observance.

## The Burderns of Observance

### AN AWARENESS OF OPPRESSION

Throughout, our interviews revealed an undercurrent of women grappling with the notion of oppression and its relevance to their lives. Often they raised the issue unprompted, reflecting a general awareness of feminist claims regarding women's roles in patriarchal religious structures. Deborah, for example, was clearly responding to this implicit discourse when, without being asked anything about oppression, she offered, "[The niddah laws are] not something that's oppressive to me." The women's awareness of feminist discourse and their desire not to think of themselves, or be viewed by others, as oppressed, deeply informed their responses to the questions we posed. Once again without external prompting, in discussing how she and her husband moderate their intimacy during the times of *niddah,* Yael, the wife of a rabbi, first raised and then attempted to exorcize the specter of oppression: "[*Niddah*] shouldn't be very oppressive. But every time, it's true—there's no doubt, there are. We go more covered, we try to go with pajamas . . . or all kinds of things that cover—there are all these things." Thus the implicit concession that though these laws *shouldn't* be oppressive, unavoidably they *are.*

Though these women seem familiar in a general way with feminist vocabulary—familiar enough, for example, to appropriate the term "oppression" for certain elements of their experience—ultimately we must ask if they are speaking the same language. To formulate an answer, we must first ask: what do these women mean when they use the term "oppression"? We suggest deconstructing the term into three subcategories: (1) the imposition of severe inconvenience (say, a job with long hours or an "oppressive" commute); (2) the stifling of ambitions and drives (say, career tracking); (3) more literal and direct forms of subjugation (sexual harassment and exploitation, systemic wage discrimination). These are, of course, soft categories, with significant overlap among them. Still, for heuristic purposes, they are useful in untangling some of the threads of our participants' discourse of oppression.

"PARTICULARLY DIFFICULT":
THE UNIQUE CHALLENGES SURROUNDING NIDDAH

Some of our participants reported experiencing the laws of *niddah* differently from other religious obligations. They found it "particularly difficult," and explained or alluded to some reasons for this distinction. Leah depicted her difficulties with *niddah* as stemming from a combination of the newness of the *mitzvah,* the newness of the relationship it circumscribes, and the area of the relationship upon which it lays claim:

> This is really the first time that you have to deal with something that is really hard. What—do you struggle over transgressing Shabbat? . . . Things that are new for us we learn, we deal, we try, we improve . . . but these are really difficult. . . . I am sure that I am not the only person who is struggling with this difficulty . . . mainly in that a relationship is new and everything is new.

By contrasting this *mitzvah* with those surrounding Sabbath observance, she distinguishes between areas of observance that have become second nature through a lifetime of acculturation, and the hardship of a new *mitzvah* to which she has become obligated through marriage.

Other women named different aspects of *niddah* observance as annoying or onerous. Chana, a mother of teenage children, spoke of the burdensome rigor of the internal checks required twice daily upon the cessation of bleeding: "Well I can say that it is certainly a burden! And the seven clean days are very difficult because you always feel that you have to be connected to the clock and see if it's time to do another check, and make sure that it doesn't get too late. That is a real pain." While Chana discussed the burdens connected to time pressures, Rivka resented the physically intrusive aspect of the obligation: "the checks are not pleasant . . . it annoys me that I have to shove something into my body." These women's complaints about the *niddah* ritual fall roughly into the category of inconvenience. This is not to dismiss or belittle their grievances, only to highlight that they are framed more in terms of logistical annoyances than as threats to identity.

Yael found the ritual more onerous. She also related directly to the particular difficulty of taking on *niddah* observance at the time of marriage, and her complaint begins with the characterization of *niddah* as an inconvenience or burden. The context in which she understands this burdensomeness, however, expands and becomes tied to other marriage-related identity hardships; these hardships, taken together, become emblematic for her of a deeper form of oppression:

> It's a certain burden, and we don't always love it. . . . At the beginning it's a horrible feeling because *they* are changing this for *you* and that for *you*— *they* change your family name, things that are difficult; that is, they do reduce a certain essence/identity [*mahut mesuyemet*]. . . . *She* has to leave the family that gave her an identity and change *her* name, *she* has to cover *her* hair—and *she* already doesn't belong to everyone as *she* did before. (emphasis added)

Yael notes that the "burden" and "difficulty" of taking on *niddah* observance at this particular juncture of the life cycle is exacerbated by the constellation of other changes imposed upon women at this time. Cumulatively, these changes brought about a "horrible feeling." Unlike Leah, she does not relate to her observance as a positive choice, but as a series of abuses "they" are imposing upon "you," "she," and "her"—absenting herself completely as a first-person voice from her own discourse (Gilligan et. al. 1988; Brown and Gilligan 1992). This dissociation bespeaks an acute inner dissonance vis-à-vis the nexus of *niddah* and marriage that, for Yael, is far from resolved.

Yosefa's displeasure with *niddah* was not limited to its effect on her life immediately following marriage:

> My problem is not just how hard it is to do the checks twice a day—not just that I can't have intercourse—it's that I can't be touched. My needs for being touched are not just sexual, they're human.

Yosefa expressed a profound sadness at the denial of nonsexual contact during *niddah*, a contact she experiences as a basic human need. After giving birth she "stained" continuously for three-and-a-half months, which, according to halakha, assigned her the status of *niddah* for that entire period. During that time she underwent frequent and acute emotional crises, which she attributed to the denial of physical contact with her husband. She was aware that, in cases of extreme emotional duress, halakha allows for leniencies. She also knew that to procure such an exemption would require petitioning a rabbi. "I know if I called my rabbi, told him I was crying all the time, he'd say okay; but why do I have to be mentally ill before I can get permission?" Yosefa felt that to enter into the legal fiction of mental illness would represent a compromise to her integrity even more damaging than the ordeal she was currently suffering. She related to the *niddah* laws as dehumanizing for the manner in which they disregarded her basic emotional needs.

Shifra was even more strident in her condemnation of *niddah:* "Not being able to touch each other is torture . . . it's hard enough that you don't have sex when you want; but the touching. . . . To go to sleep in a separate bed is just . . ." Shifra's speech became halting, her tone increasingly livid, as she described the intense frustration and inner turmoil of feeling bound inextricably to a ritual that is a source of unremitting personal torment.

To say that these women felt stifled by the *niddah* requirements would be a grave understatement; "suffocated" comes closer to encapsulating their responses. They experienced the ritually imposed cycle of separation and closeness as a series of deprivations and degradations in violent opposition to their psychological and emotional health. Knowing that they could be touched in the near future did nothing to relieve this distress; on the contrary, the absence of an intimate space within which to relate to their husbands was a key deprivation and common complaint.

LEGAL IMPOTENCE: THE REQUIREMENT TO ASK A RABBI

In addition to the significant emotional and physical difficulties presented by *niddah* observance, our participants also expressed frustration with its authoritarian structure. If a woman observing *niddah* sees a blood stain, either when she is not menstruating or on the cloth of one of the internal checks during the seven clean days before immersion, she is instructed to ask a rabbi whether this stain renders her unclean. She (or her husband) brings the cloth or her undergarments to the rabbi, who examines it and makes a ruling about her status. In this dynamic, our participants described feeling demoralized, divested of personal power—deprived not only of authority, as a passive heir to this legal code, but of an education sufficient to grant an understanding of its arcane bylaws.

Many of the participants' accounts resonated with the third category of oppression—systemic subjugation—and thus with the feminist claim that religious women's obligations, and the control of the body and sexuality constitute a patriarchal exercise of domination and social control (Turner 1996):

> I spoke to my husband and then I asked a Rabbi. I didn't really like that. To tell the truth, that was always something that really put me off in this whole matter because it's very personal and private. And to go take your physiological evidence to someone—I was never comfortable with it. (Deborah)

Deborah's words conveyed a sense of dehumanization in life's most delicate sphere, such that she felt reduced to a kind of medical exhibit. Her humiliation was exacerbated by having to petition a man for menstrual validation and sexual permission—which, in addition to being viscerally repellant, reminded her that these obligations were part of a system in which men dominate women's sexuality. Tina also expressed her experience of violation and domination in an almost physical way:

> What really bothers me are the checks that I have to do inside my body: I sometimes have this feeling that it is the long hands of the rabbis of hundreds of years literally entering my body to check me.

In recent years, the Modern Orthodox community has seen the emergence of female *Yo'atzot Niddah* (literally, *Niddah* consultants), learned women who steep themselves in the laws of *niddah* practice and take on the rabbinic decision-making role in this sphere. In the short time since the first *niddah* consultants began functioning in this role, the response within the Modern Orthodox and the more conservative Israeli National Religious communities has been extremely positive.

### RESPONSES TO RABBINIC AUTHORITY

Our participants described a range of responses to the sense of rabbinic subjugation to which *niddah* rituals give rise. Deborah maintained her observance of the *niddah* ritual itself, while eventually factoring out the rabbinic component. "I decided I had enough sense to make these decisions on my own." Yertl made a similar decision, although hers can be viewed as somewhat more subversive and extreme; her husband is a rabbi who regularly answers *niddah* questions from women in their community: "Don't you think it's strange that during twenty-five years of marriage he never asked me: 'Don't you have a question?' But I would never ask him or anyone." Like Deborah, Yertl can be seen as appropriating authority where she feels authority has been misplaced by tradition.

Another participant expressed her hostility toward this aspect of *niddah* observance by manipulating the system to the point of mockery. Whenever she would have a stain that required consultation, she would "shop around" to see who would offer her the most lenient opinion, playing the power of the rabbinic authorities against one another. While her story added a cynical twist to a common frustration, and expressed her personal rebellion against this part of the system, it is important to note that at the end of the day she remained within the system—continuing to observe the laws, and ultimately accepting a rabbinic authority (albeit the most lenient version of it she could find), rather than casting off the system as a whole or even this particular ritual.

Tina noted that over the course of history, male impurity faded as a practical halakhic category, and men's *mikveh* immersion was deemed obsolete. She related the story of a friend, strictly religious in all other aspects of her life, who ceased observing *niddah* as an act of resistance against this historical bias. "Well, too bad," Tina quoted her friend as saying, "I'm stopping."

### Bearable to Beneficial, Authority to Power: Positive Responses to Observance

Our participants accepted the obligations of halakha in their lives even when they personally disliked them, and had little hesitancy acknowledging this difficulty. At the same time, many of them spoke at length of the benefit and value which the observance of *mitzvot* in general brings to their lives and extolled the importance of upholding them. Using words like "beauty" and "enhancement," they stressed not only the voluntary and at times enthusiastic nature of their participation in halakhic ritual, but a sense of value and benefit in the particular halakhic realm of *niddah*. Some had to search to find these benefits, while others claimed to experience them naturally and vividly. Some found that they made other, unsavory aspects of *niddah* observance bearable; some made no attempt to connect the two realms; others spoke exclusively of empowerment and beauty.

RITUAL AS ROTE:

COMMITMENT TO HALAKHA AS THE BASIS FOR OBSERVANCE

One dominant strain in our interviews placed the value of *niddah* observance not locally within this particular set of rituals, but rather as a component of halakhic observance as a whole. Many of these women spoke openly about the negative elements of *niddah* observance; in the final analysis, however, they all concluded that the value of halakha as a way of life, and the benefits of membership within the religious Jewish community, outweighed these concerns. They related to the halakhic lifestyle as a whole greater than the sum of its parts.

Chava, who has been married for almost thirty-five years, made it clear that it was *only* because of her commitment to a religious way of life that she observed this *mitzvah,* and that she did so despite profoundly negative feelings toward the ritual itself: "I hated the whole thing—from beginning to end. I only did it because I had to, but my life would've been much better without it."

Similarly, Deborah "accepted [*niddah*] from the point of view that it is halakha," maintaining, "I certainly do not see the logic in it." She has a strong-enough voice to state unequivocally that she feels burdened by what to her are incomprehensible strictures; yet ultimately she chooses to subsume that voice to the goal of maintaining a religious lifestyle. In such an encompassing system, spiritual meaning and value are not necessarily to be found in every particularity of observance. Rather, the primary source of value is drawn from the choice to adhere to a lifestyle and defer to a system in which, on the whole, one believes. Deborah articulated this position very clearly:

> Why do I wait a certain number of hours between meat and milk, and why do I refrain from turning on the electricity on Shabbat, and why do I do lots of other things? From my point of view it all belongs to the same category. It's halakha. . . . It's the way I live my life. . . . Do I feel a fantastic rush every time I do something? No!

Likewise, Rachel, who has seven children, noted that when she took on the obligations of the laws of *niddah* upon marriage, she felt "a great amount of happiness because I knew I was doing the right thing." This sentiment recurred in many of the interviews.

A number of our participants placed even less stock in the *niddah* ritual per se. For those who prefer to place ritual activity—especially rituals as seemingly charged as *niddah* and *mikveh*—in contexts of valence and meaning, these women's voices are important to keep in mind inasmuch they resist placement on even a nuanced axis of oppression/empowerment. For them, *niddah* is simply internalized as one among many halakhic rituals, which themselves are indistinguishable from the other rituals of daily life. For example, Jane said, "I do not feel oppressed, for me it is not intrusive, it is a vestige of something. It is one of the things that do not have that much meaning but I do them anyway." Despite her indifference vis-à-vis meaning, Jane did claim to find benefit in the *niddah* ritual:

> I find no meaning in the ritual per se, but I do find benefit in the constant renewal of sexual interest. And there is a positive effect in having to find

other means of communication [aside from sex]. This was not the reason for it, but it is a happy side effect. The point could've been made in less than two weeks a month, but still there is something to be gained.

Interestingly, Jane feels no need to translate these "happy side effects" of her *niddah* observance into sites of religious meaning, much less project them back into the ritual's initial intent; that is, transform them into a form of apologetics. The ritual justifies itself: one divine commandment among many. No other explanation or justification is required.

ESSENTIAL VALIDATION:

THE *NIDDAH* PERIOD AND RESPECT FOR WOMEN'S NEEDS

A number of our participants appreciated the *niddah* cycle's legislation of a nonsexual sphere within married life. Shoshana framed this appreciation in terms of the ritual's intrinsic "intent":

> The meaning of the separation is that during a woman's cycle, during those two weeks a woman might be feeling more sensitive/delicate [*adin,*] and involvement in sexual relations bothers/disturbs [*mafria*] during this period. It is a period of quiet with myself.

Sara added that, in addition to respecting a woman's biological-emotional needs, the laws of *niddah* also place welcome limitations on spousal intercourse. Noting that women sometimes have difficulty refusing their husbands' sexual advances, she described as an intended benefit the imposition of an external, impartial, and inherently legitimate separation that obviates the need to rebuff a husband's desire for sex. She felt this advantage especially keenly after giving birth:

> You know, I think about couples who don't observe, and you have to start saying it's good for me now or it's not so comfortable. It's good in my view that there is time. It's not nice. At that time the woman is so concentrated on herself, and you don't want sex.

This separation allowed Sara to focus her energies internally in this time of transition and tumult, without feeling bad about doing so. It gave her the time she needed while menstruating or recuperating after birth, a time that otherwise, perhaps, her husband would not be willing to grant.

Rachel felt similar benefits. "I usually enjoy sex. But, there are times when a *woman* needs the physical and times when she doesn't want it. It's good that the laws respond to that" (emphasis added). Her account presents an interesting contrast to those of Yosefa and Shifra above, who complained precisely of the *absence* of a nonsexualized space within the *niddah* cycle's on/off sexual dialectic. Rachel's speech pattern was significant inasmuch as it reflected an unwillingness to admit—or possibly obliviousness to—this alternate perspective: she began by describing her enjoyment in the first person, but moved to an inclusive third person as she related to a feeling she assumed is common to all women.

Like Rachel, Rivka spoke of the benefit of this separation in facilitating her ability to be more of an individual within the relationship: "I needed the space. . . . I think that the *mitzvot* and the world of Torah are built with a lot of contemplation about the nature of people." By respecting her in this way, Rivka said, the laws affirm her inherent feminine sensibilities and encourage her to relate more deeply to herself and her preferences.

Among our participants who expressed sentiments consonant with those quoted above, Bruria was the most unequivocal. She felt that the *niddah* cycle enhances her marriage:

> The *mikveh* gives me a wonderful feeling; when I go, I feel like my husband is waiting for me like an honored guest, like he waits Friday night for the Sabbath angels . . . it makes me feel like our relationship moves to a higher level.

She claimed that it also enhances her sense of inner peace and self esteem:

> Every time there is this feeling of renewal, and I feel that I enter the water as a religious person who is accepted for who I am, without makeup, without colors: I have an intrinsic net worth, without any props.

Bruria introduced novel interpretations of the meaning and purpose of *niddah,* openly acknowledging that these interpretations were her own. She engaged in an inner dialogue as to whether "there is intellectual honesty in giving this modern meanings that perhaps were not the original intent." She concluded, "I think there is."

It would be possible to interpret the above characterizations as variations on the theme of patriarchal apologetics, or even false consciousness: an internalization of patriarchal demands so deep that it results in total identification, which is then formulated using a rhetoric that draws upon feminist language. It is equally possible, though, that the resonance these women find in the halakhic system's take on women's life cycles emerges from a sense of identification that is genuine and profound, based primarily upon their experience of their biological and emotional rhythms. These participants feel that their tradition embodies a feminist voice: it responds to the needs of women's bodies, minds, and souls; it is not merely prescriptive, telling them what they can and cannot do with their bodies, but descriptive of their own deepest understanding and experience of themselves.

The "truth" of these women's consciousness is, of course, impossible to know. Whether somewhere on the spectrum between oppression and validation, or simply unique to each individual woman, what was most valuable was how these participants use the tradition to articulate their needs to their partners in an authoritative manner. What is clear is that their assertion and articulation are facilitated greatly by tradition's definitive imprimatur. Halakha has given these women legitimation for a voice-that-says-no within their sexual relationships—a voice that, within both traditional and modern patriarchies, has to varying degress been silenced and denied. The law gives women the only voice that can possibly counter the invincible authority and power of men's sexual desire: the power of an oppositional patriarchial voice, the power of the Rabbis/God negotiating with the power of their male partners. Those women who do feel the need to refrain from sexuality feel that they come to the negotiating table with the only voice that can counter the voice of men's desire: the more powerful men's voice of Tradition. The voice-that-says-no becomes then a voice that bears rabbinic affirmation. Its practical efficaciousness in establishing sexual boundaries consonant with the needs of our participants is a palpable benefit for which they express profound appreciation.

### POSSESSING A VOICE IN SEXUALITY

In addition to respecting women's desire to be nonsexual, the halakhic framework, according to many of our participants, sanctions their sexual desires within the framework of marriage. The Torah (as inferred from Exod. 21:10) charges every married man with the *mitzvah* of *onah;* that is, the commandment to provide his wife with her conjugal rights. Thus, the halakhic system establishes a sexual sphere within marriage that is distinct from procreation, and encourages women to expect, enjoy, and *demand* an active and vital sexual relationship with their spouse.

Though the *mitzvah* of *onah* is separate from the directives of *niddah,* they overlap inasmuch as part of the husband's *onah* requirement obliges him to sexual relations on the night of *mikvah* immersion and encourages women to communicate to their husbands (either symbolically or verbally) when they are sexually available.

A woman can also initiate physical things. It's good to say that I want this or that, especially because the woman is supposed to enjoy. In fact, the husband is not fulfilling his commandment of *onah* if you don't enjoy. So that means that if you want sex, or whatever, then he has to agree and you have the right to ask for it. (Yael)

Contrary to Freud's (1931) image of the silent and passive woman as sexual partner, because of the *mitzvah* of *onah*, Yael feels as though "she has the right to ask" when she wants sex.

Sara echoed this sentiment:

[W]hatever the woman wants is the obligation of the husband. I remember that they [their instructors] spoke to us about how important it is that a woman should also enjoy.

This halakhic premium on women's sexual fulfillment can be seen as a stark challenge to broad-based claims that religion represses women sexually and that women's pleasure is achieved through surrender, passivity, and recognition of themselves as sexual objects (Nicholson 1994).

Jane concurred that this element of *niddah* affirms, very practically and directly, her own needs within the sexual relationship, and validates a woman's rights to sexual fulfillment and desire more generally:

The general feeling of the *mitzvah* of *onah* makes me feel that the tradition goes against the idea that sex is all about him and his needs. . . . The *mikveh* joins the larger value of what does *she* need, what does the woman deserve?

Just as many of our participants felt that the tradition speaks to them in validating their voice-that-says-no within their sexual relationships, they felt that it "joins" their "I want/I need/I desire" voice—another voice traditionally silenced by men's power. Their sexual fulfillment is validated and underwritten by a patriarchal tradition that in this instance stands and speaks unequivocally *with* them, demanding of its men, as a requirement of membership in good standing, that they listen.

POSTPONING IMMERSION:

*HALAKHIC* AUTHORITY AND SEXUAL POWER

Because women are the arbiters of *niddah* observance, it also functions as a locus of women's power. By, for example, refusing to go to the *mikveh*, or delaying their immersion, they command the halakhically sanctioned authority to withhold sex from their husbands. This authority is significant in that it turns on its head the general Western construction that "heterosexual sex means that men enact their social power over women" (Choi and Nicholson 1994, 22). Because Orthodox women are conscious of the potential to delay immersion and thereby halt sexual relations, their awareness serves as an instrument of power even when they choose not to act upon it.[4] Accordingly, these laws imbue women with a sexual standing that counters the Foucaultian notion "that the discourses associated with female sexuality specifically act to regulate and control women, and to maintain men's position of power" (Ussher 1994, 148). The women we interviewed clearly perceive themselves as, to a large extent, regulating and controlling their sexual relationships and, as such, occupying positions of power not only within the discourses associated with their sexuality, but within their actual sexual practice. A number of our participants cited instances when communities of women banded together, refusing (as a group) to go to the *mikvah,* until an injustice done by one of the men in the community against a woman peer was rectified. The historicity of these stories is far less important than what they reveal about the sense of not only individual, but *communal* influence with which Orthodox women feel empowered by the laws of *niddah.*

Miriam, a Hasidic woman and mother of eight, delayed going to the *mikvah* as a form of birth control. Having evaluated her sexual and emotional needs and decided that she "didn't want to have children too quickly," she found herself unable to get a rabbinic sanction to use contraceptives. She then took matters into her own hands, utilizing the power invested in her by the halakhic system to subvert rabbinic authority, determine her own sexual destiny, and curb her husband's sexual activity by simply waiting an extra day or two before she went to the *mikvah.*

*Mikvah* can be used as an overt tactic of power, a sexual weapon.

> There was one time that I thought not to go to the *mikvah.* There was something that was bothering me, something that was bothering us, that we hadn't resolved, so I didn't feel like going. But then I realized that that is not right. (Yael)

Despite the fact that she decided against it, that she consciously thought about delaying means that she is aware of the power she wields.

The knowledge of the subversive potential held by this aspect of *niddah* observance is something some of these women came to on their own. For others it was inherited knowledge, passed down to them by their mothers to help them find more maneuverability—and, ultimately, a kind of power—within the patriarchal system than may not at first seem apparent. The type of power these women described resonates with Perelberg's (1990) concept of "the power of the weak." This power is distinguished, first of all, from an idea of authority (Bendix 1973; quoted in Perelberg 1990) that is "linked to the idea of legitimization, the right to make particular decisions, and to command obedience." Power, on the other hand, "lies in the possibility of imposing one's will upon the behavior of other persons" (ibid., 290). Perelberg emphasizes that these "'oblique' or peripheral power strategies" are in no way equivalent to direct forms of authority, insisting:

> The fact that power can be exercised from a subordinate position is fundamental to both the way in which gender roles are constructed in different societies and the respective positions from which men and women perceive themselves (see also McCormack and Strathern 1980, who have pointed out that most societies tend to present a more complex pattern of interaction between men and women than one would perceive by examining the "official" system of rights, duties, and authority). (Perelberg 1990, 45)

### Discussion and Conclusion

The women we interviewed reported a range of attributions to the *niddah* ritual, as well as a range of responses to the same attributions and the basic *niddah* regulations. Some women felt oppressed by the practice of *niddah*. There were those who felt vehemently that the regulatory aspect of *niddah* itself impinged upon their psychological and emotional well-being in ways damaging and profound. They felt subjugated, harassed, and in some cases abused by a rabbinic authority who intruded in the most private aspect of their lives, put their bodily functions on display, and exposed their sexuality for patriarchal supervision and control. Others also described the regulatory element of *niddah* as oppressive, but seemed to mean it as a term of inconvenience, rather than the more penetrating and severe connotations implied by the systemic critique.

Complicating the picture, however, were those among our participants for whom regulation per se was not inherently oppressive. The fact that their sexuality was regulated was not a significant categorical distinction from the other requirements of their halakhic lifestyle. In fact, some expressed appreciation for the sexual regulations affected by *niddah*, the structure that it gave to their sexual practice (which they felt was deeply consonant with essential biological and emotional needs), and the cycle of abstinence and desire, of individuality and coupling, that it facilitated in their relationships with their husbands. Yet others resisted attribution altogether, relating to *niddah* strictly as a behavioral phenomenon, a series of acts to be accomplished (a "checklist," as one put it), and expressed disinterest, indifference, and even hostility vis-à-vis attempts to imbue it with different meanings.

With few exceptions, the interviewees did not relate to the fact that these regulations have been couched in traditional literature within a discourse of defilement. While aware of these voices, our participants dismissed them as antiquated remnants of a premodern consciousness. They did not see themselves as second-class citizens being segregated from a fearful or disdainful society, or from husbands skittish at the potential ill-effects of menstrual blood. Nor did observance provoke feelings of degradation or shame.[5] Indeed, many of our participants have maintained ancient practices while abandoning the ancient or medieval classifications and valuations. It seems that for these women, defilement has largely evaporated as an attribution for *niddah*, following its diminished significance in modern consciousness. What is left is a system of sexual regulations that itself elicits a wide range of alternative attributions and diverse emotional responses.

Among this wide range of accounts, some resonated with elements of more theoretical feminist analyses, some challenged them, and others seemed to hover outside of their purview altogether. It should be noted, of course, that the phenomenon of the oppressed identifying and collaborating with the oppressor is not new, and certainly could be presented as a plausible explanation for some of these women's affirmation of *niddah* as nonoppressive, beneficial, and essentially correct. These women could be interpreted as suffering from a range of cognitive-emotional disorders: false consciousness, Uncle Tom–style oppressor identification, patriarchal collaboration. We felt, however, that privileging this kind of analysis would constitute an abstraction and flattening of their experience. More to the point, I argue that overvoicing them in these ways contradicts basic feminist values, to say nothing of feminist methodologies in research.

By listening in this way, one can hear Orthodox women's thoughts and experiences move beyond the schematic abstractions of prevailing concepts, and into a highly textured range of responses. By refusing to implicate them on an axis of collaboration-resistance, or to locate them within a simple oppression-empowerment dichotomy, we are better able to hear the ways in which they manage a broad range of voices, at times in concert, at times in conflict, and at times content merely to coexist. We were able to hear not only hidden "knots of resistance" (Foucault 1980), but knots of experience more broadly. Gruenbaum (2000) is instructive and appropriately cautionary in this regard:

For the most part, Western feminists have found themselves in a dilemma. . . . To label women of a different culture as having a false consciousness . . . sounds like a delegitimization of the culture or belief of others . . . and thus too often the result has been a pedagogy of missionizing, telling others what they ought to do differently for reasons justified only by the enlightened outsiders' beliefs. (57)

Like Kaufman (1993), we found that women's lived experience of *niddah* incorporates not only diverse reactions, but a sophisticated weaving of responses. Thus we affirm the possibility of a ritual life that is deeply and authentically imbued with alternative attributions of meaning. In a broader sense, we hope to deepen the sense of texture and humanity of women who choose to live within traditional frameworks, and to encourage others to value their experience more highly.

# 6

## ROLES, RULES, AND RESPONSA

### THE BACKLASH AGAINST FEMINISM

I first met Elie Holzer, one of the founders of Shirah Hadashah, at a JOFA conference in 2001. By sheer coincidence, we had both come to speak about the same topic: Rabbis Twersky and Meiselman's responses to the phenomenon of women's prayer groups. Each of us reclaimed the intrinsic value of a person's religious subjectivity as something that cannot and should not be a priori defined by authority, whether textual or human. Elie drew his claim from an analysis of Rabbi Soloveitchik's hermeneutic and philosophy of religion and I did so from a feminist-psychological perspective. After our sessions we began brainstorming about what a serious prayer community—one that acknowledged and honored the spiritual dignity and desires of women—could look like.

In light of both our general experiences within the Modern Orthodox community, and the specific topic that had brought us to the conference, Elie and I understood quite keenly how charged this issue was. The preceding years had been characterized by intense exchanges in the Modern Orthodox world about increased women's participation in public roles, particularly around prayer and the ritual life of the synagogue. Modern Orthodox women felt an increased sense of desire—and of entitlement—in this arena, and the response of many Modern Orthodox authorities was taking the shape of a classic patriarchal backlash against feminist gains. There seemed to be much at stake for those attempting to hold the line of "no change," which was reflected in their willingness to lash out quite aggressively against those calling even for changes that appeared to pose no halahkic problem (or at least could find solid halakhic ground upon which to stand).

Elie and I both had spent many years on the ritual committees of shuls, and so we were familiar with the range of responses to this call for change. We knew that we would not be confronting a purely halakhic conversation. We knew that some would attempt to make halakhic arguments, some would stress the need to maintain a unified front within Orthodoxy, and some—inevitably the loudest—would employ a range of metahalakhic, antifeminist rhetoric. We knew of the deep discomfort of certain rabbinic authorities and their adherents in admitting that some religious needs are left unmet by the tradition in its current state.

The halakhic arguments against ritual changes could be met with counter-arguments, and this was a welcome and legitimate conversation. After all, we were not (and are not) claiming ours is the *only* halakhic way to do communal prayer, or the only way to understand traditional principles like *kvod ha-tzibur* (respecting communal dignity) and *kvod ha'adam* (respecting human dignity)—which are also the central halakhic categories employed in determining such issues as the permissibility of women reading from the Torah and leading certain parts of the service. Our intention was never to argue that ours was the only way to pray, but merely that it is a traditionally valid mode in which to stand before God.

The argument about Orthodox unity is one to which we remain sympathetic, but which we decided cannot outweigh the considerations of human dignity. Once again, we were and are perfectly willing to view this argument as a *makhloket le-shem shamayim* (a disagreement for the sake of heaven). The metahalakhic, antifeminist conversation, on the other hand, utilized tactics of recrimination, intimidation, and delegitimation that, ultimately and ironically, undermined its own purpose: exposing the extent to which increased women's participation was not *at all* a halakhic issue (why else all the fire and brimstone, with little or no halakhic content anywhere to be found?) and undermining its own credibility with hyperbolically alarmist claims. When Rabbi Meiselman says that if we accept women's prayer groups, soon women will be dancing with pagan idols in shul, the mind races until it settles upon a profound understanding that what is at stake is something other than halakhic integrity. The intent of such rhetoric is clearly to shut down conversation, to silence opposition—and, in most cases, it succeeds.

It is important to note that my claim is not that the rabbis cited below represent all of Modern Orthodoxy. There *are* other voices, and these give us hope. However, those quoted below are strong voices within the Modern Orthodox community that play a role in shaping the conversation about the legitimacy of certain kinds of change. I hope that fleshing out the stark contrast between the metahalakhic rhetoric that forms the basis for much of their rejectionist stance, and the move to express the spiritual desires of women within halakhic boundaries, will help us to recontextualze this conversation and ultimately to see it in a different light. Responses to challenges of existing cultural norms are laden with nuanced layers of signification that require close reading to unpack. What is remarkable is how distinctly broad cultural ideologies are expressed in the language of ostensibly localized critiques of discrete behaviors and campaigns. In this chapter I shall deconstruct various Orthodox rabbis' opposition to the drive for certain changes in women's roles. The particular group under discussion evinces its own distinct symbolism, but the responses resemble trends in other cultures as well. The language may appear vastly different, but the essential conversation remains resonant with other instances of backlash; the dynamics and discourse of this highly nuanced culture operate within other cultures, religious and secular, as well.

This chapter treats several instances, spanning roughly the last hundred years, in which there have been thrusts for increased participation of women within Orthodox Jewish society. These include the fight for women's suffrage and their right to hold public office in pre-state Israel (1919); the phenomenon of all-women's prayer groups in 1970s America; and the current trend toward greater women's participation in Orthodox ritual. Though separated by decades, each of these developments met with similar responses from the Orthodox rabbinical establishment: suspicion and delegitimation. The rabbis tap into collective Jewish symbology by making implicit comparisons between those petitioning for increased participation and the known cultural villians, casting an aura of suspicion on the project as a whole. They question the activists' motives, ascribing to them ulterior agendas that are foreign and inauthentic to the tradition. This claim leads naturally to accusations that proposed changes jeopardize the tradition's very authenticity, and in turn the communal stability that authenticity is understood to guarantee. This rabbinic discourse does not limit itself to deciding matters of Jewish law, but claims authority as an arbiter of both social roles and individual spiritual needs. In all these cases, the legal decision is prohibitive; an interesting discussion in itself, but not my focus. Rather, I shall analyze the metalegal discourse that emerges around women's roles, and how it gets folded into discussions about women's rules. What is the justification for the status quo? What is the attitude toward those who are asking for change? What is the perception of what that change will bring about? What are the cultural ideologies that inform all of this? Is this rhetoric echoed in other faiths, in other instances of drives for women's participation?

### Case 1. Women's Voting, Palestine, 1919

In the early twentieth century, as liberal democracies througout the world faced the issue of women's suffrage, the Jews of pre-state Israel were engaged in this conversation in their own localized terms: their debate included the question of whether women could hold public office. Rabbi Abraham Isaac Hacohen Kook, a significant spiritual leader of the time, responded separately to the questions of women's suffrage and their election to public office: the latter, in an "Open Letter to the Honorable Committee of the 'Mizrahi' Association" (1919); and the former in a "General Responsum" (1920). What is important, however, is less the negative verdict itself than the associations it evokes for him about women's nature and role in society. One need not read between the lines to speculate about his values in this area; he makes them quite explicit and beyond debate: Kook's legal discussion here is noteworthy for its brevity.

Rather than following the time-honored rabbinic method of presenting a survey of opinions and precedents, then offering a verdict based on which side seems more compelling and relevant to the case at hand, he makes the sweeping claim that these are instances of what in Jewish legal tradition is nearly unheard-of: an open-and-shut case.

> Now regarding the law I have nothing to add to the words of the rabbis who came before me. In the Torah, in the Prophets and in the Writings, in the Halacha and in the Aggadah, we hear one voice, that the duty of fixed public service falls upon men.

> I must say that the Rabbis who announced this prohibition, stemming from the law, until now, drew their opinion from the source of the *one voice* we hear from the Torah, from the Prophets and from Scripture, from the Halakha, and from the Aggadah, that . . . opposes this modern innovation [that is, women's suffrage]. (1919, 129)

It is interesting to note that other, serious legal voices claim that the legal discussion is far more multivocal, the issue far more complex; they bring a host of precedents to support this position (sources that Rav Kook, whose knowledge of Jewish legal tradition was encyclopedic, certainly would have known). What I suggest is that for Rav Kook what is at stake are not two discrete rules affecting women, but the more general and totalizing preservation of women's traditional roles. This rejection of change requires far more than a measured, negative verdict. It requires the creation of a supplemental realm of discourse. He impugns the motivations of those supporting it and decries the dangers such a move will pose for the spiritual health of Jewish individuals, families, and, in particular, the existence of the Jewish state. David Ellenson concisely characterizes the nature of Rav Kook's response:

> [I]n looking at his position on this issue, Kook did not put forth specific legal arguments, i.e., citations of Jewish legal precedents, against such extension [that is, of suffrage to women]. Instead, he composed a "meta-

legal" argument that centered on what he perceived as the nature of the Jewish people and on the need for *am yisrael* to construct a nation that would be true to its authentic character and indigenous religious-national principles. (2004, 350)

In other words, Rav Kook categorizes women's suffrage as something foreign to Jewish tradition and the values it represents, locating it definitively "outside." It can be understood only as a "modern innovation," a "European novelty—alien to the biblical spirit and to the national tradition" (1920, 132). Standing in stark opposition to the "biblical integrity and purity with which our life has been imbued since time immemorial," and derived from a "novel Irish moral quality," this foreign value runs counter to the "spirit of the whole nation" (1920, 132).

Kook rejects the premise, advanced by suffrage proponents, that equality is linked with dignity and respect. In fact, he says, the desire for equality in the secular world is a deviation from and distortion of women's true nature, resulting from their mistreatment at the hands of crass men. Because Jewish women are treated well, they require no such remedy. Therefore, the only basis for their desire to vote must be a drive to imitate non-Jews:

> If [the other nations'] family situation had been as peaceful and dignified as it generally is in Israel, the women themselves, as well as men of science, morality and high ideals would not demand what they call: "rights" of election for women. (1920, 133)

It is interesting that members of the British Parliament felt that they also treated their women well. As William (1892) wrote: "Women have no need to vote, husbands, fathers, or brothers have always protected their interests and would continue to do so."

Similarly, for Rav Kook, political equality for women has no place in Jewish tradition; it is derived either out of wrongheaded admiration of gentiles, the desire to be accepted by them, or for their own selfsame, degraded motivations. Questioning the purity of the motivations is enough to delegitimize the demand (notice he has not yet addressed the validity of suffrage itself). But casting doubt on the sources calling for it makes the whole project suspect.

This imitation of the "nations" is hardly, for Rav Kook, a neutral proposition. If its causes are confused and misguided, its effects are potentially catastrophic: not only for individuals and families, but for the Jewish people as a whole (all of which, for Rav Kook, become interconnected to the point of indistinguishability within the narrative of national redemption). The corrupting effects of public participation begin with the women upon whom these new "rights" would be foisted. Indeed, Rav Kook does not merely reject classifying as a right the ability to vote or hold public office: he claims that these putative advances actually constitute the *denial* of far more basic rights:

> Do not touch the foundation of foundations of the *rights* of our mothers, sisters and daughters. The original firm *rights,* that are founded upon the beautification of the special internal moral and natural power, and on the sacred, refined and noble value of the woman of Israel, which make deep roots in life, and bring it a lasting happiness.
>
> The Israelite woman bases her *rights* on the refined content of her unique psychical value, not on measured and limited laws, formed in a mechanical cast, which are for her iron horns, which do not suit at all her psychical refinement (1920, 134)

The figurative language Rav Kook utilizes to bolster his argument calls out for analysis. Harsh industrial imagery ("mechanical cast," "iron horns") emphasizes the antipathy between women's naturalistic, ethereal essence and the clangy metallic, nuts-and-bolts reality of this-worldly endeavors. Far from offering liberation, these laws will act on women as torturous malforming constraints. They will "embitter" and "obliterate the splendor of our sisters' lives," cast them into a "low state," and, once the damage has been done, they will "have not the power to repair that which they spoil" (1920, 133).

Rav Kook's position is reminiscent of Lord Gladstone (1892) who claimed: "voting was unfeminine and unnatural participation in the sordid affairs of the government and would sully the purity of women's character." "The fear I have," Gladstone states, "is lest we should invite her unwittingly to trespass upon the delicacy, the purity, the refinement, the elevation of her own nature." Because women are the cornerstones of family life, such a perversion of their natural station will inevitably predicate the family's collapse. According to Rav Kook, how this collapse will take place deserves special attention:

> When we demand of the woman that she go out into the political public domain, and shall become entangled in expressing her opinion in weighty and political questions in general, then we do one of two things: either she learns through this flattery, to flatter the man, and to cast her vote according to his, not according to her conscience, by which we spoil her morality and inner freedom; or through the tempest of opinions and their divisions, the status of home peace is destroyed. (1920, 133)

This speculation is especially striking in light of the putative "unique psychical value" and "special internal moral and natural power . . . sacred, refined and noble value of the woman of Israel, which make deep roots." Rav Kook does not appear to acknowledge the conflicting valences of these representations. Because of what he sees as an strict interdependency between family and nation, the breakdown of the former will lead inevitably to the latter's collapse. It is perhaps not a surprise that in the United States as well, both members of the Republican and Democratic parties were in perfect concord in their rejection of women's suffrage: "the loving comraderie [*sic*] between the willful few republicans and the willful few democrats who in normal relations do not waste time in each other's company was an amazing sight to the galleries. Mr. Lodge of Massachusets, and Mr. Martin of Virginia, Mr. Wadsworth of New York, Mr. Underwood of Alabama, as divided as the Kaiser and the King of England in most matters, were as united as twin brothers in defending the nation against the awful disaster to the nation should women be enfranchized by the federal amendment" (Kent 1990, 55).

It is this broad societal concern that preoccupies Rav Kook most deeply. "The family for us is the foundation of the nation . . . light rifts in the family must bring a great break in the nation."[1] The national unrest he predicts is not merely domestic. By "show[ing] the world that we have no original system— stemming from the content of our own spirit, which is revealed through our teachings and holy traditions," and instead making themselves into "mere followers of European culture,"[2] and "little disciples of of contemporary civilized people" (1920, 133), the Jewish nation, in the eyes of the world, forgoes its claim to a unique identity, and thus to a discrete tract of land. It gives an opening to those "enemies of Israel—both internal and external—who make use of the libel that the Young Israel has lost its link to the Holy Book, and therefore has no right to the Biblical land" (1919, 130).

Because return to the Land of Israel is bound up with a spiritual-historical narrative (which Rav Kook was renowned for explicating), the prospect of Jews' being stripped of their claim to the Land of Israel is far more than an existential threat. It is perhaps no wonder, then, that in both of his writings on the subject, Rav Kook refers to those who question this enterprise as "enemies of Israel"; he thus implicitly—but very clearly—casts as collaborators and accomplices to these enemies any and all who might support, even unintentionally, their insidious agenda. Those promoting greater participation for women in public life—those claiming that women should be able to vote, and/or hold public office—fall in perforce with this unsavory crew, standing in brazen opposition not only to Israel's covenantal past but to its existential present and national future.

In their broad strokes, the principles upon which Rav Kook makes his case—women's spiritual and psychological well-being, the strength of the family, and the health of the nation—represent values of wide consensus.[3] Thus it is perhaps doubly striking that any of these broad-based societal agendas can be construed as integrally bound up with the seemingly far more localized questions of women voting or holding public office. According to Rav Kook, cultural self-realization is closely tied to the silencing of women's public voice. Yet even if one were to accept the problematic scenarios that he speculates would result from women voting and holding public office, one would not necessarily be led to identical conclusions. If women expressing their opinions at the polls leads to family strife, perhaps deeper questions about the family structure itself should be pursued. Rav Kook, however, takes it for granted that the answer to this and the other problems he poses is simply for women to keep quiet (see Gilligan 1982; Narayan 1997). More penetrating questions of why cultural health requires the sacrificing of women's rights are left unasked by Rav Kook, except insofar as he rejects the premise that women's rights would be advanced by a greater public voice. Distinguished in his generation for qualities of spiritual depth, personal empathy, and a distinctly modern sensibility (he was nearly alone among his ultrareligious peers in integrating secular nationalism into the Jewish traditional core, and tireless in emphasizing the validity and value of various aspects of secular life), he nonetheless takes great pains to demonstrate that women's roles fall outside the pale of any such modernizing discussion; indeed, he expresses the implicit hope that, following his definitive explication of their non-negotiability, they will not be discussed at all.

### Case 2. Women's Prayer Groups

R. MEIR TWERSKY: EVES, IDOLATORS,
AND THE "TORAH-SANCTIONED DEGENERATE"

In the late 1970s, a group of women defining themselves as "Modern Orthodox" took the then-radical step of establishing all-women's prayer groups.[4] Two prominent rabbis, Meir Twersky (1998) and Moshe Meiselman (1998) responded with a litany of objections. While ultimately prohibiting such gatherings, their responses, like Rav Kook's, are far from simple legal judgments. Both concede that women's prayer groups as such do not constitute an outright violation of halakha. This concession, however, does not make their opposition any less adamant. As with Rav Kook, the halakhic discussion is a jumping-off point for an intriguing, complex discourse treating the cultural ideology of these authority figures vis-à-vis religious women's appropriate, sanctioned roles and the necessity of maintaining them. The proposed change is delegitimized and deemed dangerous to communal continuity, its proponents' motivations are called into question, and they themselves demonized by comparison with well-known upstarts (idolators, Eve)—all exclusively metahalakhic arguments. What is it about women's drive for increased public ritual participation that leads the men to generate such intricate rationales to support their objections?

Twersky defines women's prayer groups as unequivocally "other," falling squarely and clearly outside the pale of normative Jewish prayer. However, because the usual avenue of normative exclusion—that is, legal prohibition—is unavailable to him, Twersky is forced to find other other means. Thus he begins with a *meta*-metahalakhic argument: an argument for the validity of metahalakhic arguments. In addition to the letter of the law, he says, there exist "axiological principles that go beyond the strict adherence to the formal law . . . the complementarity of particulars and principles—law and spirit . . . the existential rhythm, ontological emotions and *cardinal values of halakhic living*" (7; emphasis mine). Women's prayer groups, according to Twersky, violate the "spirit of the law."

In order to make such a claim about what prayer is *not,* Twersky offers a definition of what, according to Jewish tradition, prayer *is.* He argues that classical Jewish sources define prayer as an inward religious experience inherently at odds with any kind of public display. One engaged in an act of genuine prayer would not only avoid outward exhibitions of spiritual fervor, but would actively flee the public eye. Participation in the public rituals of communal prayer does nothing to enhance the experience of prayer. Why Jewish tradition established public prayer at all, much less assigned it such a place of prominence in communal life (based on his argument, *any* public expression of prayer seems misguided and antithetical to traditional imperatives and mores) is left unaddressed by Twersky, for whom the "otherness" of public prayer seems applicable to women only.

This apparent and somewhat glaring disjuncture does nothing to curb the stark insistence of Twersky's language and tone. "The desire for and emphasis upon active participation and leadership are *antithetical* to *genuine service of the heart* and contribute to the *extroversion* of prayer" (12; emphasis added). Women's prayer groups may not be technically impermissible, but anyone desiring such a forum for worship stands in direct opposition to Jewish tradition ("antithetical"); has something wrong—something false—in her heart ("genuine service of the heart"); and maintains a superficial relationship to her own spiritual life and, ultimately, to God ("extroversion of prayer").

To illustrate this point about the potential gap between legal spirit and letter, Twersky invokes, by way of analogy, a well-known Jewish villain: the "Torah-sanctioned degenerate" (*naval birshut Ha-Torah*). "Gluttony, vulgarity and excessive conjugality inter alia are all possible without violating any particulars of Torah" (7).[5] Although drawn under the pretense of a technical point about the possibility of flouting tradition's essence while adhering to its technical requirements, the implicit resonance of the juxtaposition is impossible to ignore: while women's prayer groups may be innocuous within the halakhic realm, in the metahalakhic realm (understood to attend more authentically to tradition's telos) they occupy the same vile sphere as gluttony, vulgarity, and excessive conjugality. By implication, anyone advocating for such changes maintains a similarly shallow relationship to Jewish law and is motivated by similarly corrupt, suspicious drives.

But what could move someone ostensibly committed to tradition (that is, the letter) to act so flagrantly against it (that is, the spirit)? To explain this apparent contradiction, Twersky invokes a "false consciousness" paradigm. The emergence of women's prayer groups, he says, is not a representation of increased desire for spiritual expression among women but rather the result and expression of a religious crisis. Unwittingly, Orthodox women have absorbed—been consumed by—the values of a "secular egalitarian" culture that stands in direct contradiction to the Jewish spirit. The good news is that, having adopted these values unknowingly, women need only to be reeducated properly in order to rectify their breach. They may think they are cultivating an authentic religious urge, but in fact they have been duplicitously swindled into confusing spirituality with a "fool's paradise of religious accommodation" (p. 75). Jewish women, he argues, must be helped to internalize

> the dissimilar equality of the two genders and elucidate the vitally important heightened spiritual dimension of the feminine role, as delineated by the Torah and our sages. Such educational initiatives—will, God willing, foster genuine religious experience and satisfaction in general and enhance the *tefilla* experience in particular. The religious crisis which has spawned *tefilla* groups would thereby be authentically resolved. (16)[6]

As Twersky goes on to demonstrate, "fool's paradise" is not an accidental phrase. Coupled with the language of crisis (an odd and glaring imposition worthy of attention in its own right) the Garden of Eden allusion gives a mythic spin to what Twersky suggests is a mistake primordial in origin and potentially catastrophic in its effect. The mythic symbology works to associate a uniquely modern religious development to a familiar paradigm with deep-seated negative connotations. The association works to foreclose further discourse: if change in women's social roles is equivalent to original sin, what further elaboration or analysis is required? Interestingly, rather than spell out the nature or history of the "religious crisis" he asserts but does nothing to substantiate, Twersky instead spells out the terms of his own metaphor. If those proposing increased participation occupy a "fool's paradise," what is the sin? Who are the players? By way of background, he introduces yet another well-known Jewish villain: assimilation. Assimilation, he says, comes in two forms: one "practical or active," whose manifestations are "overt and conspicuous" to the naked Orthodox eye, and thus relatively easy to negotiate; and the other, far more insidious, which he refers to as ideological or ideational assimilation. The latter is notable for its Trojan stealth: its proposals for change can pass the halakhic litmus test, yet still subvert the spirit of the law. Like the biblical serpent, who engages Eve in seemingly innocuous small talk in order to eventually lull her into sin, ideological assimilation

> is oftentimes *subtle and beguiling*. It can be *clothed in* technical halakhic compliance, thereby *masking* the ideological deviation. . . . [It] almost always precedes and inexorably results in practical assimilation. (10; emphasis added)

For Twersky, the drive for change in women's roles ceases to be viewed as merely foreign to the tradition and begins to be construed as a threat—and that those pressing for such change cease to be seen merely as misguided or foolish and begin to be understood as enemies of the Jews. The Torah-sanctioned degenerate, while clearly a negative figure, is ultimately a danger to no one but himself. According to Twersky, however, the threat posed by those advocating for increased women's participation is far broader in scope. As the biblical story makes clear, the destruction wrought by the snake does not stop at the first woman: she turns around and passes it on to her male counterpart and by extension to all humankind. According to Twersky, those advocating for change have already been dazzled by the charms of assimilation, the charms of the snake. It is clear what he perceives his duty as rabbi to be: to protect himself and his community from allowing that second, fateful transfer to take place.

Like Rav Kook, Twersky bases his claims of otherness and dubiousness on a principle—the private, inward focus of prayer—upon which many would agree. It is not the principle itself, but his radical reification and sweeping prescriptive application of the principle that rankles common sense and makes his broad-based claim seem out of all proportion with its purported source. His harsh, dismissive language (a form of intimidation that may derive at least in part from a lack of clear legislative authority and/or faith in the persuasiveness of a more evenhanded approach) only adds to this sense of imbalance.

This polemical overreaching is reflected even in the one attempt Twersky does make to root his case in some quasi-legal ground. Perhaps bolstered by this extra measure of legitimacy, he goes even further in classifying this form of women's participation as a foreign, illegitimate, potential threat to Jewish tradition and marks its advocates as enemies. At the same time, his discourse ratchets up markedly in its alarmist pitch. Invoking the extrahalakhic principle of building legal fences to mitigate against possible *eventual* violation of the law, he invokes the ominous and necessarily vague discourse of the "slippery slope." The danger of greater women's participation in this instance is no halakhic violation per se, but rather its potential to form a link in a causal chain leading to un-halakhic behavior at some unspecified future point—a chain of events whose culmination is nothing short of catastrophic. The vagueness of the actual threat stands in stark contrast with the speculative scenario Twersky vividly depicts:

> We must recognize that the possible ramifications of this falsehood are especially frightening and particularly tragic. Propelled by negative momentum and misguided by erroneous teachings, some women, God forbid, could reject all remaining halakhic constraints in an unrestrained attempt to enhance their [inauthentic] tefilla experience in particular and religious experience in general." (14–15)

Twersky's discourse shifts definitively from merely describing a threat to casting those supporting the proposed change as enemies of Jewish tradition and unity. In addition to the generalized sense of an enemy as one who would promote "falsehood" to "frightening" and "tragic" ends, a more specific, intertextual indictment is being lodged. "Propelled by negative momentum and misguided by erroneous teachings" constitutes an allusion to the well-known (at least, to Twersky's audience) first chapter of Maimonides' Laws of Idolatry, in which the medieval luminary describes idolatrous practices as originating with modestly erroneous teachings advanced by misguided priests, which then, propelled by negative momentum, evolved into the kind of wild, unrestrained paganistic practices (child sacrifice, orgiastic rites) that for Jewish tradition define non-monotheistic worship. By way of juxtaposition, Twersky suggests an affinity between pagan practices and women's prayer groups, which both stand in diametrical and hostile opposition to Judaism's authentic core. Those advocating for such groups must perforce be viewed less than favorably in Jewish eyes.

### R. MOSHE MEISELMAN: SILENCING WOMEN'S PRAYER

R. Meiselman (1998), in his article on women's prayer groups arrives at the same conclusion as Twersky via a different, even opposite, tack. Women's prayer groups, he claims, have no clear halakhic status and as such are spiritually meaningless. While the assumptions underlying this assertion clearly require unpacking, Jewish tradition presents a host of counterexamples, ranging from the obvious to the esoteric—examples with which Meiselman would certainly have been familiar. Indeed, Meiselman's line of argument commits him to a view of prayer that runs counter to a long tradition of contemplative and ecstatic Jewish practitioners whose prayer is offered outside of the sanctioned minyan. His statement implicitly condemns or dismisses practices of, for example, such legendary rabbinic figures as the Rambam[7] and Bachaye Ibn Pakudah[8] (to say nothing of the biblical Hanna, whose private and intensely personal supplication serves in the Talmud as the halakhic paradigm of prayer). These seminal figures not only condone, but endorsed and practiced silent and private prayer as a means of inducing more elevated spiritual states. Even on its surface, it is a strange argument: if women's prayer groups have no halakhic significance, then why should its performance be considered a halakhic issue? What threat can an act of no significance pose?

Meiselman, however, has much worse to say. Because his argument is based on the nonhalakhic status of women's prayer groups, he prefers to invoke a halakhic authority within which to frame his disapproval. He finds this authority in the person of his uncle, Rabbi Joseph Soloveitchik, the father figure of late twentieth-century American Modern Orthodoxy. Like Rav Kook, Rav Soloveitchik (known colloquially as "the Rav") was a towering figure for many of those attempting to integrate religious traditionalism with a modern perspective; because of his stature, he has been widely appropriated by a wide spectrum of authorities attempting to legitimize their particular approach to achieving this balance. Because the Rav challenged and stretched traditional norms on various issues relating to modernity (including women's Torah study), the limits he set in these matters are considered especially significant: the "outer limits," as it were, of modernistic innovation that may still be considered legitimately "Jewish."

It is against this charged backdrop that Meiselman invokes the Rav in the service of his invalidation and prohibition of women's prayer groups. It is significant that Meiselman neither refers to any of Soloveitchik's published writings nor even quotes him directly from speech. Instead, he paraphrases what he says were Soloveitchik's generally held positions, to which he claims to have had privileged access via his position as family. Notwithstanding the inherent unverifiability of such claims' content, their form betrays a subtle and important subtext. The kinds of conversations Meiselman reports as having had with Soloveitchik are both rabbinic and personal in nature. One detects an underlying message that Meiselman sees himself as a legitimate heir to the tradition of Modern Orthodoxy, not only by virtue of his position as a rabbi, but as Soloveitchik's nephew.

It is in this tradition—for this tradition—that Meiselman claims to speak when he says that the Rav considered women's prayer groups among the "sundry topics that have emerged from the feminist movement." While "initially [the Rav] viewed all of the above as silly—and hoped they would pass—eventually he viewed them as dangerous" (5). Meiselman, paraphrasing Soloveitchik (or, more accurately, projecting a persona in Soloveitchik's name) attacks the legitimacy not only of women's prayer groups, but of *any* change in traditional women's roles; he dismisses all such changes under the heading of the "feminist movement." In truth, the suggestion of such change is not even worthy of mention, much less of an official rabbinic response: between the belittling "sundry" and the infantilizing "silly," Meiselman effectively conveys his "contempt" (another word used by "Soloveitchik," characterizing his stance toward anything feminist) for having to address a matter so clearly and definitively outside the normative boundaries of what is acceptably Jewish. It does not deserve a response.

Meiselman does not stop at labeling women's prayer groups as "outside"; because of the momentum they had gained by the time he was prompted to write about them, they had become "dangerous," even "pernicious." "Use of [prayer] in that context [that is, women's prayer groups] could only deceive, mislead and trivialize real religious activity" (7). The danger is not in what *is* but in what *could be:* he fears that allowing *tefillat nashim* will lead first to the desecration of the synagogue, then to dishonoring the *sefer torah,* and finally to inevitable alien practices (such as a women's *hakafot* ceremony on *Rosh Chodesh*). In the end, women will include pagan rituals and cast off the yoke of obligation in a free-for-all spiritual exploration detached from anything halakhically Jewish—and, therefore, devoid of anything spiritually authentic.

To hone and illustrate his point, Meiselman invokes the primary nemesis of Orthodoxy in his time: the Conservative movement. The Rav, according to Meiselman, felt that *tefillat nashim* lay the ground for a new and possibly "per-

nicious version of Conservative Judaism." The gravity of this comparison—
which does the double work of distancing women's prayer groups from anything Orthodox *and* casting them as a heretical and existential threat—would
not have been lost on his readers. Nonetheless, he makes the point explicit and
frames it as closely to a legal verdict as possible, given the absence of actual
legal grounding: "It violated every canon of [Soloveitchik's] halakhic and religious being."

### Case 3. Women Reading Wedding Documents, 2004

The last few years have witnessed other examples of Orthodox women's increased participation in public life. The Orthodox Jewish wedding ceremony
includes the centuries-old custom of publicly reading the wedding contract
(*ketubah*), an ancient Aramaic document. Traditionally, this reading, as well
as the whole ceremony, has been performed by a man. In recent years, however, Orthodox women, seeking areas in which to increase participation without violating halakha, have begun to read the *ketubah*. On the systemic plane,
there is a growing conversation about the issue of ordaining women to the
rabbinate. Responding to these phenomena, Rabbi Hershel Schachter (2004),
a head rabbi and revered teacher at Yeshiva University, and one of the most
influential legal authorities for the Modern Orthodox world, wrote an essay
harshly condemning and ultimately prohibiting both of these forms of participation. His argument is very much in concert with those we have examined
above, in that it eschews attempts at hard legal arguments in favor of metahalakhic and at times harshly polemical formulations. This strategy is also in
harmony with at least one other responsum Schacther wrote regarding increased women's ritual participation. Rachel Adler offers a thorough examination of Schachter's response to women's prayer groups, in which he employs
"an unprecedented diversity of extralegal sources" (2001, 5):

> The body of the work, unlike classical, nonpolemical responsa and unlike
> scholarly articles, offers no arguments pro and con, no possible objections
> or contrary perspectives. It consists simply of a list of twelve reasons why
> women's communal worship is out of the question. Like other polemical
> responsa, the document consists not of, an introductory statement of the
> problem, a body of text debating it, and a conclusion rendering a decision,
> but of one massive conclusion. (ibid., 16)

Schachter begins his response to *ketubah*-reading and women's ordination
with the former, acknowledging that "from the perspective of the laws of '*sid-
dur kiddushin*' [the wedding ceremony], there's nothing wrong" (2). Schachter

then makes a rhetorical move that he repeats several times over the course of the essay: "Yes, even if a *parrot or monkey* would read the *ketubah,* the marriage would be one hundred percent valid" (ibid.; emphasis added). Schachter's invocation of parrots and monkeys—natural mimics that imitate human speech and activity without any consciousness of what they are doing—is ostensibly technical. This point is emphasized by the online editor of Schachter's essay, in an attempt to respond to "various communications" he received from correspondents (who apparently missed the comparison's ostensibly technical intent):

> The statement about monkeys or parrots reading the *ketubah* was clearly intended to dramatize the *halakhic* insignificance of the reading of the *ketubah* from the standpoint of the marriage ceremony. It was not intended to imply or insinuate anything else. (1)

Though it is impossible to guess intent, the reading of the parrot/monkey comparison as a dehumanizing slight against women who seek increased ritual participation was sufficiently manifest to cause a minor uproar within the Orthodox community. It is possible that what sparked this response was not merely the use of the comparison, but its repetition. After giving a historical-legal account of the *ketubah*-reading practice, Schachter concludes:

> So it is a correct observation that if one only studies [those areas of Jewish law treating the marriage ceremony] there's absolutely no mention whatsoever that anything is wrong with a woman reading the *ketubah.* Yes, a monkey could also read the ketubah! (3)

Like the first animal comparison, this one comes immediately on the heels of an acknowledgment of the legal permissibility of women's *ketubah*-reading. The repetition of the comparison, coupled with this pointed juxtaposition, suggests an attempt at rhetorical counterbalance. The permissibility of *ketubah*-reading for women, Schachter seems to imply, should not be viewed as a victory or even an opportunity for women, any more than it would be viewed as a victory or opportunity for an animal. Who would want to participate in an act when her participation has no more significance than that of a parrot or monkey? Furthermore, when a woman actually does read a *ketubah,* there is the implication that she more closely resembles a parrot or monkey—repeating what she has seen done by higher beings (read: men), with no consciousness or will of her own—than another human.

And yet a third instance of the comparison/juxtaposition:

Of course the [marriage validity] will not be affected in the slightest! An animal can also read the *ketubah* without affecting the [marriage validity]! The truth of the matter is that no one has to read the *ketubah!*

By now, the local implications begin to seem less significant than the repetition itself, which takes on a kind of punishing, Pavlovian cast. Again, without guessing at Schachter's intent, rhetorically one is being conditioned to associate the permissibility of a ritual act with that act's emphatic (note the liberal use of exclamation points), almost contemptuous emptying of significance or worth. In this case, by the end of Schachter's essay, the time-honored custom of reading the *ketubah* (which over centuries of homiletic interpretation has become saturated with layers of meaning) has effectively been reduced to an act requiring no consciousness and no will, thus commanding little respect. How much value or honor are we likely to assign to a ritual that could just as easily be performed by a parrot or monkey? In short, Schachter chooses to divest Jewish custom of meaning rather than allow women to participate in a public ritual technically open to them.

Notwithstanding the ritual's irrelevance, Schachter goes on to develop a comprehensive and insistent metahalakhic argument for why women should refrain from reading the *ketubah* under the wedding canopy. In order to do this, he draws Jewish tradition down a single, simple axis:

All people were created [in the image of God], and the Torah has instructed each of us to preserve his [Godly image]. One aspect of [Godliness] is the fact that God is a "Hidden God," He always prefers to hide [in private]. Therefore, we assume that part of our mitzvah of preserving our [Godly image] is for all of us to lead private lives. (4)

Based on this speculative, contingent principle regarding the importance of leading "private lives"—no more than an assumption, and only "part" of the much larger (by definition infinite) endeavor of *Imitatio Dei*—Schachter draws sweeping conclusions about ritual life and women's place in it (and, primarily, out of it). He does not acknowledge any inconsistency between the blanket inclusiveness of his verdict—to say nothing of its binding force—and his own admission regarding the highly provisional character of his claim. In addition to his openly qualified language, Schachter quotes no sources to support his leap from the general insight about God's hiddenness to the blanket theological requirement of every human being to live as privately as possible.

Commitment to his reductivist principle requires him, for example, to view *all* public ritual as both regrettable and inexplicable[9]

> Sometimes the *halakha* requires of us to act in a public fashion . . . as for example to have [public prayer, public reading of the Torah], etc. . . . We only require and demand of the men that they compromise on their [modesty] and observe certain *mitzvos* in a public fashion. We do not require this of women. They may maintain their [quality of hiddenness], just as Hashem (most of the time) is a [Hidden God] (Isaiah 45:15). (4)

Schachter makes no attempt to explain why men were chosen to suffer and women spared these lamentable "compromises," "requirements," and "demands." Nor does he elaborate on why these public rituals have been assigned such places of pride within Jewish communal life. He radically limits the Jewish God to a being defined principally by hiddenness, relegating traditions of communal and individual revelation to a flip parenthetical, and does not acknowledge Him as being in any way complicated, much less problematic. For Schachter, these questions appear to be insignificant or perhaps simply eclipsed by the irresistible force of his unified theory of Judaism. Once it is understood that women's exemption from public ritual is actually a privilege that allows them to remain in line with Judaism's defining value ("they alone, unlike men, are given the opportunity to maintain their [quality of hiddenness] at all times" [8]), what question could one possibly have?[10]

Schachter does, however, tacitly acknowledge that some questions (or at least some questioners) may remain. This acknowledgment comes in his attempt to undermine not the arguments of those pressing for greater women's participation (which he has already conceded are halakhically sound) but their motivations and personal character. On this point Schachter is quite blunt:

> Clearly the motivation to have a woman read the *ketubah* is to make the following statement: the rabbis, or better yet—the God of the Jews, has been discriminating against women all these millennia, and has cheated them of their equal rights, and it's high time that this injustice be straightened out! (5)

Schachter makes no attempt to support, or even explain the basis of, his condemnation. Nor does he elaborate on his equation of God with "the rabbis." Rhetorically, of course, it clearly works in his favor: consolidating rabbinic (and thus his own) authority by overt identification with the divine, and by extension classifying all who would disagree with him in the issue of ordaining women as heretics. The suggestion is not incidental and does not remain implicit for long. Schachter goes on to identify those pressing for increased women's participation with a virtual "who's who" of Jewish heretics and splinter groups. Of the pre-Talmudic Sadducees, he writes, citing no evidence: "One of their big issues was this issue of discrimination against women" (6). Following in their footsteps, the early Christians also "felt that the rabbis had discriminated against women" (6). More recently, "the Reform and the Conservative movements have expressed this same complaint against the rabbis, or better put—against the God of the Jews: Discrimination against women!" Interestingly, and in contrast to their use by Meiselman, these misguided Jews are invoked by Schachter not as threatening enemies of Jewish community and tradition but as obvious missteps whom history has already—unfavorably—judged: "Look what has become of the [Sadducees], the early Christians, the Reform, and the Conservatives." For Schachter these figures, quaint historical footnotes at best, are mentioned as cautionary tales for anyone considering diverting from the rabbinic party line, embracing the "silly misunderstanding" of feminism and thus unwittingly cutting themselves off from Jewish history and destiny.

All this is not to say that Schachter lacks an enemy with whom to associate those advocating for women's increased participation in public life. He simply reserves this role for an especially contemporary, and especially contemptible, nemesis:

> Our generation is so much into publicity that this [quality of hiddenness] is totally unappreciated. We live in a generation in which there is no sense of shame. People will do the most intimate and the most private acts in a most explicitly and most demonstrative fashion. (8)

It is here that Schachter's polemical thrust becomes at once most explicit and most bizarre. He identifies women reading an ancient marriage document under the wedding canopy with shameless sexual exhibitionists performing publicly "the most intimate and the most private acts." Those who champion women's increased participation are, either intentionally or unwittingly (Schachter does not say which, but it does not seem from his tone that innocence would in any way lessen the severity of the crime), in league with the shameless self-promoters whose

> arrogant attitude has led them to believe that if they were God they would always be bragging, boasting, and showing off, always "making a statement." They don't have the slightest notion that God exists. (8)

## Conclusion

Taken broadly, the discourse of backlash can be reduced to an exhortation for women to remain in the private sphere. It functions not on the local, legal level of evaluating women's rules, but on the sweeping, metalegal level of defining and restricting women's roles. Collectively, the array of rhetorical strategies these rabbis employ—defining the desire for anything beyond the status quo as foreign and dangerous to tradition, attacking the motivations of those petitioning for such change, associating them with classic cultural villains, and defining them as enemies of Jewish stability and continuity—all point to one cultural fact: the only way for the community to survive is for women's roles not to change. This amounts to an all-or-nothing strategy and must be understood in strategic terms. Why take such an extreme tack? Because cultural authorities understand on some level that when women petition for greater participation, they are expressing deeply held desires and needs. They also understand that there is, as it were, no reasoning with these women: all that is left is to invalidate, castigate, ridicule, ostracize, and threaten all in the hope of intimidating them into silence. All of the rabbis discussed above emphasize the importance of women not having a voice, be it a political voice (Rav Kook), a religious voice (Twersky/Meiselman), or a literal public voice to read a document out loud (Schachter). This silencing is cast in variations of the language of modesty, privacy, internality: squelching of their voices by confining their bodies to discrete physical spaces. The silencing of Orthodox Jewish women promoted by rabbinical authority figures resonates with themes found in other cultures' discourses of backlash as well.

Ultimately, what makes the examination of backlash interesting is not merely what it reveals about authority figures' stances vis-à-vis women's roles but what it reveals about the gender dynamics within a given community. Faludi (1991) claims that antifeminist backlash in America is a product not of "women's achievement of full equality," but rather "an increased possibility that they might win it. It is a preemptive strike that stops women long before they reach the finish line" (xx). In this light, the "slippery slope" arguments raised by all of the rabbis under discussion, which consistently seem out of proportion with the proposed change, begin at least to seem sensible on their own terms. They are not intended as rational workings-out of possible consequences but as "preemptive strikes. " They betray a perception of slippage in the consolidation of patriarchal control, always "triggered by the perception—accurate or not—that women are making great strides" (xix). Miller (1976) points out that "backlashes occur when advances have been small, before changes are sufficient to help many people" (xv); indeed, with the exception of Rav Kook, the types of change being advocated for religious women seem small-scale both in their demands and in the breadth of population they would affect. The Orthodox women who choose to attend women's prayer groups or publicly read the *ketubah* are careful to limit their "advances" to words and actions that are permissible according to Jewish law. Without invoking the paradigm of backlash, how may one understand the characterization of their worship with verbs like "deceive" and "trivialize"; adjectives like "dangerous," "vulgar," "perverse"; and nouns like "deviation" and "contempt"?

The analyses of the rabbinic responsa presented above all share the sense that, for these authority figures, there is something at stake much greater than a particular, minor change in women's communal participation. It is important to view them not merely as manifestations of a generalized "bedrock of misogyny," lashing out reflexively against any deviation from the norm. Rather, they should be contextualized with other instances of backlash, as specific patterns of strategic responses to

> the specific efforts of contemporary women to improve their status, efforts that have been interpreted time and time again by men—especially men grappling with real threats to their economic and social well-being on other fronts—a spelling of their own masculine doom. (Faludi 1991, xix)

Reactions to change expose something very raw about the nature of a given relationship in its "pre-change" status quo. I argue that the discourse of backlash, with its fierce alarmist rhetorical bluster, is actually just an articulation of oppression that had been taking place all along: a long-submerged iceberg breaking the surface for the first time, aggression made overt. One might propose a working definition of backlash as a spelling-out of the specific systems of oppression that are no longer able to preserve the status quo through unspoken means.

What threat could be considered severe enough to prompt this authoritarian showing-of-cards, this laying-bare of the patriarchal scaffolding? In all of the cases examined above (as in instances of backlash more generally), the risk authorities are rushing to quarantine is a desire for change, however small, in the nature and level of women's participation within the culture. This desire is perceived, often rightly, as reflecting dissatisfaction with the scope and/or content of women's assigned roles, and it is this movement toward greater self-definition of needs that sends communal leaders into their rhetorical tailspins. In this sense, those deeply invested in preserving status quo as a value in itself have it right: the desire for change says that traditional norms are no longer meeting a community's needs, and thus the contract through which women have been bound within certain roles is being opened for renegotiation. If these traditional roles are viewed as indispensable to maintaining cultural stability, political viability, and the word of God, then any change, however seemingly innocuous, is every bit as radical and threatening as the rabbis claim. The need to articulate this threat, and to do so as stridently and compellingly as possible only arises from the need to squelch it; that the threat has arisen already bespeaks a destabilization of the status quo. Backlash is thus the patriarchy's weakest place: it both gives voice to the unwritten inequality that has been so long taken for granted, and shows the extent to which it has ceased to be taken for granted, to which traditional authority has lost control. The anger of these responses belies their putative dismissal of women's claims as "silly," betraying the seriousness with which these claims are being taken and the depth to which they are perceived to threaten the social core. The status quo is no longer holding, but cultural authorities are trying to hold on—desperately, violently, with great rhetorical throes and pangs—to their power.

# 7

GO
AWAY
AND
CHANGE

I was once giving a talk at a Jerusalem hotel about the inception of Shirah Hadashah, explaining its conceptual underpinnings, and explaining how many of the ideas, later developed in this book, led us to try to create a traditional prayer space that respected and embodied religious feminist values. At the time, I had recently been through a divorce. When I finished my talk at the hotel, a rabbi in the audience stood up and said, with a kind of triumphant and dismissive matter-of-factness: "Yes—women in bad marriages often speak this way."

This kind of attack is inevitably jarring. By that point in the shul's evolution, however, it was not particularly surprising. As I had mentioned in the talk that night, the shul arose out of a belief that spiritual needs cannot be defined a priori by an outside authority, and that spiritual yearning and desire should be central to the practices of prayer and communal living. In particular, we wanted to make it possible for the spiritual needs and experiences of women, so long excluded from communal conversation and public life, to be expressed by women and men in the context of the halakhic and spiritual practices of the community. By the time I stood up to speak that night, I had come to understand how profoundly objectionable these simple (and, to the shul's founders, reasonable) shifts were perceived to be by certain religious authority figures and their adherents—a circle with surprisingly wide reach. I had come to understand the extent to which honoring women's spiritual needs, and bringing women's voices and women's ways into the public sphere, was identified in certain corners of the Orthodox gestalt with betrayal, anarchy, and a subversion of Jewish values and Jewish life.

Indeed, when I began to raise the idea of the shul to friends and family, although some understood and supported me, the antagonism from many others came fast and furious. I was consistently taken aback by the character, vehemence, frequency, and sources of opposition to an idea that seemed to me neither particularly inspired nor particularly radical. Even those who did not attack it outright took a guarded, wait-and-see approach, or simply circled the wagons (or, if you prefer, shuttered the windows) within their own communities: *Not here.* Some, especially those with some public stature or role, personally supported the project but rejected it publicly, for fear of damaging their credibility among right-leaning elements and compromising their political efficacy. In one way or another, they understood, perhaps better than I did, that there was something *extremely* radical about starting this little shul; further many—who were not afraid to take liberal and even radical stands on other issues—felt anxious and uncomfortable. By the time I started informally talking up the idea of starting a new kind of shul, I was no longer the effervescent ingénue. I believed I was going into the venture with open eyes. I could not have known how much wider, with each new stage of the opening of the shul, my eyes would be opened as well—at times in pain, at times in wonder, and at times in simple acknowledgment of the irrepressible complexity of women and men at the nexus of religion and gender.

---

In her book *On Being a Jewish Feminist*, Susannah Heschel (1983) offers an interpretation of Kafka's famous parable "Before the Law" and applies it to the condition of women within the patriarchal structures and strictures of Jewish law:

> By assuming a posture like that of the man from the country, women continue their relation to Judaism as outside or Other—even if they walk past the guards and through the doors. . . . But Judaism is not an edifice lying behind doors and guards. . . . There are no doors, there are no guards. Through theological exploration Judaism can belong to all who desire it. (xxxiii)

In other words, if you want to make change, just do it; no one will stop you. Those figures who look like guards are to some degree illusory, apparitions lacking in real power. In fact, they may even be waiting for you to come and take the law into your own hands.

Even if we were to accept Heschel's optimistic reading of Kafka, we are left with a claim about the nature of patriarchal religious authority whose implications are quite troubling. First, the notion that patriarchal power is "all in our heads" is countered by the daily and historical experience of women everywhere. To put it bluntly: not only have religious institutions across time and space maintained sentries at the gates to agency and power; they maintain thousands of years of tradition about how to respond to various challenges. This tradition constitutes a repertoire of tactics from which to choose, keeping in mind the particular nature of the challenge at hand and the limitations imposed by cultural mores. Some guards use overt sanctions, like marginalization and excommunication (to say nothing of capital punishment) to consolidate their power, enforce their agenda, and deter potential opposition. Some guards are subtler, employing charged imagery and employing discourse to shape the cultural landscape, embedding its values in language itself. Some guards take hostages, or threaten to: every woman knows the price of not being a good-enough wife or mother and the unwritten rules about the consequences of these "failings" for her children (particularly her girls). I would argue that even contemporary women have internalized the knowledge of these guards and their strategies, which form part of our psychic DNA. Following Matina Horner (1972), I suspect that the dynamic of "learned helplessness" has not only personal resonance but a broader cultural application. While I do not mean to suggest that women's knowledge of the strict resistance awaiting any challenge to the patriarchal status quo makes them passive or helpless—the guards are strong, but they are not invincible—I do feel that it must be acknowledged as the starting point for any conversation about the possibilities of change.

It should go without saying that it is not only traditional religious cultures that maintain these strictures or these sentries. For centuries, women who challenged the norms of behavior and identity prescribed for them were secreted away in mental asylums (see Chesler 1972). When Karen Horney (1939; 1967), in the 1930s, rejected the theory of penis envy and replaced it with a theory of womb envy, she was promptly kicked out of the New York Psychoanalytic Society. Freud (1931) himself pathologized women who did not conform to the feminine expectations of his day, diagnosing them with a damning condition he dubbed the "masculinity complex." At different points in history, women who practiced alternative forms of medicine were hunted as witches and burned at the stake. In other words, the law does not lie dormant, waiting to be claimed. Those who have treated it as if it were have paid for their mistake in blood and tears; their example serves as a standing rebuke across history and culture for others who would consider taking the law into their own hands.

---

Given this legacy, the claim that the barriers to patriarchal power for women are essentially figments of their imagination begins to seem strange indeed. The problematics of the claim are compounded when we consider its rhetorical effect. For one thing, it divides women into two highly charged moral categories: those who are changing things and those who aren't. This dichotomy is both propelled by and gives rise to a discourse of blame, assigning to the latter category the responsibility that things are not changing as much or as fast as they should. This, of course, is the real myth: that if you are not actively working to change things, you either endorse the status quo or are weak and acquiescent, a collaborator. It is a myth that has had its proponents both within feminism and among feminism's critics since the movement's inception, and it has hurt a great many women throughout that time (Dinnerstein 1976; Friday 1977; Rich 1976; Kaplan 1992; Herman 1989).[1]

The imperative simply to "go change things" seems informed by a Western myth of individualism, self-sufficiency, and unlimited agency—the assumptions of which has been one of feminism's main goals to question and subvert. As Gilligan has so compellingly argued, "The most basic questions about human living—how to live and what to do—are fundamentally questions about human relations, because people's lives are deeply connected, psychologically, economically, and politically" (1993, xiv). Our lives and choices are not made within a vacuum; despite powerful cultural messages to the contrary, we are not completely autonomous beings. The adjuration to "go change it" assumes a world where everything is open and everything is possible, where there really are no guards. But the actual landscape, as demonstrated in chapter 3, is far more complicated—and more treacherous—than this rosy picture allows. Notwithstanding the Talmudic dictate that seems to affirm Heschel's reading of Kafka, "*Torah munachat bekeren zavit kol harotzeh litol yavo veyitol*," (The Torah rests on the corner. Anyone who wishes to study it, let him/her come and study) (Kiddushin 66a), Jewish feminists have long understood that there are mechanisms for "legitimate" change and that these mechanisms are for the most part inaccessible to women. Thus they have felt largely and understandably disempowered to bring about change.

It is particularly telling to me that this discourse of "if you don't like it, go change it" finds heavy usage among those who are in power and clearly wish to maintain the status quo. Indeed, this presumed invitation is precisely what led me to join the synagogue ritual committees on which I spent so many hours and years lobbying for change. Whenever I would mention something that I felt should be different, either in casual conversation or to someone in a position of power at a shul, I was met with this response again and again. It was only when I did, in fact, attempt to change things, banging my head against the brick wall of these committees year in and year out, that I began to realize that I had, somewhat naively and somewhat tragically, misread the discourse to begin with. "If you don't like it, go change it," was *not* an invitation to a conversation about change. I should have paid more attention to the verb being used. "Go change it" really meant, "Go *away* and change it;" that is, go take your ideas somewhere else. It was the protective gesture of a hierarchy that did not want to be challenged, of a system that did not want to be tinkered with. In short, it was an invitation to leave.

"Go away and change" exemplifies the subtler and more insidious discursive tactics of the guards mentioned above. It reflects an assumption, and asserts the shaming claim, that everyone else is perfectly happy with the status quo. It says, "This is not our problem, it is *your* problem, and yours alone. What's wrong with you that you're so unhappy?" (see chapter 2). As such, it both asserts and reifies the sense of those in power that things really are fine the way they are, liberating them from taking seriously any challenges or critiques. It pretends to be descriptive—everything is fine—when in fact the discourse itself works actively to *prescribe* the status quo, to isolate all potential dissatisfaction and dissent, and present the illusion of a homogenized, satisfied mass, a united front. Who would dare try to change anything when everyone else is so satisfied with the way things are? "Go change it," then, rather than a positive invitation, is actually the opposite: a patronizing dismissal from communal life. Nobody says, after all, "Come, let us change." Imagine what a vastly different dynamic such a small shift in discourse would create!

There is another seemingly minor shift in discourse that has, I think, major consequence for the conversation of women and change. There may be a bottom-line truth to the claim that if women don't change things, things won't change. But there is a very big difference between acknowledging this unfortunate aspect of realpolitik and blaming women for not pulling themselves up by their bootstraps and bettering their own situation. To tell us to "Go away and change"—when change more often than not means leaving communities in which, despite certain sharp fissures, we feel deeply, deeply rooted—is nothing short of cruel.

---

Because the tradition of the guards can be so subtle and beguiling, I shall briefly outline some of the tactics they use to consolidate their power. One of the most prominent of these is marshaling the authority to define our religious needs, and sanction with disapproval and shame any needs running counter to traditional offerings. It is not enough to maintain consistent normative practice; one's internal religious stance must also conform with the norm. Furthermore, authenticity of needs is subjected to a battery of litmus tests that squelch process-oriented religious exploration. A woman who expresses the desire for an aliyah is grilled: Are you willing to get up and come to *minyan* every morning at 6:00 A.M.? If not, your need is obviously not serious. Meanwhile, a man who comes to shul once a year for a *yahrtzeit* is offered cake and schnapps.

It is understood, perhaps rightly, that expressing a need that differs from communal standards may create (or expose) cracks in the systemic edifice. These cracks may resonate with others, causing a chain reaction that may eventually predicate large-scale shifts in religious sensibility and practice. Responding to changing needs requires an organizational sophistication, suppleness, and vitality that Jewish tradition has proven itself ready and willing to evince in many areas. Feminism is simply not one.

In the event that a person does insist upon expressing such a proscribed need, the tactic often used is one of quarantine: to isolate it as that person's personal quirk, which cannot, and should not, be shared. I remember very vividly the countless conversations I had while planning my older daughters' bat mitzvahs. At that time Shirah Hadashah had not yet started and there was no shul that would allow us to hold the kind of service that I wanted to mark this moment in Nomi and Racheli's lives. The resistance I encountered gave me a taste of what later was to become a fixture of my life. The most common "criticism" I heard was, "This isn't Nomi's agenda, this is your agenda"; or "Racheli doesn't need this, you need this." On first hearing, this accusation cuts deeply into the conscience of any conscientious parent. The thought that one might be making choices for her children that reflect not their best interest, but her own political agenda—that she is sacrificing the former for the latter—would cause any mother some measure of anxiety and second-guessing. In short, there is a deep rhetorical power to this line of attack that could easily intimidate a mother into silence.

Of course, a deeper reflection reveals the fallacy of such rhetoric. No one asks such questions, say, about math. Yet whose agenda is it that my child learn arithmetic? Whose agenda is it that she study Bible, or that she pray at all? Indeed, this question is not asked about any other part of our children's education, secular or religious. We supply our children with the materials and create the environments in which, using our best judgment, we feel they will absorb the skills and values we believe are important. As powerful as the rhetoric of such a question is, even more powerful is the act of asking it in the first place: for it is in the asking that one kind of education is defined as normative and another is defined as marginal, questionable, and in need of justification. The rhetoric, of course is just another version of "go away and change": the status quo is fine, everyone is happy with it except you—including your children. If you are not happy with this part of her education, you must have a problem, and it is in her best interest that you keep it to yourself.

Questioning a person's needs, then, and causing her to question her own needs, whether vis-à-vis her children's education or her own religious yearning, constitutes one of the guards' major strategies. As mentioned above, the decision to start the shul was a clear assertion that there is dignity in our own religious needs. It was also an acknowledgment that one of the functions of leadership is not simply to respond to the overtly expressed needs of the community, but, as it were, to *create* need: that is, to offer the opportunity for people to connect to needs they have previously been unable to explore. I shall never forget the image of an elderly woman (who grew up in the ultra-Orthodox neighborhood of Meah She'arim, and remained quite observant) dancing with the Torah scroll on Simchat Torah at Shirah Hadashah. She looked, literally, like a madwoman, dancing wildly, frenetically, the hair of her *sheitel* (wig) lashing to and fro. She would not stop dancing, and could not stop crying, and would not let anyone else touch the Torah Scroll she cradled in her arms. I spoke to her after services; she said that she remembered as a child wanting to dance with the Torah. She also remembered that when she realized it would never be possible, she stopped allowing herself to want it. She told me to ask other women in the community when they stopped wanting what they wanted, when they gave up.

Though striking, in fact this was just an extreme example of what at the shul has become an extremely common occurrence. Older women regularly walk out crying after holding the Torah, reading from the Torah, or simply receiving an aliyah to the Torah. Often an "old-timer" will approach such a person sympathetically and ask her, with a touch of humor, "First time?" This outpouring of emotions, this overwhelming religious resonance, begs to be interpreted. If you gave a survey beforehand, many people would never have expressed a need for this kind of ritual possibility. We must begin to ask ourselves: What does it mean to awaken the long-dormant hearts and minds of so many?

———

Another underlying motif of the guards' rhetoric is what we have previously referred to as "compartmentalization": that women's issues, while acceptable for discussion in the secular realm, are constituted within religious discourse as qualitatively "other." Rosa Parks can be celebrated as a cultural hero and be brought to the front of the bus; but when religious women ask to be brought up from the back to the front of the shuls (to say nothing of being brought down from the chandeliers and out of the coat closets), far from being lauded as cultural heroes, they are repelled in no uncertain terms and branded as insatiable kvetches.

It is the guards, then, that define what is to be constituted as normative, which kinds of cultural advances are to be celebrated, which decried and sanctioned, and which kinds of penalties are to be applied. Now, it should be acknowledged that all cultures must negotiate the introduction of new values into their own core understandings and beliefs. I am certainly not advocating anarchy. One of Jewish tradition's strengths has been not only its system of rules but the system's relative transparency. "The rest is commentary—go learn." My point, then, is not that there is a system, and that the system has rules, but that how the rules are used constantly shifts in ways that are less than transparent—and less than coherent. If a change is suggested based on an educated layperson's reading of the halakha, the person and the suggestion run the risk of being dismissed for not having garnered rabbinic support. If a local rabbi comes along and endorses the change, he will be dismissed for not being "great" enough. Even a respected communal leader with impeccable scholarly credentials is not immune; if he endorses change, he risks being impugned for some religious or character flaw, and derided for "going against the *gedolim*." Power rests neither within local authority nor with the masters of the sources; the rules of the game have shifted from a discourse of legality to one of legitimacy. For anyone who follows the arcane communal politics of Modern Orthodoxy, the vicissitudes of legitimation and delegitimation are dizzying to behold.

———

I hope I have demonstrated that the notion that there really are no guards—that the Torah is "there for the taking" and no consequences are levied against those who actually try to come and take it—is quite problematic. There *are* guards, who *do* define the frame of reference for cultural legitimacy and punish in different ways those who propose to challenge or alter their dominant paradigms.

At the same time, societal developments have created a situation in which the power of the guards, while real, is not all-encompassing. Western culture, at least, places limits on the power of the guards to enforce their law. The guards can hurt; they can even scream and lash out; they can threaten and impose cultural sanctions; but they cannot, except in rare instances, literally ostracize. They cannot literally put people in jail. This limitation on their power has given even Modern Orthodox adherents an autonomous sensibility that is sometimes surprising in its manifestations. By way of analogy, the guards can force someone to wear a scarlet letter—but not everyone will read that letter the same way. Some will read it as a quaint relic divested of its shaming force; some, as a badge of courage; some barely notice it at all. Similarly, a shul can start without the sanction of many religious authorities, and still touch the hearts and minds of hundreds of Modern Orthodox congregants who want to pray in its services.

This porousness in the authority of the guards' ability to define what counts as in or out, and the interesting social dynamic that this porousness yields—Orthodox Jews accepting the aegis of that authority on the whole, while challenging or ignoring it on certain issues—provides a potential staging ground for a feminist reengagement of Orthodoxy that is constructive, vital, and popular in every sense of the word. This stance vis-à-vis authority is a direct response (some would say an affront) to the rhetoric of "Go away and change." It says, I am going to change and I am going to stay right here. It says that despite certain leaders' protestations to the contrary, I believe feminism has a place within Modern Orthodoxy, and I shall remain within this community and insist upon it. It says, Perhaps you would like me to go away, but ultimately that decision is not yours: I shall negotiate it directly, with the community at large.

What does it mean for a traditional person to stop asking for certain kinds of permission, and yet to maintain an investment in religious authority? What does it mean at once to remain committed to traditional halakha and to believe that what is considered "home" for Modern Orthodox Jews is larger than what rabbinic authorities have traditionally allowed? For me, joining with others in starting the shul was a religious act signifying this refusal to allow certain people to define exclusively where home is, a refusal to accept a particular frame of reference for what we are trying to do. It was an assertion of the right to say: we are not going to make a revolution, we are going to change certain things. And we say that it is possible to change, within the parameters of traditional halakha. In short, we are going to change, and we are going to stay.

---

As much as the principles upon which the shul was founded, this work of staying—not passively sitting and waiting for things to get better, but *actively* staying and changing—has been foundational to our identity. It was through a process heavily weighted toward doing, rather than deliberation, that we set out to create, experience, and learn what it means concretely for men and women to strive for holiness and dignity within a communal context. This activist focus may have derived in part from frustration with years of committee-ing, or simply from our restless nature. It may have derived in part from a pressing sense among all of us with daughters of formative ages that it was now or never; we were running out of time to right the dissonance between our feminism and our religious practice. For their sakes as much as our own, the split between the praying self and the inner self felt no longer viable. Moreover, we wanted to model for them a religious responsiveness, the possibility of a live conversation between tradition and subjectivity—the notion that when there is something you perceive as a problem, you notice it, name it, create a vision within which to address it, and try to make that vision real.

This is not to say, of course, that we did not deliberate and formulate principles. For example, we could not have imagined ourselves building a religious community without establishing and accepting the boundaries of halakha—after pushing it to what we understood to be its limits. We were cognizant that in recognizing these limits we were making compromises with our feminist understanding that women and men are completely equal. This acceptance of unresolved imperfection, this affirmation of multiple commitments, was (and remains) at the heart of our founding "values." At times we feel frustrated; at times we find ourselves deeply appreciating these compromises and their effects.

At the same time, it has been important to make explicit, to emphasize and constantly remind ourselves, that the search for serious and well-grounded halakhic openings was only the beginning—the scaffolding, if you will—of our emerging home. The shul is about much more than seeking halakhic opportunities to get women more involved in the performance of synagogue ritual. At its core, it is nurtured by religious sensibilities, and responsibilities, from three different sources: recognition of feminism as a core value; awareness of the challenge of creating meaningful prayer that connects to people's subjective experience; and understanding that values should be institutionalized as norms (halakha).

*Recognition of feminism as a core value.*—We must recognize that the claim of feminism is a religious claim, and it constitutes a valuable lens through which to read the tradition, enhancing its moral and spiritual aspects. Such recognition acknowledges that women's inclusion in public life goes beyond giving women access to men's behaviors. It affirms Erickson's (1964) insight that inviting women into public life means inviting women's ways of doing and being, and doing the work of translating those ways from the private to the public sphere:

Political equality . . . goes beyond the active participation in politics and government. In this sphere, too, the influence of women will not be fully actualized until it reflects without apology the facts of the "inner space" and the potentiality and needs of the feminine psyche. It is as yet unpredictable what the task and roles and opportunities and job specifications will be once women are not merely adapted to male jobs but when they learn to adapt jobs to themselves. Such revolutionary reappraisal may even lead to the insight that jobs now called masculine force men, too, to inhuman adjustments. (604)

Conversely, it means demystifying and decentralizing male roles in shul and thus extending to men the more private sphere that precedent has reserved for women. Ultimately it means extending a greater range of emotional and spiritual possibilities to both men and women.

*Awareness of the challenge of creating meaningful prayer that connects to people's subjective experience.*—Perhaps more then anything else, feminism has made us aware and sensitive to women's subjective experiences in societies. Thanks to feminism's impact upon religious women, we have also become very sensitive to and aware of women's religious subjectivity and the ways it may claim, connect to, and be infused by religious ritual practices. Yet worship in prayer is in general and inherently the place of a similar challenge for Orthodox Jews. Prayer is the place par excellence where religious praxis is called to meet, nurture, and resonate in the "subjective" hearts. Similar to feminism's view of human identity, prayer appeals to the participation of the whole person: it attempts to create an inner dialogue between what one says, feels, and knows and what one imagines, uniting the person one is and the person one would like to be. Yet mandatory and public prayer has many elements that can easily turn it into a "disembodied" routine (prayer is mandatory; it is based on a fixed text, it is set up for fixed time). Feminism inspires us to attend more carefully to this challenge, not only in relation to women in the synagogue but in relation to the entire congregation. At Shirah Hadashah, we therefore challenge ourselves by asking and trying to develop venues and opportunities by which those who come to pray in our synagogue might regain a renewed and meaningful intimate connection with prayer, beyond its mandatory and/or social aspect. To be sure, creating a place and a culture where people learn over time to take part in meaningful prayer is an ongoing challenge of many Orthodox synagogues nowadays. We join them in this challenge and feel blessed to be nurtured in this process by some of the lofty values of feminism.

*Understanding that values should be institutionalized as norms (halakha).*—
We must learn to ask, how can we translate Judaism's interpersonal obligations (*mitzvoth bein adam le-havero*) *internally* into actual shul practice, beyond the more outwardly focused machinations of the *hesed* (that is, charity)
committee? Implementing our values must not be left to the vagaries of individual goodwill.

We did, then, sit and talk. We talked through our founding principles; what
we did *not* do was dwell on them. Instead, we attempted to dwell *in* them, to
live them out. Our ideas were tested and refined by our actions. In other
words, our modus operandi was praxis: establishing a living, concrete reality
and learning by experiencing it.

It is no coincidence that the core group had met only twice before deciding
to launch the new *minyan*. Having agreed upon central principles, we then
studiously avoided slipping into long conversations about self-definition. This
decision was largely conscious as these conversations invariably slip into questions of differentiation from other groups and take on some aspect of negative identification. The longer the conversation, often the more negative the
identification. We tried to keep our attention trained on what we wanted to *do,*
rather than who we were in relation to other groups or *minyanim*. There was
plenty of negative identification to go around, plenty of traditionalists eager
to see us fail. We decided that our focus would remain inward rather than outward, toward nurturing and growth rather than justification or recrimination.

Nor did we set up a lot of planning committees. We knew that there was no
simple, linear way to get from theory to practice. Our fundamental educational and community-building principle has been to give people concrete alternatives by which they can learn through deep experience. We understood
that the many nuances of this complex endeavor could only be worked out
through the process of praxis: piecemeal, ad hoc, and often painfully slow to
unfold. This focus on praxis, with its qualitative, experiential texture, echoes
both trends in feminist methodology and Jewish normative insights. The
same can be said for the method of reengagement as a whole—of which, we
should be reminded, the shul is but one example (though an admittedly large-
scale, and exciting one). In this, as ideally in all cases, the medium was, and remains, the message.

———

One of the things that makes "Go away and change" so powerful and intimidating a statement is that the isolation it prescribes is multilayered. On the
first level, it says: You are completely alone in wanting change; everyone else is

happy with the way things are. Even if one manages to demonstrate that other people are unhappy with the status quo, those others remain isolated as a group—a group with no authoritative voice within the community, a group still subject to the sanctions of the guards, rhetorical and otherwise. In short, as long as feminist concerns remain a "woman's problem," the guards remain powerful and threatening.

Understanding this isolation was, I think, the key to the philosophy of Shirah Hadashah. The shul was founded by a community of people, men *and* women, and the concerns underlying its founding were understood by this community to be not solely the concerns of women, but of the Jewish People as a whole. This full communal participation was far from a foregone conclusion. When we were starting, everyone said, You'll never get any men to come. I was always more optimistic. First of all, many men have daughters. Many also have moral religious instincts. True, not everyone gives up power easily, but not everyone resists the sharing of power—and even those who do resist don't all do it in the same way. To those who founded the shul, religious feminism was not merely a women's issue. The problem of gender inequality within traditional Judaism, heavily guarded though it may be, was recognized as a problem for everyone. Armed with this common understanding and common purpose, we walked, and continue to walk through the guarded tradition together.

*Aggada* — narrative, non-legal sections in classical Jewish sources.

*Agunah* (plural, *agunot*) — literally "anchored," a woman whose husband refuses to give her a Jewish divorce and is therefore not free to marry anyone else.

*Aliya* — literally "ascent," the synagogue honor of approaching the dais, upon which the Torah scroll is being publicly read, and saying the blessings before and after the reading. In mainstream Orthodox practice, this honor has traditionally been restricted to male congregants.

*Beit Midrash* — literally "hall of study," where traditional Jewish texts are studied, usually by males.

*Brit* — covenant.

*Gedolim* — literally "great ones," honorific assigned to religious leaders of mainstream Orthodox Jewish society who carry great authority to decide matters of religious law and to set social norms for the community.

*Gehenna* — hell, as depicted in popular Jewish sources.

*Gittin* (singular, *get*) — Jewish divorces.

*Hakafot* — literally "goings around," the symbolic marching around with the Torah scroll in the Jewish festivals of *Sukkot* and *Simchat Torah*, celebrated each fall.

*Halakha* — Jewish law.

*Halakhic* — connected to Jewish law *(Halakha)*.

*Halitza* — performance of levirate obligations (by the brother of a deceased husband, thereby releasing the widow to remarry; see Deuteronomy 25:5–10).

*Hatznei lechet im elohecha* — literally "walk humbly with Hashem your God"; verse from Micah 6:8, used in Talmudic and later rabbinic literature as basis for the imperative to conduct oneself modestly.

*Hesed* — expansive kindness, generosity of spirit.

*Heter* — permission from a rabbinic authority.

*Kavanah* — proper intention, especially in prayer.

*Ketuba* — Jewish marriage contract.

*kevudah bat melech penima* — literally "the honor of a woman is interior," Jewish religious concept based on Psalm 45:14 that the true expression of female spiritual identity is found in private, domestic spaces (primarily the home) and not in public expression.

*Kidushin* — Jewish marriage.

*kol isha* — literally "woman's voice," Jewish legal prohibition against hearing a woman's voice in song.

*Kvod ha'adam* — literally "honor of humans," a rabbinic principle asserting the dignity of every individual.

*Kvod hatzibur* — literally "honor of the community," a rabbinic principle sometimes used to prohibit women from partaking in public roles.

*Mechitza* — literally "divider," the prayer partition separating men's and women's section in Orthodox synagogues.

**Men of the Great Assembly** — a rabbinic-like gathering of scholars described in rabbinic sources as existing in the late biblical period, before the rise of the rabbis.

*Midrash* — "exegesis"; broadly, a Jewish method of biblical interpretation/commentary.

*Mikveh* — a Jewish ritual bath. Many traditional women immerse themselves in a *mikveh* at the end of their period or at a later date, allowing them to have intercourse and other intimate contact with their husbands.

*Minyan* — a quorum of ten adults needed to recite certain special prayers. In Orthodox Judaism, only males count toward the *minyan*.

*Mipnei darkei shalom* — literally "because of the ways of peace," a rabbinic principle that takes into consideration issues of domestic happiness in rendering decisions.

*Mishnah* — an early collection of Jewish law, completed ca. 200 CE.

*Mitzvot ben adam lechaveiro* — literally "commandments between people," the aspects of Jewish Law that apply to interpersonal (as opposed to ritual) matters.

*Mitzvah* (plural, *mitzvot*) — commandment.

*nashim da'tan kala* — literally "women are weak-minded/weak-willed," Talmudic expression used to justify women's exclusion from certain intellectual activities such as Torah study.

*Naval bireshut hatorah* — literally "boor with the Torah's permission," rabbinic designation for a person who follows the letter of Jewish law but remains crude and vulgar in his/her appetites, attitudes, and actions.

*Niddah* — menstrual ritual impurity.

*Onah* — the biblical and rabbinic obligation upon the husband to provide his wife with her conjugal rights.

**Rambam Maimonides** — the medieval Jewish polymath (1135, or 1138–1204).

*Rav* — rabbi.

*Rosh Chodesh* — the Jewish new moon, celebrated for one or two days.

*Sefer torah* — a Torah scroll, namely a parchment copy of the Pentateuch used in synagogues.

*Shabbat* — the Jewish Sabbath, from Friday evening through Saturday night.

*Sheitel* (Yiddish) — a wig worn for the purpose of modesty.

*Shekhinah* — the spirit of God, imagined as especially immanent (and feminine) in many sources.

*Shul* — synagogue.

*Simchat Torah* — the fall festival when the annual cycle of reading the Torah is completed and begun anew, and *hakafot* are performed.

*Talmud* — literally "study," the central collection of Jewish oral tradition, edited and canonized after 500 CE; basis for Jewish Law.

*Talmid Chacham* — Torah scholar.

*Tefilla* — prayer.

*Tefillat nashim* — literally "prayer of women," a Hebrew designation for women's prayer groups.

*Tikkun Olam* — literally "Repair of the World," the imperative to contribute to the betterment of humankind through positive acts.

*Tzniut* — modesty.

*Yahrzeit* (Yiddish) — literally "year-time," the annual commemoration of the death of a close relative.

*Yesh Miayin* — creation ex-nihilo.

*Yeshiva* — an advanced academy of Jewish learning, traditionally for men only.

*Yo'atzot Halakha* — female Jewish-law consultants.

*Yo'atzot Niddah* — literally "*niddah* consultants," women who give other women advice concerning halakhic (Jewish legal) matters pertaining to *niddah* (menstrual impurity).

# NOTES

PREFACE (PP. IX – XIV)

1. The Pardes Institute in Jerusalem under the leadership of Judy Klitzner held Friday evening services in which women led Kabbalat Shabbat. The Leeder minyan in Jerusalem, which met monthly, gave women aliyot. The Drisha High Holiday minyan in New York did the same.

1. FEMINISM AND MODERN ORTHODOXY (PP. 1–19)

1. The religious authorities I speak about are both those who define themselves as Modern Orthodox, and those who would resist such a label; these latter indeed oppose many aspects of Modern Orthodoxy, defining themselves rather as "centrist" Orthodox. I refer to both of these different types of leaders not because I discount the important distinctions between them, but rather because both exert significant authority within the Modern Orthodox world. Many centrist Orthodox rabbis teach in Modern Orthodox yeshivot (Yeshiva University being the most prominent example) and serve as the local rabbis of Modern Orthodox communities.

2. I thank Yehuda Gelman for this incisive characterization.

3. See also Lamm 1990; Sagi 1996b; Ravitzky 1996; Kaplan 1980; Safrai 1999; Goldman 1996; Terner 1996; Bulka 1991; Sacks 1991, and Zivan 2005 for definitions of Modern Orthodoxy. While nuances exist among the definitions, all follow similar lines.

4. See Lamm 1990, Berman 2001, Ravitzky 1996 and 1999.

5. For an insightful discussion of the genesis of the Modern Autonomous Man from a feminist perspective see Bordo 1987: "The particular genius of Descartes was to have philosophically transformed what was first experienced as estrangement and loss—the sundering of the organic ties between the person and the world—into a requirement for the growth of human knowledge and progress" (100). Descartes's new conception of the world and self "as decisively separated appears, not merely as the articulation of a positive new epistemological ideal, but as a reaction-formation to the loss of 'being-one-with-the-world' brought about by the disintegration of the organic, centered, female cosmos of the Middle Ages and the Renaissance" (106).

6. Kimmel (1997), for example, drawing upon the implications of the psychoanalytic theory that boys must separate from their mothers early in order to identify with the father, speaks about traditional male or "masculine" identity as being essentially a negative identity, inasmuch as the rejection of the female is constitutive to the very core of what it means to be a man.

7. See Bordo 1987; Kristeva 1982; Irigaray 1977 and 1974; Gilligan 1982; Fox-Keller 1985.

8. See Chodorow 1978; Gilligan 1982 and 2002; Brown and Gilligan 1992; Josselson 1987 and 1996; Gergen 2001; Benhabib 1992; Flax 1990 and 1993; Baker-Miller 1976; Benjamin 1988, 1995, and 1998; Yanay and Birns 1990.

## 2. FACING THE LEGACY OF THE CANON (PP. 20–44)

1. Liberal feminism claims at its core that women must be considered entitled to the same natural rights as men.

2. "Women have been defined out and marginalized in every philosophical system and have therefore had to struggle not only against exclusion but against a content which defines them as subhuman and deviant" (Lerner 1993, 5).

3. See for example Lerner 1993 and Weiler 1988.

4. For example, Karen Horney, who presented an alternative model of psychosexual development, was removed as a permanent member of the New York Psychoanalytic Institute (see Sayers 1991).

5. See, for example, Freud 1925; Chasseguet-Smirgel 1976, Chodorow 1978 and 1989, and Gilligan 1982.

6. The letters are taken from Masson 1985.

7. In addition, Freud himself refers to Eckstein as an analyst (letter, December 12, 1897; in Masson 1985).

8. Gilligan, in her theory of adolescence, highlights the process that young girls go through. She claims that in order for them to adapt to the prevailing attitudes and culture around them, girls go out of relationship with themselves in order to be in relationship with their surroundings (1990). Elsewhere, she writes, "The paradoxical sacrifice of relationship for the sake of relationships is the core dynamic of initiation into a patriarchal social order" (1997, 159).

9. Avineri (1968), in his analysis of the thought of Karl Marx, distinguishes between the early Marx and the late Marx. He shows that establishment communism was very threatened by his earlier writings and therefore let only his later writings be known.

10. Sprengnether (1990) claims, "Dora stands for all that Freud could neither understand nor simply allow to be on its own terms in the other sex" (71).

11. See Bernheimer and Kahane 1985 and Masson 1992.

12. White ink is the term that Adrianne Rich (1976) uses for women writing in their own voice.

13. It is important to note that the women's issue is not only an issue for educators of girls; it has serious ramifications for the education of boys as well. If a certain portrait of a woman is painted, then who is the man, her partner? Who is the man in relation to this woman? What are the ramifications concerning malehood in the religious worldview?

14. Maimonides, the great twelfth-century codifier of Jewish law, elaborates on the rationale behind this policy as follows:

> A woman who studies Torah will be recompensed, but not in the same measure as a man, for study was not imposed on her as a duty. One who performs a meritorious act which is not obligatory will not receive the same reward as one upon whom it is incumbent and who fulfills it as a duty, but only a lesser reward. And notwithstanding that she is recompensed, yet the sages have warned us that a man shall not teach his daughter Torah, as the majority of women have not a mind adequate for its study but, because of their limitations, will turn the words of the Torah into trivialities. "He who teaches his daughter Torah, it is as if he taught her wantonness." This stricture refers only to instruction in the Oral Law. With regard to the Written Law, he ought not to teach it to her; but if he has done so, it is not regarded as teaching her wantonness. (M.T., Laws Concerning the Study of Torah, I:13)

Maimonides' ruling became the accepted norm so that even when organized educational institutions for women were established, the curriculum consisted of Bible (the Written Law) and not Talmud (the Oral Law).

15. It is interesting to compare this story as well to the Oedipus story, where at the end the mother commits suicide and the father blinds himself (his daughters then take care of him). Jocasta takes real responsibility for her actions; she is the "man."

16. Popper (1945) claims that democracies change by piecemeal social engineering. The radical approach to the Jewish culture claims that there is no more room for piecemeal social engineering, but rather the whole system must be changed: its foundations, its goals, and foremost its authors.

17. Following Berger, who claims "Max Weber's caveat on what he called 'ideal types' applies here. No typology exists as such in the world; it is always an intellectual construct. Thus it can never be found in pure form, and there will always be cases that do not fit into it. But this does not matter. The typology will be useful to the extent that it helps discriminate between empirically available cases, and in consequence to make possible both understanding and explanation." (1979, 56).

18. Mitchell (1974) uses the term *re-described* when presenting another reading of Freud (7).

### 3. MODESTY AND THE RELIGIOUS MALE GAZE (PP. 45–61)

1. Concentration camp victim.

### 4. THE PATERNAL VOICE IN LITURGY (PP. 62–80)

1. Of course, it is also possible to read the Men of the Great assembly's response to the prophets as saying that this is "always" what the words "awesome" and "powerful"

meant. However, this reading would have to be considered extremely weak in light of the fact that they reference contemporary events: the oppression of the Jews at the hands of the wicked, and their uncanny survival.

2. It should be noted that while the "liturgical change" approach is represented in the text by two prophets, Jeremiah and Daniel, it would be more accurate to say that their approaches, reflected in prooftexts from their respective biblical books, are appropriated by the rabbis to stand for one side in the rabbis' own internal, contemporary debate. Liturgical change seems to have been for them a more radical, "prophetic" approach; the reinterpretive approach, more conservative and community-minded. It is noteworthy that in the text itself Jeremiah and Daniel are referred to as "Rabbanan," or "Our Rabbis."

### 5. THE HANDS OF RABBIS (PP. 81–98)

1. Kandiyoti's (1991) structural analysis examines the differences between the lived experiences of Islamic women in different Muslim countries and their roles and position in the modern nation-states of the Middle East. Unlike the present work, her focus is on the effects of the political projects of states on women's lives. Kaufman (1993) gives voice to the experiences of newly religious Jewish women, individuals who have chosen to reject their upbringing in a feminist and secular environment and move to a life of commitment to religious teachings. Similar to our work, she interviews these women about how they understand their lives within the context of what is considered an oppressive patriarchal system, and gives voice to their wide range of experiences. However, she assumes a dichotomy between their lives before becoming religious (with an emphasis on individual freedom and feminist opportunity) and their lives after the choice to live in a closed and patriarchal system, asking questions of how and why they chose to embrace this way of life, rather than simply allowing them to speak in their own categories of meaning.

2. This chapter was published in an earlier version in *Gender and Society* together with my student Naomi Mormon.

3. The basis for *niddah* practice is found in Leviticus (chaps. 15, 18, 20). According to rabbinic tradition, a woman remains in *niddah* for a minimum of twelve days—five for the period of the menstrual flow, and seven "clean" days thereafter. During this time, sexual intercourse and any physical intimacy are forbidden. At the end of the seven clean days a woman must immerse in the *mikvah;* husband and wife are then free to resume sexual relations.

4. The use of the laws of *niddah* as a source of women's power is consistent with Rahel Wasserfall's (1992) findings in an ethnographic study of *niddah* in the Israeli-Moroccan community. She notes: "*Niddah* is also a symbolic site where the division of power between husband and wife is enacted" (309). In the Moroccan society, it is the

man's duty to send his wife to the *mikvah*. As an assertion of their power women sometimes demand that their husbands "beg" them to go. "Women tell of putting off their
visits to the *miqve* [*sic*] and not paying heed to the constant demands of their husbands
to go to the ritual bath. Indeed, delaying the *miqve* and thereby sexual relations seem
in the eyes of these women to be the principal source of feminine power" (322).

5. This can be contrasted with Shweder's (1991) account of Oriya Brahman society,
in which menstruating women share with men the belief that during menstruation
they are unclean and untouchable.

### 6. ROLES, RULES, AND RESPONSA (PP. 99–120)

1. Kook 1920, 133.

2. Kook 1919, 130.

3. The trope of "family values" consistently, and cross-culturally, has been wielded
as a justification for prohibiting women from participating in public life. That this
usage is at best rhetorical, and at worse cynical, is easily exposed. No one, for example,
in the name of family values supports giving money to single mothers or shelter to
abused women in order to help their families. Rather, the rhetoric of family values is
always used to keep women in their place, to prevent them from altering in any way the
status quo.

4. Normally women pray with men but aren't counted in the minyan; nor can they
perform public ritual functions like reading from the Torah and so forth.

5. Twersky is quoting/paraphrasing Nachmanides, the medieval commentator, in
his interpretation of Leviticus, chap. 19.

6. Interestingly, when the previous pope justified the Church's exclusion of women
from the priesthood, he uses a similar argument regarding men's and women's differences as being part of God's plan: "Furthermore, the fact that the Blessed Virgin Mary,
Mother of God and Mother of the Church, received neither the mission proper to the
Apostles nor the ministerial priesthood clearly shows that the non-admission of
women to priestly ordination cannot mean that women are of lesser dignity, nor can it
be construed as discrimination against them. Rather, it is to be seen as the faithful observance of a plan to be ascribed to the wisdom of the Lord of the universe. . . . The
presence and the role of women in the life and mission of the Church, although not
linked to the ministerial priesthood, remain absolutely necessary and irreplace-
able . . . today their role is of capital importance both for the renewal and humaniza-
tion of society and for the rediscovery by believers of the true face of the Church" (John
Paul II, 1994).

7. Maimonides 1953, 3: chap. 51.

8. See Bachaye "Duties of the Hearts."

9. This reductiveness is similar to the bind in which Twersky finds himself vis-à-vis public prayer, though on a much greater scale.

10. In a similar vein when explaining why women cannot be priests, the reason recalled is the Church's imitating of God's choice not to call women to be part of the Apostles: "The position of the Catholic Church: 'She holds that it is not admissible to ordain women to the priesthood, for very fundamental reasons. These reasons include: the example recorded in the Sacred Scriptures of Christ choosing his Apostles only from among men; the constant practice of the Church, which has imitated Christ in choosing only men; and her living teaching authority which has consistently held that the exclusion of women from the priesthood is in accordance with God's plan for his Church. . . . In calling only men as his Apostles, Christ acted in a completely free and sovereign manner. In doing so, he exercised the same freedom with which, in all his behavior, he emphasized the dignity and the vocation of women, without conforming to the prevailing customs and to the traditions sanctioned by the legislation of the time" (John, Paul II, 1994).

### 7. GO AWAY AND CHANGE (PP. 121–133)

1. It is, I think, analogous to the myth of abuse—if you don't like it, leave—and reflects a similar lack of empathy. Battered women themselves, of course, know that the situation is far more complicated; they know how much is really at stake in resisting. They know, for example, that for all they sacrifice by remaining in abusive relationships, at least they are unlikely to be killed. They know that when they leave they are at greatest risk for being murdered. They know that their children have a roof over their heads and that the fastest-growing segment of the homeless population is single mothers.

# BIBLIOGRAPHY

Adler, R. 1983, "The Jew who wasn't There." In Heschel, S., ed. 1993, 12–18.

———. 1998. *Engendering Judaism: An Inclusive Theology and Ethics.* Philadelphia: Jewish Publication Society.

———. 2001 "Innovation and Authority: A Feminist Reading of the Women's Minyan," Responsum. In Jacob and Zemer 2001, 3–32.

Ahmed, L. 1992. *Women and Gender in Islam.* New Haven: Yale University Press.

Apter, T. 1990. *Altered Loves: Mothers and Daughters During Adolescence.* New York: Ballantine Books.

Ariel, Y. 2000. "Women and Modesty." In Shwartzbaum and Sadan 2000, 61–69.

Aristotle. 1908–1931. *The Works of Aristotle.* Translated and edited by W. D. Ross, Oxford: Clarendon Press.

Arthur, L. 1999. *Religion, Dress and the Body.* Oxford: Berg.

Aviner, S. 1983. *Am Klavi.* Jerusalem: Kiryat Noar a Ierushalmi. (In Hebrew.)

Avineri, S. 1968. *The Social and Political Thought of Karl Marx.* Cambridge, Mass.: Harvard University Press.

Bachya, ben Joseph ibn Paqoda. 1965. *Duties of the Heart.* Translated by J. Tibbon (from Arabic to Hebrew) and M. Hyamson (from Hebrew to English). Jerusalem: Boys Town Jerusalem Publishers.

Bartky, S. 1990. *Femininity and Domination: Studies in the Phenomenology of Oppression.* New York: Routledge.

———. 1998. "Foucault, Femininity, and the Modernization of the Patriarchal Power." In Weitz, ed. 1998, 21–45.

Baskin, J. 1985. "The Separation of Women in Rabbinic Judaism." In Haddad and Findly, eds. 1985, 3–18.

Baum, C, P. Hyman, and S. Michel. 1976. *The Jewish Woman in America.* New York: New American Library.

Bendix, R. 1973. *Max Weber.* London: Methuen.

Benhabib, S. 1992. *Situating the Self: Gender, Community, and Postmodernism in Contemporary Ethics.* New York: Routledge.

Benjamin, J. 1988. *The Bonds of Love : Psychoanalysis, Feminism, and the Problem of Domination.* New York : Pantheon Books.

———. 1995. *Like Subjects, Love Objects: Essays on Recognition and Sexual Difference.* New Haven: Yale University Press.

———. 1998. *Shadow of the Other: Intersubjectivity and Gender in Psychoanalysis.* New York: Routledge.

Berger, P. 1979. *The Heretical Imperative: Contemporary Possibilities of Religious Affirmation.* Garden City, N.Y: Anchor Press.

Berman, S. 2001. "The Ideology of Modern Orthodoxy." *Sh'ma* February.

Bernay, T., and D. Cantor, eds. 1989. *The Psychology of Today's Woman: A Psychoanalytic Perspective*. Boston: Analytic.

Bernheimer, C., and C. Kahane, eds. 1985. *In Dora's Case: Freud—Hysteria—Feminism*. New York: Columbia University Press.

Biale, R. 1984. *Woman and Jewish Law*. New York: Schocken Books.

Bordo, S. 1987. *The Flight to Objectivity: Essays on Cartesianism and Culture*. Albany: State University of New York Press.

———. 1993. *Unbearable Weight: Feminism, Western Culture, and the Body*. Berkeley and Los Angeles: University of California Press.

———. 1997. *Twilight Zones: The Hidden Life of Cultural Images from Plato to O.J.* Berkeley and Los Angeles: University of California Press.

———. 1999. *The Male Body: A New Look at Men in Public and in Private*. New York: Farrar, Straus and Giroux.

Boyarin, D. 1993. *Carnal Israel: Reading Sex in Talmudic Culture*. Berkeley and Los Angeles: University of California Press.

Brown, I. 1997. "Women and Talmud Torah" M.A. thesis. The Hebrew University of Jerusalem.

Brown, L. M., and C. Gilligan. 1992. *Meeting at the Crossroads: Women's Psychology and Girls' Development*. Cambridge, Mass.: Harvard University Press.

Buber, M. 1923. "Jewish Religiosity." In *Teuda va Yehud* 1. Jerusalem: Zionist Library.

Bulka, R. 1991. "The Future of Modern Orthodoxy." In Sacks, ed. 1991, 30–47.

Bynum, C. W., S. Harrell, and P. Richman, eds. 1986. *Gender and Religion: On the Complexity of Symbols*. Boston: Beacon Press.

Chasseguet-Smirgel, J. 1990. "Feminine Guilt and the Oedipus Complex." In Zanardi, ed. 1990, 88–131.

Cherazi, S. 1987. "Female Psychology: A Review." In Walsh, ed. 1987, 22–38.

Chesler, P. 1972. *Women and Madness*. Garden City, N.Y.: Doubleday.

Chodorow, N. 1978. *The Reproduction of Motherhood: Psycho-Analysis and the Sociology of Gender*. Berkeley and Los Angeles: University of California Press.

———. 1989. *Feminism and Psychoanalytic Theory*. New Haven: Yale University Press.

Choi, P. and P. Nicholson, eds. 1994. *Female Sexuality: Psychology, Biology, and Social Context*. London: Harvester Wheatsheaf.

Connell, R. W. 1982. "*Class, Patriarchy, and Sartre's Theory of Practice.*" *Theory and Society* 2: 305–320.

———. 1983. *Which Way Is Up? Essays on Sex, Class and Culture*. Sydney, Australia: Allen and Unwin.

———. 1987. *Gender and Power*. Sydney, Australia: Allen and Unwin.

———. and J. W. Messerschmidt. 2005. "Hegemonic Masculinity: Rethinking the Concept." *Gender and Society* 19: 829–859.

Daly, C. 1999. "The 'Paarda' Expression of Hejaab among Afghan Women in a Non-Muslim Community." In Arthur, ed. 1999, 147–159.

de Beauvoir, S. 1949. *The Second Sex*. Translated by H. M. Parshley. New York: Vintage Books, 1989.

Dinnerstein, D. 1976. *The Mermaid and the Minotaur.* New York: Harper and Row.

Douglas, M. 1966. *Purity and Danger.* London: Routledge and Kegan Paul.

Dworkin, A. 1974. *Woman Hating.* New York: Dutton.

Eilberg-Schwartz, H., ed. 1995. *People of the Body.* Albany: State University of New York Press.

Ellenson, D. 2004. *After Emancipation: Jewish Religious Responses to Modernity.* Cincinnati: Hebrew Union College Press.

Ellinson, G. 1992. *The Modest Way: A Guide to the Rabbinic Sources.* Translated by R. Blumberg Jerusalem : Eliner Library.

Erikson, E. 1964. "Inner and Outer Space: Reflections on Womanhood." *Daedalus* 93:582–606.

———. 1968. *Identity: Youth and Crisis.* New York: Norton.

Faludi, S. 1991. *Backlash: The Undeclared War Against American Women.* New York: Doubleday.

Falk, E. P. 1998. *Modesty, An Adornment for Life: Halachos and Attitudes Concerning Tznius of Dress and Conduct.* Nanuet, N.Y.: Feldheim Publishers.

Feuerbach, L. 1851. *Lectures on the Essence of Religion.* Translated by R. Manheim. New York: Harper and Row.

Fine, M. 1992. *Disruptive Voices: The Possibilities of Feminist Research.* Ann Arbor: University of Michigan Press.

Firestone, S. 1971. *The Dialectic of Sex: The Case for Feminist Revolution.* New York: Bantam.

Flax, J. 1990. *Thinking Fragments: Psychoanalysis, Feminism, and Postmodernism in the Contemporary.* Berkeley and Los Angeles: University of California Press.

———. 1993. *Disputed Subjects: Essays on Psychoanalysis, Politics, and Philosophy.* New York: Routledge.

Forrester, J. 1992. "Freud's Female Patients/Female Analysts." In ed. 1992.

Foucault, M. 1977. *Discipline and Punish: The Birth of the Prison.* Translated by Sheridan. New York: Pantheon Books.

———. 1980. *The History of Sexuality.* New York: Vintage Books.

Fox-Keller, E. 1985. *Reflections on Gender and Science.* New Haven: Yale University Press.

Freud, S. 1905. *Dora: An Analysis of a Case of Hysteria.* New York: Macmillan, 1963.

———. 1925. "Some Psychical Consequences of the Anatomical Distinction Between the Sexes." In Strachey, ed. and trans. 1953–1974, 19.

Freud, S. 1931. "Female Sexuality." In his *Sexuality and the Psychology of Love,* 194–211. New York: Collier.

Friday, N. 1977. *My Mother My Self: The Daughter's Search for Identity.* New York: Delacorte.

Gadamer, H. G. 1986. *Truth and Method.* New York: Crossroads.

Garner, S. N., C. Kahane, and M. Sprengnether, eds. 1985. *The (M)other Tongue: Essays in Feminist Psychoanalytic Interpretation.* Ithaca: Cornell University Press.

Gergen, M. 2001. *Feminist Reconstructions in Psychology: Narrative, Gender and Performance.* Thousand Oaks, Calif.: Sage.

Gergen, M., and Davis, S., eds. 1997. *Toward a New Psychology of Gender.* New York: Routledge.

Gilligan, C. 1982. *In a Different Voice: Psychological Theory and Women's Development.* Cambridge, Mass.: Harvard University Press, 1993.

———, et al. 1988. *A Guide for the Reader.* Cambridge, Mass.: Harvard University Press.

———. 1990. "Joining the Resistance: Psychology, Politics, Girls and Women." *Michigan Quarterly Review* 29: 501–536.

———. 1993. *In a Different Voice: Psychological Theory and Women's Development,* second ed. Cambridge, Mass.: Harvard University Press.

———. 1997. "Remembering Iphigenia: Voice, Resonance, and a Talking Cure." In Shapiro, ed. 1997, 143–168.

———. 2002. *The Birth of Pleasure: A New Map of Love.* London: Chatto and Windus.

Gladstone, W. E. 1892. "Female Suffrage: A Letter from the Right Hon. W.E. Gladstone to Samuel Smith, M.P."

Goldman, E. 1996. *Expositions and Inquiries: Jewish Thought in Past and Present.* Edited by Sagi, A., and D. Statman. Jerusalem: Magness Press. (In Hebrew.)

Greenberg, B. 1981. *On Women and Judaism: A View from Tradition.* Philadelphia: Jewish Publication Society.

Gruenbaum, E. 2000. *Female Circumcision Controversy: An Anthropological Perspective.* Philadelphia: University of Pennsylvania Press.

Haddad, Y., and E. Findly, eds. 1985. *Women, Religion, and Social Change.* Albany: State University of New York Press.

Halbertal, M., and T. Hartman Halbertal. 1998. "The Yeshiva." In Rorty, ed. 1998, 458–470.

Hampson, D. 1990. *Theology and Feminism.* Cambridge: Blackwell.

Hartman T., and Samet. (Forthcoming). "Uncovering Private Discourse: Sex Education in Iraeli Jewish Religious Schools." *Curriculum Inquiry.*

Heilbrun, C. 1988. *Writing a Woman's Life.* New York: Ballantine Books.

Helmreich, W. 1982. *The World of the Yeshiva.* New Haven: Yale University Press.

Herman, J., and H. Lewis, 1989. "Anger in the Mother-Daughter Relationship." In Bernay and Cantor, eds. 1989. 139–166.

Heschel, A. J. 1954. *Man's Quest for God: Studies in Prayer and Symbolism.* New York: Scribner.

Heschel, S. 1983. *On Being a Jewish Feminist.* New York: Shocken Books.

Heywood, L., ed. 1997. *Third Wave Agenda: Being Feminist, Doing Feminism.* Minneapolis: University of Minnesota Press.

Horner, M. 1972. "Towards an Understanding of Achievement-Related Conflicts in Women." *Journal of Social Issues* 28: 157–175.

Horney, K. 1939. *New Ways in Psychoanalysis.* New York: Norton.

———. 1967. *Feminine Psychology.* New York: Norton.

Hyman, P. 1976. "The Other Half: Women in the Jewish Tradition." In Koltun, ed. 1976.

Ilan, N., ed. 1999. *A Good Eye: Dialogue and Polemic in Jewish Culture: A Jubilee Book in Honor of Tova Ilan.* Tel Aviv: Hakibbutz Hameuchad Publishing.

Irigaray, Luce. 1974. *Speculum of the Other Woman.* Translated by G. Gillian. Ithaca: Cornell University Press.

———. 1977. *This Sex Which is Not One.* Translated by C. Porter and C. Burke. Ithaca: Cornell University Press.

———. 1993. *Je, Tu, Nous: Toward a Culture of Difference.* Trans. by Alison Martin. New York: Routledge.

Irvine, J. M., ed. 1994. *Sexual Cultures and the Construction of Adolescent Identities.* Philadelphia: Temple University Press.

Jacob, W., and M. Zemer, eds. 2001. *Gender Issues in Jewish Law: Essays and Responsa.* New York: Bergham Books.

John Paul II. 1994. "Apostolic Letter Ordinatio Sacerdotalis of John Paul II to the Bishops of the Catholic Church on Reserving Priestly Ordination to Men Alone." Vatican City.

Josselson, R. 1987. *Finding Herself: Pathways to Identity Development in Women.* San Francisco, Calif.: Jossey-Bass.

———. 1996. *Revising Herself: The Story of Women's Identity from College to Midlife.* New York: Oxford University Press.

Kandiyoti, D. 1991. *Women, Islam and the State.* Philadelphia: Temple University Press.

Kaplan, E. A. 1992. *Motherhood and Representation: The Mother in Popular Culture and Melodrama.* London: Routledge.

Kaplan, L. 1980. "The Ambiguous Modern Orthodox Jew." *Tefutsot Israel* 18(1): 31–41. (In Hebrew.)

Kaufman, D. 1993. *Rachel's Daughters: Newly Orthodox Jewish Women.* New Brunswick, N.J.: Rutgers University Press.

Kent, K. S. 1990. *Sex and Suffrage in Britain, 1860–1914.* Princeton: Princeton University Press.

Kimmel, M. 1996. *Manhood in America: A Cultural History.* New York: Free Press.

———. 1997. "Masculinity as Homophobia: Shame, Fear, and Silence in the Construction of Gender Identity." In Gergen and Davis, eds. 1997, 223–242.

Kohlberg, L. 1976. "Moral Stages and Moralization: The Cognitive-Developmental Approach." In Lickona, ed. 1976.

———. 1981. *The Philosophy of Moral Development.* San Francisco, Calif.: Harper and Row.

Kolodony, A. 1985. "A Map for Reading; or, Gender and the Interpretation of Literary Texts." In Garner, S. N., C. Kahane, and M. Sprengnether, eds. 1985, 241–259.

Koltun, E., ed. 1976. *The Jewish Woman: New Perspectives.* New York: Schocken Books.

Kook, A. I. HaCohen. 1919. "On the Election of Women." In *Women and the Jewish Tradition.* Translated by M. Lorberbaum, 1997, unpublished source book. Jerusalem: Shalom Hartman Institute.

———. 1920. "On Women's Voting." In *Women and the Jewish Tradition.* Translated by M. Lorberbaum, 1997, unpublished sourcebook. Jerusalem: Shalom Hartman Institute.

Kristeva, J. 1982. *Powers of Horror: An Essay on Abjection*. New York: Columbia University Press.

Lamm, N. 1990. *Torah Umadda: The Encounter of Religious Learning and Worldly Knowledge in the Jewish Tradition*. Northvale, N.J.: Jason Aronson.

Leibowitz, Y. 1976. "Education for Mitzvot" (in Hebrew). Pp. 57–67 in *Judaism, The Jewish People, The State of Israel*. Jerusalem: Shocken.

Lerman , H. 1986. *A Mote in Freud's Eye: From Psychoanalysis to the Psychology of Women*. New York: Springer.

Lerner, G. 1993. *The Creation of Feminist Consciousness: From the Middle Ages to Eighteen-Seventy*. New York: Oxford University Press.

Lickona, T., ed. 1976. *Moral Development and Behavior: Theory, Research, and Social Issues*. New York: Holt, Rinehart, and Winston.

MacKinnon, C. 1987. *Feminism Unmodified: Discourses on Life and Law*. Cambridge, Mass.: Harvard University Press.

———. 1989. *Toward a Feminist Theory of the State*. Cambridge, Mass.: Harvard University Press.

———. 2005. *Women's Lives, Men's Laws*. Cambridge, Mass.: Belknap Press of Harvard University Press.

Maimonides, M. 1953. *The Guide of the Perplexed of Maimonides (1135–1204)*. Translated by M. Friedlaender. New York: Hebrew Publishing.

———. 1993. "Letter to Ovadyah." Translated by M. Loberbaum, 1993. *Svara* 3(1): 57–66.

———. [n.d.]. *Mishnah Torah: The Laws Concerning the Study of Torah*, I:B.

Manolson, G. 1997. *Outside, Inside: A Fresh Look at Tzniut*. Jerusalem: Targum.

Masson, J., ed. 1985. *The Complete Letters of Sigmund Freud to Wilhelm Fleiss (1887–1904)*. Cambridge, Mass.: Belknap Press of Harvard University Press.

———. 1992. *The Assault on Truth: Freud's Suppression of the Seduction Theory*. New York: Harper Perennial.

Meiselman, M. 1998. "Feminism, and Public Policy." *Tradition* 32:3.

Mill, J. S. 1954. *On Liberty, Representative Government, the Subjection of Women: Three Essays*, with an introduction by Millicent Garrett Fawcett. London: Oxford University Press.

Miller, J. B. 1976. *Toward a New Psychology of Women*. Boston: Beacon Press.

Mitchell, J. 1974. *Psychoanalysis and Feminism*. New York: Pantheon Books.

———. 1986. *The Selected Melanie Klein*. New York: Free Press.

Moharty, C. T. 1988. "Under Western Eyes: Feminist Scholarship and Colonial Discourses." *Feminist Review* 30: 65–88.

Muffs, Yochanan. 2005. *The Personhood of God: Biblical Theology, Human Faith, and the Divine Image*. With a Foreword by David Hartman. Woodstock, Vt.: Jewish Lights.

Narayan, U. 1997. *Dislocating Cultures: Identities, Traditions, and Third-World Feminism*. New York: Routledge.

Nicholson, P. 1994. "Anatomy and Destiny: Sexuality and the Female Body." In Choi and Nicolson, eds. 1994, 7–26.

Ozick, C. 1983. "Notes Towards Finding the Right Question." In Heschel, S., ed. 1983, 120–151.

Perelberg, R. J. 1990. "Quality, Asymmetry, and Diversity: On Conceptualization of Gender." In Perelberg and Miller, eds. 1990.

Perelberg, R. J., and A. Miller, eds. 1990. *Gender and Power in Families*. London: Routledge.

Plaskow, J. 1983. "The Right Question is Theological." In Heschel, S., ed. 1983, 223–233.

———. 1990. *Standing Again at Sinai: Judaism From a Feminist Perspective*. New York: Harper.

Polhemus, T. 1978. *The Body Reader: Social Aspects of the Human Body*. New York: Pantheon Books.

Popper, K. 1945. *The Open Society and Its Enemies*. London: Routledge.

Priesand, S. 1975. *Judaism and the New Woman*. New York: Behrman House.

Rapoport, T. A. Penso, and T. Hartman Halbertal. 1996. "The Artistic Selfhood of Adolescent Girls: Two Improvisations of Cultural Scripts." *Journal of Contemporary Ethnography* 24: 438–461.

Ravitzky, A. 1996. "New From the Torah? On Orthodoxy and Modernity" (in Hebrew). In Sagi, ed. 1996a, 445–460.

———. 1999. *Freedom Inscribe: Diverse Voices of the Jewish Religious Thought*. Tel Aviv: Am Oved. (In Hebrew.)

Rich, A. 1976. *Of Woman Born: Motherhood as Experience and Institution*. New York: Norton.

———. 1979. *On Lies, Secrets, and Silence: Selected Prose, 1966–1978*. New York: Norton.

———. 1980. Afterword to *Take Back the Night*, ed. L. Lederer, 313–320. New York: Morrow.

Rorty, A., ed. 1998. *Philosophers on Education: New Historical Perspectives*. New York: Routledge.

Ross, T. 1999. "Can We Still Pray to Our Father in Heaven?" In *A Good Eye: Dialogue and Polemic in Jewish Culture*, a Jubilee book in honor of Tova Ilan. Hakibbutz Hameuchad Publishing House, Ltd, 264–278.

———. 2004. *Expanding the Palace of Torah: Orthodoxy and Feminism*. Waltham, Mass.: Brandeis University Press.

Ruddick, S. 1989. *Maternal Thinking*. New York: Ballantine Books.

Sacks, J. 1991. *Orthodoxy Confronts Modernity*. Hoboken, N.J.: Ktav Publishing.

Safrai, Z. 1999. "Religion, Halakha, Tradition, and Modernity" (in Hebrew). In Ilan, ed. 1999, 582–602.

Sagi, A., ed. 1996a. *Emunah biZmanism Mishtanim*. Jerusalem: Elinor Library.

———. 1996b. "HaRav Soloveitchik: Jewish Thought in Light of Modernity" (in Hebrew). In Sagi, ed. 1996a, 461–500.

————. 2003. *A Challenge: Returning to Tradition.* Jerusalem: Shalom Hartman Institute.

————. 2006. *The Jewish-Israeli Voyage: Culture and Identity.* Jerusalem: Shalom Hartman Institute.

Sanday, P. 1982. *Female Power and Male Dominance.* Cambridge: Cambridge University Press.

Sayers, J. 1991. *Mothers of Psychoanalysis.* New York: Norton.

Schachter, H. 2004. *Can Women Be Rabbis?* www.torahweb.org.

Seidler, V. J. 1997. *Man Enough: Embodying Masculinities.* London: Sage.

Shapiro, E., ed. 1997. *The Inner World in the Outer World: Psychodynamic Perspectives.* New Haven: Yale University Press.

Sharma, A., ed. 1987. *Women in World Religions.* Albany: State University of New York Press.

Shoemaker, L. 1997. "Part Animal, Part Machine." In Heywood, ed. 1997.

Shwartzbaum, O., and A. Sadan. 2000. *K'tnot Or,* Jerusalem: Mofet Institute. (In Hebrew.)

Shweder, Richard A. 1991. *Thinking through Cultures: Expeditions in Cultural Psychology.* Cambridge, Mass.: Harvard University Press.

Smith, J. I. 1987. "Islam." In Sharma, ed. 1987, 235–250.

Sokol, M. 1996. "Master or Slave? On Human Autonomy in Front of God in Rabbi Soloveitchik's Thought" (in Hebrew). In Sagi, ed. 1996a, 403–443.

Soloveitchik, J. B. 1966. "Sacred and Profane." *Gesher* 3 (Sivan 5726) 5–29.

————. 1983. *Halakhic Man.* Translated by L. Kaplan. Philadelphia: Jewish Publication Society.

————. 1986. *The Halakhic Mind: An Essay on Jewish Tradition and Modern Thought.* Ardmore, Pa.: Seth Press.

Sprengnether, M. 1990. *The Spectral Mother: Freud, Feminism and Psychoanalysis.* Ithaca: Cornell University Press.

Stake, R. 2000. "Case studies." In *Handbook of Qualitative Research,* edited by N. Denzin and Y. Lincoln, 435–454. 2d ed. Thousand Oaks, Calif.: Sage.

Steinberg, J. 1997. "From a 'pot of filth' to a 'hedge of roses' (and back): Changing Theorizations of Menstruation in Judaism." *Journal of Feminist Studies in Religion* 13 (2), 5–26.

Strachey, J., ed and trans. 1953–1974. *The Standard Edition of the Complete Psychological Works of Sigmund Freud.* 24 vols. London: Hogarth Press.

Swidler, L. 1976. *Women in Judaism: The Status of Women in Formative Judaism.* Metuchen, N.J.: Scarecrow.

Terner, Y. 1996. "The Religious Act according to the Rav Soloveitchik: God's Commandment or Human Creation?" (in Hebrew). In Sagi, ed. 1996a, 383–402.

Tolman, D. 1994. "Daring to Desire: Culture and Bodies of Adolescent Girls." In Irvine, ed. 1994, 250–283.

Trible, P. 1995. "Eve and Miriam: From the Margins to the Center." In Trible et al. 1995, 5–26.

————, et al. 1995. *Feminist Approaches to the Bible*. Washington, D.C.: Biblical Archaeology Society.

Turner, B. 1996. *The Body and Society*. London: Sage.

Twersky, M. 1998. "Halakhic Values and Halakchic Decisions: Rav Soloveitchik's Pesak Regarding Women's Prayer Groups." *Tradition* 32(3):5–17.

Ussher, J. 1994. "Theorizing Female Sexuality: Social Constructionist and Post-Stucturalist Accounts." In Choi and Nicholson, eds., 1994.

Walsh, M. R., ed. 1987. *Psychology of Women: Ongoing Debates*. New Haven: Yale University Press.

Wasserfall, Rahel. 1992 "Menstruation and Identity: The Meaning of *Niddah* for Moroccan Women Immigrants to Israel." In *People of the Body: Jews and Judaism from an Embodied Perspective*, ed. Howard Eilberg-Schwartz, 309–327. Albany: State University of New York Press.

Weiler, K. 1988. *Women Teaching for Change: Gender, Class and Power*. With an introduction by Henry A. Giroux and Paulo Freire. South Hadley, Mass.: Bergin and Garvey.

Weitz, R., ed. 1998. *The Politics of Women's Bodies: Sexuality, Appearance, and Behavior*. New York: Oxford University Press.

Wright, E., ed. 1992. *Feminism and Psychoanalysis: A Critical Dictionary*. Cambridge, Mass.: Blackwell.

Yanay, N., and B. Birns. 1990. "Autonomy as Emotion: The Phenomenology of Independence in Academic Women." *Women's Studies International Forum* 13:249–260.

Yanay, N., and T. Rapoport. 1997. "Ritual Impurity and Religious Discourse on Women and Nationality." *Women's Studies International Forum* 20(5–6):651–663.

Zanardi, C., ed. 1990. *Essential Papers on the Psychology of Women*. New York: New York University Press.

Zivan, G. 2005. *Religion Without Illusion—Facing a Post-Modern World: An Inquiry into the Thought of Soloveitchik, Goldman and Hartman*. Hakibbutz Hameuchad Publishing. (In Hebrew.)

# INDEX

Adler, Rachel, 62, 113
Akiva, R., 34–35
*Aliyot* (call to read Torah), x
Anthropomorphism and God, 63, 71–72, 78–79
Apologetics on women's role, 74, 92–93
Aristotle, 50
Assimilation, 103, 109, 121
Authority of canonical texts, 21–25, 33. *See also* Power relations; Rabbinic authorities
Autonomous vs. relational views of human nature, 12–14, 124, 137n5

Babylonian Talmud, 63
Backlash against feminism. *See* Responsa to women's public role
Beauty standards, oppressions of, 52, 57, 58, 60, 92
Berger, Peter, 79
Berman, Saul, 10
Beruriah, 37–41
Biblical sources: Eve and dangers of female gender, 49–50, 108–9; modesty's equality in, 61; for niddah, 140n3. *See also* Torah
Blessings. *See* Prayer
Bloom, Harold, 43
Body, human: vs. inner (spiritual) life, 48; men's discomfort with women's bodies, 26; women's natural grounding in, 50–51. See also *Niddah*; Objectification of women's bodies; *Tzniut*
Bordo, S., 58
Boyarin, D., 39, 41
Bynum, Caroline Walker, 74

Canonical texts: and authorities' resistance to women's participation, 32–37, 41–42; psychoanalytic texts as canonical, 21–32; reaffirmation model, 37–38, 41–42; reinterpretation model, 38–39, 42–43, 44; rejection model, 39–41, 43–44; significance and meaning relationship, 29–30; silencing of women in, 20–21
Chodorow, N., 28–29
Christianity, 18, 141n6, 142n10
Collaboration-resistance, cooperation with *niddah* as, 97
Community: communal narratives and women's status, 32, 33–35; egalitarian *shul*'s basis for, 121, 129–32; inclusion of women's spaces in, 16; and influence of women in *mikveh* observance, 95; observance of *mitzvot* as commitment to, 89–90; and *shul* as spiritual center for men, 45
Compartmentalization strategy for integrating modernity, 8, 9, 11, 124–25
Connell, R. W., 76
Conservative Judaism, 62, 112–13
Containment as motivation for covering, 49–51
Contextual issues. *See* Cultural context
Conversion, reinterpretation of language for, 65–67
Covering, motivations for, 49–59, 84, 97
Creation stories, 49–50, 108–9
Creativity, human, 12
Cultural context: Freud's attachment to, 26–27, 29; and power of language, 62–63, 69, 74, 79, 80; prayer, 64, 69–70; and reinterpretation of canonical texts, 38–39; religion's influence on, 43–44. *See also* Community; Patriarchal social order

De Beauvoir, Simone, 50

Defilement vs. modern attitudes about *niddah*, 97

Discrimination against women. *See* Marginalization of women

*Divrei Torah* (public reading of), x, 100

Domestic sphere. *See* Private sphere

*Dora: An Analysis of a Case of Hysteria* (Freud), 30

Dworkin, Andrea, 52

Eating disorders, 60

Eckstein, Emma, 22–25

Education: feminist agenda for equality in, 138n13; and reinterpretive model for canonical texts, 43; study of Torah, 33, 40, 139n14; women's access to, 32, 35–41

Egalitarianism, 11, 62, 81, 121–33. *See also* Equality

Ellenson, David, 102–3

Emotional nature of women and exclusion from power, 33, 37, 49–51, 82

Equality: and biblical sources, 61; as feminist agenda, 21, 138n13; and gender essentialism, 108; and responsa to women's suffrage, 103; in synagogue rituals, 52–53. *See also* Egalitarianism

Erickson, Erik, 130–31

Essentialism, gender: as argument for status quo, 104–5; and equality, 108; flaws in, 77–78; Freud's, 26; and impulsive passion in women, 33, 37, 49–51, 82; male, 50, 76; post-biblical origin of, 33–34, 37; and power, 33, 37, 40, 49–51, 82; Western continuation of, 58–59; and women's physicality, 50–51

Ethical sensibilities: autonomy of man vs. relational ethic, 12–14, 124, 137n5; complexities of response to changes, 100–101; and feminism, 67, 81–82; human dignity as overriding value,

100; modesty's twisted ethic, 48; power to define, 10–11, 123–24, 128; and religious truths, 20; selective integration of secular norms, 8–12; universal, 13, 78, 100; and Western obsession with women's bodies, 45–46; and women as sexual gatekeepers, 51–56

Eve, sin of, 49–50, 108–9

False consciousness, 92–93, 97–98, 108

Faludi, S., 118, 119

Family structure, women in public sphere as threat to, 104, 105, 141n3

Feminine sensibilities: as argument for status quo, 104–5; fluidity of, 77–78; and idealization of women, 20, 34–35, 45, 47, 51–56, 104–5; and image of God, 70–72; male gaze as central to, 57; and modesty as virtue, 48–49; *niddah* as supporter of, 91–93; and passionate nature of women, 33, 37, 49–51, 82; and prayer language change, 68–72; self-sacrifice ideal, 34; Western version, 57–59. *See also* Women

Feminism: creation of respectful space for, 121–33; critique of, 2–4, 81–82, 83, 124; ethical stance of, 67, 81–82; as gift from God, 9–10; and *halakhah*, 15, 16; holistic view of human identity, 131; modesty as neofeminist empowerment, 46–47; and objectification of women's bodies, 45, 58; vs. Orthodoxy, 1–7, 10–12, 14–16, 21, 81, 101–17, 138n13; vs. patriarchal social order, 2, 16, 18, 119–20; and psychoanalysis, 21–32; reengagement with Orthodoxy, xi–xii, 3–4, 6, 16–18, 72, 129–32; as religious claim, 130–31; as threat to Jewish identity, 103, 109, 121

Feuerbach, L., 79

Fine, Michelle, 59

Firestone, Shulamith, 27

Foucault, M., 48
Freud, Sigmund, 21–32, 123
Fusion of horizons concept, 29–30

Garden of Eden story, 49–50, 108–9
Gender roles: canonical support for traditional, 32–33; equality in, 61; fluidity of, 74, 76–78; Freud's biases, 26–29; and God imagery, 74; metahalakhic defense of status quo, 100, 102–17; *niddah*'s impact on, 92–96; and sexual desire, 51–56; Talmudic inconsistency on, 35–41. *See also* Essentialism; Men; Private sphere; Public sphere; Women
Gilligan, Carol: adolescent relationship to identity, 138n8; as author's mentor, 1–2; ethic of care, 13; on importance of human relations, 124; on masculinity and femininity, 77; on psychoanalysis, 27, 31
Gladstone, W. E., 104
God: depersonalized vs. relational, 71–72, 73–74; feminism as gift from, 9–10; gender of, 70–72, 75–76; as hidden, 115–16; human representation of, 63, 71–72, 78–79; as immanent, 72; as Other, 71, 72; as Place, 75; representation vs. reality of, 70–72, 79; Torah study as encounter with, 33; transcendence of, 70
Goddess-based revisionism, 70–72
Greenberg, Blu, 3
*Guide of the Perplexed* (Maimonides), 73

*Halakhah:* and feminism, 15, 16; inconsistent gender interpretations in, 35–41; as perspective on gender roles, 32; and prayer language, 63–64, 69; and reading of wedding documents, 113–14; and resistance to egalitarian worship, 62; and response to modernity, 5, 7, 12; Shirah Hadashah's respect for, 132; and women's participation in *shul*, x, 100; women's prayer groups' legitimacy, 106–7, 111; women's study of, 17, 139n14. *See also Niddah;* Torah; *Tzniut*
Hampson, Daphne, 18
Harmonization with modernity, 8–12
Hartman, David, 73
Hartman, Tovah, 1–2, 4–7
Hegemonic masculinity, 76
Heilbrun, C., 30–31
Heschel, A. J., 67–68, 69
Heschel, Susanna, 41, 122
Hierarchical society, 16, 77. *See also* Patriarchal social order
Holzer, Elie, 99
Horner, Matina, 123
Human dignity as overriding value, 100

Idealization of women, 20, 34–35, 45, 47, 51–56, 104–5
Identity: autonomous vs. relational views of, 12–14, 124, 137n5; collective, 16; and commitment to mitzvot, 83; feminist/Orthodox tensions in, 1–7, 103, 109, 121; feminist view of human, 131; fluidity of gender, 67, 74, 76–78; and importance of women's voice, 44; modesty's distortions of, 54; negative, 14–16, 132; *niddah*'s distortions of, 86–87; spiritual facet of, 18–19; subjective internal truth of, 25, 30–32, 41–42
Immersion (*mikveh*), 89, 90, 92, 93, 94–96, 140–41n4
*In a Different Voice* (Gilligan), 77
Individualism, Orthodoxy's integration of, 12–14
Inequality, 16, 76, 77, 89, 133
Innate nature of gender differences. *See* Essentialism
Irigaray, Luce, 43
Israel, 5, 105–6

Jacobs, Mary, 30–31
Jewish Orthodox Feminist Alliance
    (JOFA), xi, 6
Judaism, accessibility of, 122. *See also*
    Modern Orthodoxy

Kandiyoti, D., 140n1
Kaufman, D., 98
*Kavanah* (intention), 68
Kent, K. S., 105
*Ketubah* (wedding contract), 113–17, 119
*Kibbutz ha-dati*, 5
Kohlberg, Lawrence, 13
*Kol isha* (sensuality of woman's singing), 45
Kolodny, A., 43
Kook, R. Abraham Isaac Hacohen, 101–6

Lamm, R. Norman, 8, 11
Language: creative power of, 80; and
    cultural context, 62–63, 69, 74, 79,
    80; God as independent of, 79; as
    path to transcendence, 69. *See also*
    Prayer
Law, religious. See *Halakhah*
Law of Idolatry, Maimonides, 110
Learned helplessness, 123
Learning. *See* Education
Leibowitz, Yeshayahu, 12
Lerman, H., 21
Liberal feminism, 21
Liberalism and Orthodoxy, 10, 12
Liturgy. *See* Prayer

MacKinnon, Catherine, 13
Maimonides: on exclusion of women
    from learning, 34, 139n14; on God's
    nature, 71, 73; Laws of Idolatry, 110;
    reinterpretive method for sacred lan-
    guage, 65–67; and women's passion-
    ate nature, 50–51
Male gaze, 20, 45–47, 51–59, 60
Marginalization of women: and isolation
    of change agents, 125, 126–27, 132–33;

and language, 71–72; and men's fears
    of lustful thoughts, 53; and Torah
    study, 33. *See also* Objectification of
    women's bodies; Oppression
Marriage: *niddah*'s impact on, 85, 86,
    90–91, 93–94; wedding contracts,
    113–17, 119
Masculine sensibilities: fluidity of, 77–78;
    and image of God, 73; in language of
    prayer, 63; male gaze, 20, 45–47, 51–59,
    60; and maleness, 75–76. *See also* Men
Masson, J., 25
Matchmakers, 59–60
*Maternal Thinking* (Ruddick), 77–78
*Mechitza* (gender divider in shul), 45
Meir, R., 35–41
Meiselman, R. Moshe, 100, 111–13
Men: as definers of women, 20–21,
    25, 26, 32–33, 52–56, 60, 123–24; fears
    of own passions, 51, 52–53, 55–56,
    59–60; fears of women's powers, 26,
    38, 41, 46, 82, 118–20; feminism as
    issue for, 133; gender confusions in
    Western society, 58–59; and gender
    essentialism, 50; lack of equal obli-
    gation with women, 89; modesty
    for, 48; need for feminist education,
    138n13; in private sphere, 131; *shul*
    as spiritual center for, 45; as victims
    of gender hierarchies, 77. *See also*
    Masculine sensibilities
Men of the Great Assembly, 63–64, 66, 74
Menstruation rules. See *Niddah*
Messerschmidt, J. W., 76
Metahalakhic defense of gender status
    quo, 100, 102–17
*Mikveh* (immersion), 89, 90, 92, 93,
    94–96, 140–41n4
Mill, John Stuart, 13
Miller, J. B., 118–19
Mishnah, 33–34
Mitchell, J., 26, 27–28
*Mitzvot:* and autonomy of man, 12–13;

benefits of observance, 89–96; as commitment to community, 89–90; gender inequality in requirements, 89; and identity, 83; *mikveh,* 89, 90, 92, 93, 94–96, 140–41n4; *onah,* 93–94; study of Torah, 33, 40, 139n14. See also *Niddah; Tzniut*

Modernity, Orthodoxy's selective adoption of, 7–16. *See also* Western secular society

Modern Orthodoxy: commitment to sacred language, 73; vs. feminism, 1–7, 10–12, 14–16, 21, 81, 101–17, 138n13; feminist reengagement with, xi–xii, 3–4, 6, 16–18, 72, 129–32; negative identity, 14–16; resistance to egalitarian worship, 11, 62; response to modernity, 7–16; unity vs. human dignity, 100; value of, 18–19. See also *Niddah;* Prayer; Rabbinic authorities; *Shul* (synagogue) rituals; *Tzniut*

Modesty (*tzniut*). See *Tzniut*

Monotheism, and feminine images of deity, 70–71. *See also* God

Moral sensibilities. *See* Ethical sensibilities

Muff, Yochanan, 73

Muslim women, 140n1

Narratives, communal, as basis for women's status, 32, 33–35

*Nashim d'atan kalah* (women are weak-minded) argument, 18, 33–34, 37

Nation, changes in gender roles as threat to, 105–6

Negative identity, 14–16, 132

Neo-Kantian tradition, 12–13

*Niddah* (purity and immersion): blessings of, 84, 89–96, 140–41n4; burdens of, 84–89; complexities of observance, 96–98; overview, 82–84; Torah sources for, 140n3

Norms, societal. *See* Ethical sensibilities

Objectification of women's bodies: beauty's oppressions, 52, 57, 58, 60, 92; and Orthodox power relations, 51–56; in Western society, 45–46, 56–59

Obligations, religious. See *Mitzvot*

Observance, ritual. See *Niddah;* Prayer; *Shul* (synagogue) rituals; *Tzniut*

Onah (husband's sexual obligation to wife), 93–94

*On Being a Jewish Feminist* (Heschel, S.), 122

Oppression: beauty standards as, 52, 57, 58, 60, 92; feminist vs. traditional views, 81–82; and Freud, 28–29; and modesty, 48–49, 54, 59–60; *niddah* as, 82, 84–85, 96; protection of women as, 55–56; responsa to women's public participation as, 17–18, 119; in Western secular society, 57–59. *See also* Marginalization of women

Oral Law, 17, 35–41, 63–64, 139n14

Ordination of women, 113–17

Orthodox Judaism. *See* Modern Orthodoxy

Other: God as, 71, 72; women as, 21, 39, 107, 122

Ozick, Cynthia, 71–72

Paganism, 110–11, 112

Pantheism, regression into, 71–72

Patriarchal social order: canonical texts' embeddedness in, 21, 38, 39–40; vs. feminism, 2, 16, 18, 119–20; and gender role education, 32; and God as male, 75–76; Judaism as embedded in larger, 44; liturgy as reinforcer of, 62; Orthodox women's awareness of, 84; power of, 122–24; and sexuality control, 47, 82, 87–88; support for women in relationship, 93; women's subversion of, 95–96

Perelberg, R. J., 96

*The Personhood of God* (Muff), 73

111–13; overview, 99–101, 118–20; Schachter on women in public sphere, 113–17; Twersky on women's prayer groups, 106–11

Revelation, divine, 9–10, 33, 127

Revisionist model, 25–30, 38–39, 42–43, 44

Rich, Adrienne, 43, 54, 70

Rituals. See *Niddah;* Prayer; *Shul* (synagogue) rituals; *Tzniut*

Ross, Tamar, 9, 68

Ruddick, Sara, 77–78

Schachter, R. Hershel, 113

Scientific knowledge, Modern Orthodoxy's integration of, 8

Secularism. *See* Western secular society

Seduction theory, Freud's, 27

Self. *See* Identity

Sexuality: desires and gender roles, 51–56; husband's obligation to wife, 93–94; men's fears of own passions, 51, 52–53, 55–56, 59–60; men's fears of women's, 26, 38, 41, 46, 82, 118–20; patriarchal controls on, 47, 82, 87–88. See also *Niddah; Tzniut*

Shame as motivation for covering, 49–51, 97

Shapiro, R. Mendel, x

Shirah Hadashah, x, 45, 81, 99, 121–33

Shoemaker, L., 58

*Shul* (synagogue) rituals: creation of women's home in, x–xi, 16; egalitarian participation, 52–53, 121–33; independence of, 129; resistance to women's participation in, xii–xiii, 17–18, 32–37, 41–42; separation of women in, 20, 45, 52–53; spiritual importance for women, 127; Torah reading, x, 100

Slippery-slope theory and antifeminism, 110–11

Smith, J. I., 47

Soloveitchik, R. Joseph B. (the Rav), 12, 111–13

Spirituality. *See* Religion

Status of women: and communal narratives, 32, 33–35; and exclusion from power, 33, 37, 49–51, 82; feminist challenge to, 21; and idealization of women, 20, 34–35, 45, 47, 51–56, 104–5; legal and cultural aspects of, 32; participation in public sphere as elevation of, 119; rabbinic resistance to change in, 100, 102–17, 125. *See also* Marginalization of women

Steinberg, J., 83

Study of Torah, 33, 40, 139n14

Subjective experience: as basis for identity, 25, 30–32, 41–42; as basis for spiritual fulfillment, 121; prayer as, 64–67, 131–32; religion as, 2–3, 127; and respect for women's sexuality, 93

Suffrage, women's, 101–6

Synagogue. See *Shul* (synagogue) rituals

Systemic subjugation and *niddah,* 87–88

Talmud, 17, 35–41, 63–64, 139n14

*Tefillah* groups (prayer groups). *See* Prayer

Temptresses, women as, 49–51, 82

*Tikkun Olam* (Repairing the World), 78

Torah: Eve and dangers of female gender, 49–50, 108–9; modesty's equality in, 61; niddah ritual's origins in, 140n3; public reading from, x, 100; spiritual experience of, 127; study of, 33, 40, 139n14

"Torah-sanctioned degenerate," 108

*Torah Umadda* (Lamma), 8

Touching and *niddah,* 86–87

Tradition, religious. *See* Modern Orthodoxy; Rabbinic authorities

Trible, Phyllis, 3–4

Twersky, R. Meir, 15, 106–11

*Tzniut* (modesty): motivations for covering, 49–59; overview, xii, 45–46; and prohibition on women as scholars, 35; as response to Western culture, 46–49, 59–61

Ultra-Orthodoxy (*haredi*), 14
Universal norms, 13, 78, 100

Values. *See* Ethical sensibilities
Victimization, and protection of women
as oppression, 55–56
Virtue, women as paragons of. *See* Idealization of women
Voices of women: canonical silencing of,
20–21, 32–33, 38–39; feminist vs. traditional, 81–82, 83; *niddah*'s empowerment of, 91–96; rabbinic authorities'
resentment of, 106, 118–20, 121; sexual
norms as silencing agents, 82; as sexual temptation, 45; spiritual importance of, 44
Voting rights, 101–6

Wasserfall, Rahel, 140–41n4
Wedding contract (*ketubah*), 113–17, 119
Western secular society: challenge of
sexual gaze in, 45–47, 49, 56–59;
consequences of objectification
of women in, 53; as corrupting
influence on women, 108; and
limits on rabbinic authority, 128–29;
men as definers of women in, 60;
Modern Orthodoxy's selective integration of, 7–16; myth of unlimited
agency, 124

Women: Catholic church's exclusion
from priesthood, 141n6, 142n10; challenging Freud's canon on, 21–32; education access of, 32, 35–41; emotional
response to Torah access, 127; and
family structure, 104, 105, 141n3; idealization of, 20, 34–35, 45, 47, 51–56,
104–5; men as definers of, 20–21, 25,
26, 32–33, 52–56, 60, 123–24; men's
fears about, 26, 38, 41, 46, 82, 118–20;
and modesty as neofeminist empowerment, 46–47; *niddah*'s empowerment of, 91–96; ordination of, 113–17;
as Other, 21, 39, 107, 122; passionate
nature of, 33, 37, 49–51, 82; as sexual
gatekeepers, 51–56, 59; subversion of
rabbinic authority, 88–89, 95–96;
value of ways of being/doing, 130–31;
as weak-minded, 18, 33–34, 37. *See
also* Feminine sensibilities; Feminism; Status of women; Voices of
women

Yanay, N., 83
Yehoshua ben Levi, Rabbi, 63
Yeshiva, 33
*Yo'atzot Halakha* (female Jewish law
consultants), 17, 88

Zionism, 5–6, 10